CONTEMPORARY PORCELAIN

CONTEMPORARY PORCELAIN

MATERIALS, TECHNIQUES
AND EXPRESSIONS

PETER LANE

A & C BLACK · LONDON   CHILTON BOOK COMPANY · RADNOR, PENNSYLVANIA

Dedication

To the memory of my mother, Freda Margaret Lane (1906–1994), whose courage, fortitude and caring good humour was a shining example to everyone during her final, painful illness.

First published in Great Britain 1995
A & C Black (Publishers) Limited
35 Bedford Row, London WC1R 4JH

ISBN 0-7136-3956-3

Copyright © 1995 by Peter Lane

A CIP catalogue record for this book is available from the British Library.

First published in the USA by Chilton Book Company, Radnor, Pennsylvania 19089
ISBN 0-8019-8635-4

Jacket illustrations
Porcelain Vessel, wheel-thrown carved and pierced, by Horst Göbbels. *Photograph by Wolf Böwig.*

Frontispiece
Vessel form in bone china, slipcast, carved and altered, 20 cm high, by Angela Verdon, 1992.

Designed by Bob Eames
Typeset by August Filmsetting, St Helens
Printed in Singapore by Tien Wah Press (Pte.) Ltd

'Sphere Protrusion', porcelain, 45 cm high by Peter Masters, 1991. The strong rhythmic raised pattern is built up from individually applied elements; sodium vapour glaze fired to 1280°C in a natural gas kiln.

CONTENTS

Acknowledgements

Any author of a book of this kind must rely heavily upon the goodwill and cooperation of many people. I am deeply indebted to all the porcelain makers who have so generously given of their time and expertise in helping me to gather material for this book. I am especially grateful for the loan of photographs willingly provided by so many potters around the world and to the photographers for allowing their reproduction as illustrations for the text. In particular, I would like to thank Wolf Böwig, of the Keramik Galerie Böwig in Hannover for taking great care in photographing the work of several important artists for me. Hein Severijns (Holland), Jan Schachter (California), Curtis Benzle (Ohio), Bill Hunt (Editor of *Ceramics Monthly*), Janet Mansfield (Editor of *Ceramics: Art and Perception*), Sandra Black (Western Australia), Erik Pløen (Norway), and others were all extremely helpful in providing me with addresses of potters working in porcelain. My sincere thanks are due also to Chris Hogg and Harry Fraser for their helpful technical notes on the search for porcelain and bone china bodies with good working properties. Many potters, gallery owners and collectors at home and abroad have all given me the encouragement needed to produce a completely new book on contemporary studio porcelain. My thanks are also due to my editor, Linda Lambert, who persuaded me that it was time to address the subject again. To my wife, Jean, for her patience and tolerance while I spent long hours communicating only with my word processor, and who regularly interrupted her own creative work to keep me supplied with good food and endless cups of coffee, a very special thank you.

Peter Lane, 1994
New Alresford, Hampshire

INTRODUCTION

There have been many exciting developments in the field of contemporary ceramics since my first book on the subject was published in 1980 under the title of *Studio Porcelain*. This was an attempt to examine an area of the discipline which, despite its long history, had been largely neglected by studio potters. This new book endeavours to address the subject afresh and to investigate what changes in attitude or in approaches to design and making, if any, may have occurred during the intervening years. In the course of my research, I have consulted a large number of ceramicists who regularly work with porcelain and tried to discover something of their personal philosophy towards their art and its place in modern society. Particular emphasis is given in the book to the enormous diversity and rapid development which has taken place over the latter part of the 20th century in international studio porcelain and considers some of the aesthetic concerns, technical achievements and working methods of these ceramicists working with porcelain and its close relative, bone china.

Porcelain offers a far wider range of options and applications than those most popularly perceived for it. The basic qualities usually associated with or required of high-fired porcelain such as delicacy, translucency, fineness, whiteness, density and purity remain available, of course, but many potters have chosen to break with traditional expectations of the medium. Their primary concern is more likely to be the exploration and realisation of three-dimensional form, using porcelain as the most appropriate plastic material, and incorporating various techniques for their purposes. Often, those singular physical properties will be still evident in a porcelain object but the emphasis on any or all of these will depend upon the manipulative processes employed at various stages from wet to dry; the thickness of sections; the application of colour in oxides, stains, slips or glazes; and on the final firing.

It has generally been accepted that porcelain, as a material, can be somewhat daunting both to use and control until one becomes familiar with certain unique aspects of its character. In *Studio Porcelain* I tried to clear away much of the fog and mystique surrounding the successful making of

porcelain and to offer advice and suggestions for its imaginative use. Today, there appear to be virtually no boundaries which cannot be stretched and few rules that can remain inviolate in this area of human invention as can be seen by the immense variety of forms and surface treatments in the work of porcelain potters from around the world which have been assembled together in this book. Originality, flair and skill combine in the best work to present us with numerous stimulating images: vessels, tiles, wall panels, figurative sculptures, and abstract objects all

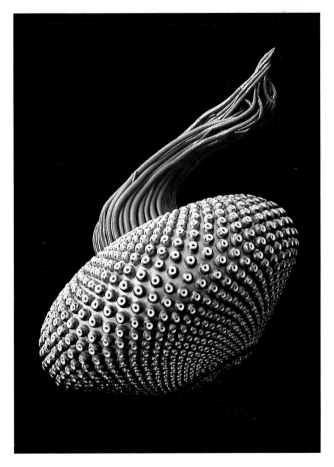

'Sphere Protrusion', porcelain, 45 cm high by Peter Masters, 1991. The strong rhythmic raised pattern is built up from individually applied elements; sodium vapour glaze fired to 1280°C in a natural gas kiln.

  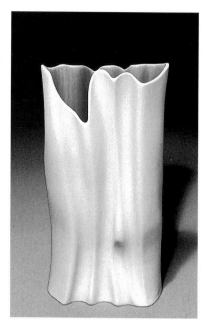 

created in an unusually 'unforgiving' medium. It must be acknowledged that a number of potters who became well-known after several successful years working with porcelain have turned to earthenware clays because they found that the lower firing temperatures presented them with greater control, but others have preferred to continue using this fine, white body while gaining fresh inspiration through pushing the material to the very limits of their ability.

Not all the pieces illustrated will be immediately recognisable as porcelain because they seem not to fit into any of the familiarly held perceptions. One might question, therefore, whether porcelain was the proper medium to use for them, but for one reason or another, it was decided that a different clay body would fail to satisfy all the practical and aesthetic requirements which the artist deemed essential for his/her personal expression. In each case, porcelain acts as the common denominator linking all the works chosen to illustrate this book. Techniques and processes described are, in many instances, similar to those identified with other branches of ceramics adapted, where necessary, to suit individual needs.

The work of the contemporary ceramicist has grown out of a long and glorious history. It seems that countless generations of potters have already explored every practical, technical, social, cultural and aesthetic aspect from the preparation and composition of clay bodies and glazes to the construction and firing of many different types of kilns in producing the vast wealth of ceramics which we all inherit. In truth, it is often stated that since so much has gone before, there is little scope for truly fresh invention.

Goblet form on tall, angular stem made from wheel-thrown and handbuilt elements and fired to 1280°C in a gas kiln with a reducing atmosphere, 38.5 cm high, by Maria Bofill, 1993.

Second left Porcelain pot, 11 cm high, by Geoffrey Swindell, 1989. Wheel-thrown, with textured surface made at the leatherhard stage by imprinting marks with a wire brush. This texture is enhanced later by a feldspathic glaze overloaded with vanadium. Fired to 1250°C in an oxidising atmosphere.

Second right Slipcast porcelain vessel form with carved rim by David Fink (USA), 1993. Colour glazed inside but with the exterior polished. The inspiration for this piece came from eroded rock formations.

Far right Porcelain Vase with 'gosu' brush decoration in blue, 28 cm × 15 cm, by Alistair Whyte, 1993.
Photograph by Avon Colour Studio.

Nevertheless, ceramics continues to offer us the appropriate, and universally understood, visual and tactile means to express individual thoughts, ideas and feelings. In this respect one can make an analogy with words or with musical notes in that they, also, are infinitely reworked to communicate anew.

Few clays can be used 'as dug' in the making of refined ceramics. Therefore we refer to the clay mixtures as bodies. Varying amounts of clays and certain other materials such as quartz, flint, feldspar, nepheline syenite, Cornish stone, whiting, silica sand and talc are combined together to make workable plastic bodies to suit a whole range of purposes and firing temperatures. Porcelain bodies, however, are usually composed of just three main ingredients: kaolin (China clay), feldspar and quartz with smaller amounts of ball clay or bentonite added to ensure plasticity. Unfortunately, ball clays can impair the whiteness and affect translucency whereas bentonite is less likely to do so. However, bentonite (a highly plastic, colloidal substance with a very fine grain size), which is widely used for preparing porcelain with good throwing properties, can increase problems of shrinking and cracking if more than six per cent exists in the composition.

Porcelain is simply a composition of fine, relatively similar sized particles of kaolin, silica and feldspar which achieves a more complete fusion than stoneware or earthenware clays that tend to be made up with additional ingredients including sands or grog. It is the extra silica content of porcelain which contributes its glassy translucent quality but, at the same time, makes it more susceptible to stress due to its high rate of expansion and contraction. All potters are aware of the importance of slow cooling following a kiln firing but porcelain is especially vulnerable to dunting, if cooled too quickly, at those points where the silica inversion take place at 570°C and 226°C respectively.

Despite differences in composition, most porcelain bodies possess the potential to be translucent but the degree to which that state is achieved depends on the thickness, or rather thinness, of the clay. Nevertheless, if translucency alone is held to be the key to defining 'true' porcelain, it may be argued that many of the bodies currently available are no more than white porcellanous stonewares. Therefore, the definition of porcelain is open to question. However, this is not an issue that concerns us here. My researches have discovered an extremely wide range of applications for white, porcellanous bodies having a very high content of the essential kaolin, feldspar and silica supplying the main qualities expected of porcelain. Some body compositions are considerably more translucent than others but that particular property may be of little interest to the ceramicist for whom form, surface, colour or texture is sufficient for their expression and communication. Porcelain bodies generally become vitrified when fired to temperatures well above 1200°C and the higher this is, the greater the proportion of glass that will be formed in the body. This is the main factor assisting the passage of light through it, although complete vitrification is not necessary for this to occur.

There are many potters for whom those delicate and varying degrees of translucency, which can only be revealed after the final firing, will be the supreme attraction and ultimate goal. The interplay of light onto and through a finely-made piece provides one of the most satisfying experiences in both seeing and touching. Yet this aspect may not appeal to everyone. Instead, some ceramicists

Porcelain bowl with extremely thin walls, thrown, turned, and decorated with brushed and trailed slip over latex resist, 44 cm diameter, by Arnold Annen, 1992.
Photograph by Reto Bernhardt.

may be attracted to porcelain more for its smooth, dense texture which allows it to accept the finest incising, piercing and carving at various stages from wet to dry. Others will prefer to exploit whiteness for its own sake or as a 'canvas' for colour. For there is no doubt that much of the appeal of porcelain (and even more so with bone china) as a material in which to produce forms of diverse kinds owes a good deal to that particular quality of clean brightness uncontaminated by iron or other impurities. The full, unblemished colour spectrum is thus made available for unhampered use.

Often, porcelain has been chosen to form the whole or a significant proportion of the body composition for making quite low-fired ceramic objects. In such instances, the potters are not concerned with meeting the normal requirements for domestic use (e.g. to hold liquids) so they do not need the extra strength and durability afforded by firing the body to maturity. All porcelain bodies must be fired to temperatures in excess of 1200°C if they are to become impervious to water. But, even, when fired as low as 1000°C, porcelain still offers an extra-fine, smooth, white body, superior to most others, that provides such excellent opportunities for surface treatments that they compensate for any physical weakness. In some cases, potters have chosen to use porcelain in the form of slips to coat and conceal any coarser clays they have used to create the piece. Porcelain-based slip gives them a good, white ground for colour while a thicker application can be compacted and burnished to a silky-smooth sheen.

Potters, perhaps, are more intimately occupied with and, to a certain extent conditioned by, the materials, techniques and processes of their discipline than any other artist-craftsmen. They have to understand sufficient of the practical physics and chemistry involved if they are to avoid frequent frustrations. Even the most experienced suffer disappointments from time to time when results are not quite what had been intended. The search for personal ideals is continuous and, in most cases, their appetite for

Top Jug and bowl forms slipcast in bone china and decorated with airbrushed ceramic stains by Sasha Wardell, 1992.

Middle Vase, 'Autumn', 35 cm high, by Judith de Vries, 1992. Constructed from separately made 'leaves' of laminated, coloured porcelain built up piece by piece. Fired to 1200°C in an electric kiln. *Photograph by Claude Crommelin.*

Bottom 'Desert Night', porcelain bowl, 29 cm diameter × 18 cm high, by Pippin Drysdale, 1993. Wheel-thrown, with painted coloured stains on top of a white (tin/zirconium) glaze, fired to 1200°C in an electric kiln.

Opposite 'Chalice of Promise', handbuilt porcelain, wood-fired in an anagama type kiln, 26.5 cm high, by Catharine Hiersoux, 1990.

11

technical understanding is voracious. This interest has spawned an enormous number of books which have been published on every aspect of ceramics during the years following the Second Word War but the demand for yet more information about technicalities remains undiminished.

Despite the inveterate curiosity of most potters, I have discovered a surprising number who admitted that they have little or no interest in ceramic chemistry for its own sake. They obtain all their commercially-prepared materials from reliable sources knowing how they will perform in use so that they can concentrate all their creative energies to procure fairly predictable results. Above all it is the expression that matters. During more than 30 years of making and teaching ceramics, my own interest in and respect for the diverse ways in which individual artists around the world resolve technical as well as aesthetic problems of design remains strong. I firmly believe that as experience grows so does the realisation that there is so much more than anyone can possibly comprehend in a single lifetime. Therefore, we have to be selective, concentrating upon particular aspects that appeal to us and, in that continuous enquiry, we are limited only by the time we can devote to it and by our own capacity to understand. This fact, for me, contributes to the continuing excitement of ceramics and of porcelain in particular. The main aim of this book, therefore, is to examine and explain some of the personal thoughts, feelings, approaches and techniques currently employed by individual ceramicists in the specialised field of porcelain. However, it is important to stress that those techniques can never be a satisfying end in themselves. They are only the *means* employed to achieve that end. Any discussion about techniques, therefore, must be directly related to the more significant aesthetic achievements of the work illustrated.

It is highly unlikely that the reader will find that *all* the works depicted in this book appeal to his or her personal taste. Nor has it been possible to include reference to every notable potter working in porcelain at the time of writing. Nevertheless, I believe that, as an author, it is essential to exercise a broadly catholic choice which gives a reasonably wide representation of studio porcelain in the late 20th century. I have consulted a great number of ceramicists working in porcelain and bone china around the world all of whom have been most generous in providing me with information about their thoughts, feelings, aims and processes. Direct quotations from them are frequently used to amplify the text. In this way, I have been able to include

'Huntly', porcelain plate, 29.5 cm diameter, by Peter Minko (Australia), 1993. Wheel-thrown and burnished at the leatherhard stage before bisque firing to 920°C. Hand painted with finely ground pigments (mainly metallic oxides) and fired twice to 1280°–1300°C in oxidation to fuse the colours to the unglazed surface. Gold lustre is then applied in a further firing to 760°C.

Porcelain Bowl, 38 cm × 7 cm, by Russell Coates, 1993. Wheel-thrown, with painted underglaze blue decoration under a clear/white glaze fired to 1270°C and then enamelled with the design of a cross in a red circle surrounded by paired cormorants, geometric border and dolphins.

details of the working methods of many potters from different social and cultural backgrounds. These are illustrated and discussed throughout the book. The materials potters use in the execution of their art are common to all, but their stimuli, influences, approaches and objectives cover a very wide spectrum.

My own personal preference is for making 'vessel' forms, especially bowls, since they are open to infinite variation both subtle and extreme and whether or not concerned with function. Although countless millions of container forms have been produced in ceramics to serve a multitude of purposes from the humble to the sublime,

pure craftsmanship? Indeed, to what extent can critical criteria remain constant in the face of continuing development? the unrelenting speed of change affects us all. What one generation adores the next often *abhors* as in other areas of visual expression. It would seem virtually impossible to identify a definitive kind of 'public' taste that might indicate what should be expected of ceramic art today. We do not *need* individually produced, handmade ceramics. They are not essential for everyday, practical purposes. Of course, there will always be those who prefer not to use industrially-made ceramics, or glass, or plastics, etc. in a domestic situation and, doubtless, their needs will continue

Bowl in multi-coloured (yellow, blue, black and brown), laminated porcelain, fired to 1320°C in a reducing atmosphere, 16 cm diameter, by Rainer Doss, 1993.

Porcelain Sculpture, untitled, with aluminium tubes and steel wire, 19 cm × 19 cm × 15 cm, by Wil Broekema, 1991. *Photograph by Dick Huizinga.*

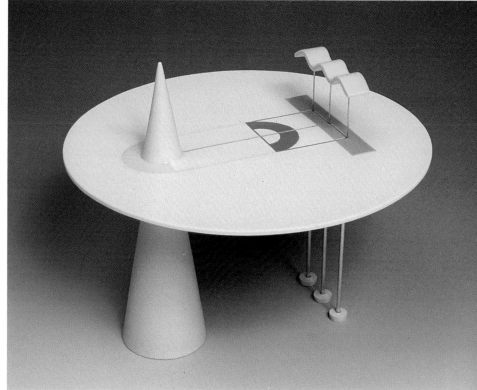

there will never be an end to their aesthetic possibilities. The best of these objects transcend utilitarian needs to become the purest form of three-dimensional art.

Throughout history, ceramics presents us with a magnificent kaleidoscope of human expression, functional, figurative and abstract. But too many art critics tend to dismiss sculptural work executed in clay as being of little relevance to the field of 'fine' art and arguments concerning its status remain unresolved. Uncompromising attitudes raise questions as to whether criticism of any ceramic work can be truly objective other than in matters of fact, that can be judged in those measurable, quantifiable aspects such as

to be supplied, but the modern potter is not *bound* to cater for them. Therefore, the only certain restrictions, apart from economics or individual sensibilities, are those imposed by the potters's own ability to control the material processes of his or her art. One can choose to build upon tradition or fly in the face of it. Above all else, contemporary ceramics should be accepted as a prime vehicle for tactile, visual expression.

Many questions came to mind during my enquiry into contemporary studio porcelain, some of which relate to ceramics in general. Although some answers may be found in the following pages, most will remain open to discussion and reassessment. It is extremely difficult to attempt a definitive analysis of a discipline in a state of constant flux, but by questioning, examining and observing developments around the world one can arrive at some small understanding and appreciation of the wonderful diversity to be found in modern ceramics. We can look at a piece and ask ourselves in what way it relates to traditional ceramics or how it fits within the context of the late 20th century? Whether it has the power to evoke a sympathetic or antipathetic response in us? Are there references to, or influences from, any other branches of the visual arts? Does it seem to reflect a moment in time like the present or does it echo past moods, expressions or cultures? How 'original' is it and does it matter if it is not? Is it so esoteric that it only belongs in an exclusive gallery setting?

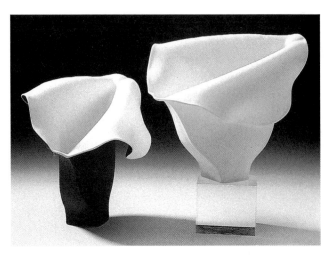

Two slipcast and altered bone china vases with sprayed ceramic stains and fired to 1240°C in an electric kiln, 20 cm high, by Angela Mellor, 1993.

'Bloom', handbuilt, wood-fired porcelain, 33 cm high, by Catharine Hiersoux, 1992.
Photograph by Richard Sargent.

Porcelain Bowl, 30 cm diameter, by Greg Daly, 1993. With etched surface and lustre decoration. This piece has just one glaze containing copper carbonate, but one half is green where the kiln atmosphere was predominately oxidising and the other is red where a reduction has taken place. This is caused when one burner out of four has a reducing flame resulting in a localised reduction occurring.

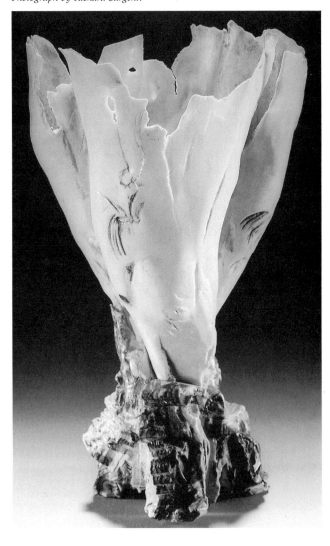

We are constantly bombarded with images from so many different sources that few can fail to be affected by them. The natural world has long provided inspirational material for creative expression in ceramics but experiences of travel, transport, architecture, urban environments, etc. in addition to aspects of the human condition such as war, famine, social injustice and even family relationships can also act as trigger points for intensely personal work.

I have been fortunate in being able to select examples of porcelain ceramics to illustrate the text from ceramicists whose earlier work has been included in my previous books and to have discovered and made contact with many others whom I did not previously know. For my part, I found the research involved to be both invigorating and frustrating. The frustrations were constant because the gathering and collating of material together with the concentrated effort of writing allowed no time for me to respond in my own ceramic work to the surge of creative energy aroused by such an amazing diversity of images, or the richness of invention and ingenuity, demonstrated in the work of so many ceramicists included in this book. It is my hope that the selection presented will prove both stimulating and thought provoking. In an ideal world all the illustrations would be published in full colour but, where this has not been possible, dimensions, colours or other detailed information has been provided in the captions to enable the reader to visualise the objects as they really are.

As can be seen in this broad survey of contemporary studio porcelain, there are at least as many women as there are men engaged in ceramics at every level but, for reasons of economy throughout this book, terms such as potter, artist, craftsman, ceramicist should be read as synonymous and applicable equally to either gender.

Porcelain sculpture (unglazed), 'Zone Series 12', thrown, altered and assembled, 18 cm by 12.8 cm approximately, by Margaret Realica, 1990. The slabs are made from finely thrown cylinders which are cut open when they have stiffened slightly. Electric kiln fired to 1260°–1300°C.
Photograph by Robert Aude.

'Container Form', by Lara Scobie, 42 cm × 37 cm × 21 cm. Constructed by building up layers of thinly rolled porcelain (Harry Fraser porcelain body). The textures are achieved by pressing the clay into Indian printing blocks. Oxides and underglaze stains are applied to the texture and then sponged off to leave a residue of colour in the impressions. Fired to 1300°C in a reduction atmosphere.

Laminated and assembled porcelain bowl, 15 cm × 17.5 cm × 17 cm approx., by Thomas Hoadley, 1993.
Photograph by Paul Rocheleau.

QUALITIES AND PROPERTIES OF PORCELAIN

Composition of porcelain bodies

Despite an abundance of fairly reliable materials available from commercial sources, the search for the ultimate porcelain body free from any disadvantages continues. The ideal would probably be a supremely white body which would be very plastic, easy to throw or handbuild, be able to support itself when wet, have minimal shrinkage, resist cracking or splitting at every stage from wet to dry, be translucent when relatively thick, be strong when fired, and to mature around 1200°C while performing to perfection in any kind of kiln or atmosphere. Even with the advanced technology available to the ceramics industry today, it is unlikely that all these requirements can ever be met but we continue to explore possibilities.

A translucent porcelain body recipe, specially developed for use by the late Audrey Blackman (well-known for her rolled modelled porcelain figures), was published in *Ceramic Review* (No. 100) in 1986. It remains popular with a number of British potters and is as follows:

Standard Porcelain China Clay (English China Clays)	50%
Westone – H (sodium activated white Texas bentonite)	5%
FFF Feldspar	27%
Quartz (300s mesh)	17%
Whiting	1%

Another recipe for a throwable bone china body was made for Anne Hogg (see page 46) and this, also, appeared in *Ceramic Review* (No. 113) in 1988.

Bone ash	50%
Super Standard Porcelain China clay	25%
MF4 flux	25%

2.5% Westone – H white bentonite is added to this recipe.

Both these bodies were developed by Anne's husband, Dr Christopher Hogg, and I am indebted to him for the following information.

Both of these bodies use a particularly white and pure bentonite from Texas. The company producing it was owned by English China Clays, but it was sold to Laporte at Redhill in Surrey a couple of years ago. Whether they still import the bentonite into England, I do not know, but it is now called Bentolite H (yes, with an 'l').

From a scientific point of view, whiteness and translucency of porcelain are well understood to the extent of being calculable, given the right information. The properties are dependent on two fundamental properties: light absorption and light scatter. (I am here ignoring the influence of thickness, which, although very important, I take as being obvious.)

Light is absorbed by colouring metal ions, usually iron and titanium in clay bodies. Light is scattered at interfaces between the glassy matrix and the crystalline phases present such as mullite from the clay, and undissolved quartz. Colouring metal ions reduce both translucency and whiteness. Crystalline phases reduce translucence but increase whiteness. The whiteness and

Porcelain Bowl, diameter 12 cm × 10 cm high, by Karl Scheid, 1992. Wheel-thrown porcelain with diagonal relief carving under a feldspar-petalite copper red glaze fired to 1360°C in reduction.
Photograph by Tomoki Fujii.

translucency actually achieved are the result of the balance between these two parameters.

To make a porcelain that is both white and translucent requires the minimum of colouring metal ions and a fairly low level of crystalline phases. This means using pure clays, no ball clay for example, and a high feldspar content to give plenty of glass on firing and only a small quantity of crystalline phases. Needless to say, these requirements conflict with the plasticity required for throwing, and stability during firing. Compromises are inevitable.

Firing porcelain in reduction helps, converting yellow ferric iron to pale blue ferrous iron that is less strongly colouring, provided that no titania is present to interact with it. Cornish china clays contain little titania, but many china clays from other parts of the world can contain as much as in many English ball clays.

Another technique is to add something that reacts with the iron and bleaches it. This is what happens in bone china, where the phosphate from the bone ash in effect bleaches the iron. The result is an almost pure white body that is very translucent. Unfortunately, a lot of bone ash is needed to ensure that all the iron is combined with the phosphate, and a bone china body can be described as a porcelain body mixed with an equal weight of bone ash. This halves the clay content and so greatly impairs the plasticity.

Bowl in multi-coloured laminated porcelain, fired to 1320°C in a reducing atmosphere, 15 cm diameter, by Rainer Doss, 1993.

Three vessel forms, 'Composition', handbuilt with laminated, multi-coloured porcelain, fired to 1280°C in an electric kiln, 22 cm, 20 cm and 15 cm diameter, by Mieke Everaet, 1992.

In the extreme, the two properties of whiteness and translucency are conflicting: a material is either extremely white and opaque or extremely translucent and not white. If nearly all the light is reflected back to you, there is none left to pass through, and conversely if much of the light passes through, less is reflected back. White opaque glazes are opaque because they are white; window glass is very translucent but not at all white. In practice, things are not that extreme, and most people have an appreciation of what is white and translucent in porcelain, compared to what is not.

In addition to all that, there is the property of plasticity that I have mentioned only in passing. Here, I'm afraid science has still a long way to go in understanding the fundamentals. There is plenty of practical experience and many empirical tests for plasticity, but not much science. The simplest solution to poor plasticity is to add a little bentonite, and use the purest you can get. A sodium-activated bentonite is best, acidified after mixing it in to ensure good flocculation. Preferably use an organic acid that burns away, such as acetic acid (vinegar). Mineral acids give off unpleasant fumes during firing. An alternative method of flocculating is to add a very little slaked lime (and I mean a very little, if you value the skin on your hands). Some China clays produced in Czechoslovakia and much used in German porcelain are flocculated this way.

A good, reliable porcelain body introduced to many potters in Britain during the 1960s and 1970s and which became extremely popular was the David Leach Porcelain Body. I used it almost exclusively for several years. This body is still available from commercial sources today and can be obtained in many parts of the world as indeed, can most other prepared bodies. The porcelain from Limoges in France is the preferred vehicle for the work of several potters whose work is illustrated in this book. Others use a porcelain based on the Zettlitz kaolin from Czechoslovakia. My own current preference is the the Harry Fraser Porcelain Body produced by Potclays Limited in Etruria, Stoke-on-Trent, England. I have found this body to be generally most reliable to use. It throws well, fires white and, although it has a reasonably wide firing range, it is translucent when potted thinly enough at temperatures as low as 1220°C. Harry Fraser explained the process of developing this particular porcelain for me as in the following notes.

There are many recipes for porcelain bodies. Most of them are blends of kaolin with a flux (usually feldspar) and free silica in the form of flint or quartz. Some recipes include additions of ball clays, bentonite or other plasticisers. The incorporation of ball clay is very desirable from a plasticity viewpoint but, if present in any significant amounts, tends to prevent translucency. Consequently, its use in porcelain bodies is usually confined to recipes where translucency is not a requirement — for example, in porcelain insulators.

Development of a plastic, throwable but white firing and translucent porcelain is very dependent upon the type of kaolin used. Grolleg features in many recipes and indeed was the basis of the well-known David Leach Porcelain Body formulation in the 1960s and 1970s. However, an even more plastic kaolin was then produced by English China Clays and known as Standard Porcelain China Clay. This China clay has a very slightly lower iron content than Grolleg and thus fires slightly whiter as well as being slightly more plastic. I, therefore, selected it as the basis for a new porcelain body, using FFF Feldspar as the flux and 200s mesh quartz to develop thermal expansion. Preliminary mixes were not sufficiently plastic and so Quest white bentonite was progressively introduced until the plasticity seemed to be reasonably good — and certainly as good as any other porcelains then available.

A problem is that we all know what plasticity is but nobody has yet succeeded in devising an instrument that can properly measure it. Plasticity is closely linked to green strength and that we can measure by means of a Modulus of Rupture machine. MOR tests done on clay samples of the new body showed that green strength was well up to that of other porcelains. However, previous experience had indicated that the handling properties could, perhaps, be further improved by slight flocculation. This also would enable filter pressing times to be significantly reduced and thus lower production costs.

Trials were done using whiting and other flocculants as a part replacement for feldspar in the body recipe. Whiting does, however, become a very vigorous flux at high temperatures — especially where a glassy matrix is developed — and so refractoriness tests had to be carried out to quantify the extra fluxing effect. In this way, an optimum flocculant addition was incorporated which produced a slightly better throwing body, the clay

Three Vessel Forms, tallest piece is approximately 25 cm high, by Anne Hogg, 1993. Wheel-thrown bone china with carved decoration. Rust particles were kneaded into the plastic body used for two of these pieces to provide the black speckles. Fired in an electric kiln to 1270°C.

Two porcelain bowls, 12 cm and 6 cm high, by Suzanne Bergne, 1993.
Thrown and altered on the wheel, with poured glazes and fired twice
to 1220°C in an electric kiln.
Photograph by Andra Nelki, Indigo Studio.

Handbuilt ceramic form combining an earthenware base with
supporting a porcelain vessel decorated using the neriage technique.
60 cm high. This piece is the result of collaboration in design and
execution by two Belgian artists, Frank Steyaert and Chris Scholliers
in 1993.

Porcelain sculpture 'Zonder Titel', constructed from extruded coils of Limoges porcelain body (TM10) fired in reduction to 1260°C to obtain a colder, more bluish white colour, 70 cm × 40 cm, by Netty Van Den Heuvel, 1992.

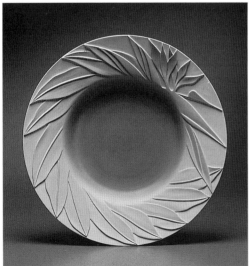

'Bird of Paradise', 28 cm diameter, by Rolf Bartz, 1990. Porcelain platter, wheel-thrown and carved, with airbrushed underglaze colours (orange and pale blue). Fired 1260°C in an electric kiln, unglazed but polished with silicon carbide paper after the final firing.

seeming more flexible and standing up better. It was incidentally interesting that the improvement in throwing properties of the clay body could not be detected on the MOR machine. Flocculation also reduced the filter pressing time from around ten hours to about seven, enabling production in the normal working day.

The quartz grain size was also important. In porcelain bodies, the effect of the quartz content on thermal expansion depends on its particle size, and this is influenced by the firing temperature and amount of glass formation which takes place. Glass formation dissolves the free silica, converting it to silicate which lowers thermal expansion and thus has an opposite effect to free quartz. The finer the particle size the more effective free silica becomes in promoting thermal expansion but also the more easily it can be taken into glaze solution by the solvent action of the fluxes. A 200s mesh grade of quartz was selected which, in trials, gave the best combination of craze resistance and fineness.

The new porcelain body was then sampled to porcelain users whose production trials confirmed that it threw exceptionally well and fired to a good colour and translucency.

A most important consideration was the production plant upon which to produce the new porcelain. Hitherto, production of studio porcelain bodies had been by slotting the production in between batches of other white firing bodies, e.g. white earthenware and white stoneware types. In a sliphouse system one can clean out blungers, agitation arks and pugmills but not very easily, and it is impractical to clean out interconnecting pipework to the pumps etc. In a factory, therefore, it is likely that when switching from one body to another

there will be some degree of contamination with what was previously processed. For this reason, the practice of rejecting the initial production and progressively feeding it back into the system is generally used to minimise any contamination with the previous body. Nevertheless, this procedure cannot be as good as the use of plant dedicated only to porcelain production.

Production of the new body was, therefore, withheld until dedicated plant could be made available. Two years later, suitable plant became available at Potclays Limited and the body was launched into production.

Bowl Form, 15 cm × 12.5 cm, by Dorothy Feibleman. Laminated parian, built as a flat slab, pressed in to a mould and then 'thrown' upside down to close the foot and compress the laminations. Fired to 1120°C in an electric kiln.
Photograph by Thomas Ward, courtesy of Bonhams, London. This piece is in the collection of Galerie Hunteregger St. Polten, Austria.

Porcelain 'Yo Yo' Jar, freely decorated with metallic oxides and wash and lines drawn through the glaze, 25 cm × 17.5 cm, by Tom Coleman, 1993.

Body recipes

Many potters choose to make their own porcelain bodies to recipes with which they have become familiar over a long period of time. In this way, they can avoid some of the problems encountered in the use of commercially-prepared bodies when ingredients are altered for one reason or another. **Tom Turner** (USA) uses a body which he has made up from the following recipe for more than 18 years:

Tom Turner Porcelain *(cone 9–10)*

Vee Gum-T	4
OM4 ball clay	12
Tile 6 kaolin	75
Kaopaque-20	38
Custer feldspar	60
Silica (200s mesh)	70
Epsom salts	0.25

Translucent porcelain bowl, by Patrick Piccarelle (Belgium), 1993. Wheel-thrown and trimmed several times, carved and bisque fired and then engraved with dental tools. The holes are filled with a high viscosity glaze (Cornish stone 85, whiting 15) and then glazed overall with a palette of feldspathic glazes. Fired in reduction to 1280°–1300°C (gas kiln).

Porcelain Sculpture, untitled, with glass marbles, and steel wire and steel tops applied to the tapering porcelain column, 34 cm × 30 cm × 15 cm, by Wil Broekema, 1993. The porcelain is fired to 1240°C in an electric kiln before assembling with adhesive. *Photograph by Wil Broekema.*

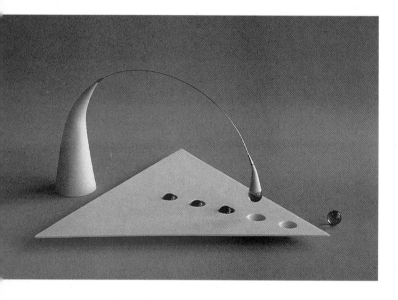

Vessel Form, with resist pattern towards the rim sponged away in relief, and the lower section painted in colour, 8.5 cm × 11 cm diameter, by Astrid Gerhartz (Germany), 1993. *Photograph by Wolf Böwig.*

'Vee Gum-T is the whitest and most plastic material I've ever found. It is a plasticiser and lubricant that doesn't burn out. The Epsom salts are essential for throwing as a flocculated body will stand up and a deflocculated body will not.'

Turner mixes the above body in a particular order. Firstly, the Vee Gum-T is blunged in warm water or hot water and then he proceeds down the list of ingredients and, by adding the most plastic materials first, maximum plasticity is achieved. This body matures at cone 9 and will survive up to cone 10 but then begins to deform. For handbuilding, the Vee Gum-T content should be increased to between 2% and 3%. To lower the maturation point, 1% of talc is added for each lower cone number required.

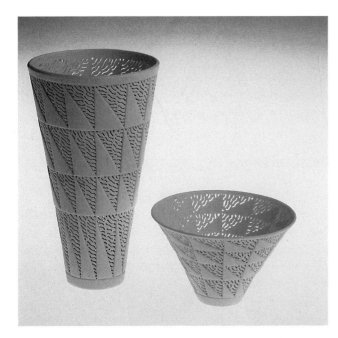

Two triangular vessel forms, by Sandra Black. Slipcast porcelain, carved and pierced at the leatherhard stage and cleaned up when dry. Fired to cone 7 in an electric kiln.
Photograph by Victor France.

Sandra Black (Australia) suggests a porcelain body recipe developed by Mike Kusnik in Western Australia:

No. 1	Cresta B.B. kaolin	60
	Potash feldspar	40
	Zinc oxide	3

She altered this recipe in 1983 in order to improve the whiteness as follows:

No. 2	Cresta B.B. kaolin	30
	Eckalite No. 1 kaolin	30
	Potash feldspar	40
	Zinc oxide	3
	Zircon	2.5

Another variation provided by Black also comes from Mike Kusnik:

	Cresta B.B. kaolin	40
	Eckalite No. 1 kaolin	32
	Zinc oxide	3
	Silica	26
	Bentonite	3

'This clay is a very white and plastic porcelain. The feldspar, zinc oxide, silica and bentonite are milled for 12 hours. After 12 hours, add the kaolin and mill for a further four hours.'

Black prepares her porcelain in batches of ten kilos dry

weight, firstly making it into a slip which is stirred and sieved through a 100s mesh. 'The clay is then ball milled for between 16–24 hours. This removes any iron spots and grinds the clay to a fine consistency before it is poured into cloth bags to be hung up to dry in a shaded area. When the right consistency is obtained, the bags are dampened down with a water hose to remove dirt and to soften hardened slip around the opening. The clay is removed from the bags and wedged before storage. It is usable after its first wedging but storage is recommended to improve plasticity.'

Derek Clarkson (UK) uses the 'Audrey Blackman' porcelain body referred to earlier in this chapter for his very translucent bowls with incised decoration. For his crystalline glazes, however, he prefers to use the Special Porcelain body (firing range 1300°–1400°C) from Limoges (available in Britain from Reward-Clayglaze) because it combines well with the glaze recipes and firing cycles he has developed. (This is described in greater detail in Chapter Five.) He reclaims the trimmings produced when turning his pots by putting them into a plastic bucket and moistening them with water from a fine hand sprayer to bring them to a soft, throwing consistency. The full bucket is left for two or three weeks and then the contents are thoroughly wedged to a good condition for throwing.

I have found it essential not to allow porcelain clay trimmings to dry out completely if I intend to re-use them for thrown work. When reconstituting the clay by hand wedging, it is difficult to rid it completely of air pockets which can prove fatal in thinly thrown bowls. My preferred method is to let the trimmings fall into my wheel tray containing slip from the previous throwing session and then mix this up thoroughly before removing it to stiffen on a large, two inch thick plaster batt resting on the bench beside my wheel. After one or two hours this reclaimed clay is turned over on the batt to stiffen further. It is then kneaded and wedged ready for throwing. I do not possess a de-airing pugmill but, although this method does work for me, the reclaimed body cannot compare with fresh clay. As a consequence, I often prefer to mix the 'old' clay with an open textured, stoneware clay and use it for handbuilding.

Paper porcelain

An increasing number of ceramicists have been experimenting with porcelain bodies mixed with other materials such as paper or textiles. Soaking textile fabric in slip enables them to wrap thin flexible sheets around a form and the organic matter is burnt away in the kiln to leave the 'skin' of fired clay behind. Cotton paper pulp mixed 50/50 with dry clay produces a heavy slip that can be poured on to plaster batts to make flat sheets or it can be cast to shape in plaster moulds. Stiffened sheets can be rolled out so that the surface resembles leather. These sheets can be torn or cut with scissors and assembled into various forms in the normal way. Firing should be carried out in a well-

'Pots with Minoan Influences, (Pots No.51)', 20 cm × 6 cm, by Paul Scott, 1993. Etching printed on paper porcelain with cobalt oxide under a transparent glaze fired to 1200°C.
Photograph by Andrew Morris.

ventilated area to allow for the pungent gases that the mixture releases. **Paul Scott** (UK) is one who has explored the possibilities offered by mixing paper pulp with porcelain. He uses a mixture consisting of two parts porcelain to one part paper pulp. This proportion gives the material

remarkable strength in both the leatherhard and dry states and it is possible to produce literally paper-thin sheets with it. Although Scott uses these ceramic sheets rather like a printmaker would use ordinary paper for making etchings (see page 143 for a description of this technique), others have created sculptural expressions with similar material.

Translucency

The translucency of porcelain is an essential ingredient in the work of a number of ceramic artists including **Arnold Annen** (Switzerland). Having worked with different clays and firing processes in Switzerland, France, Japan, Holland and Germany between 1970 and 1989, he returned to set up his studio in Basel. There he began to develop a unique technique for making his distinctive, paper-thin porcelain bowls in 1991. His methods demand a disciplined approach and an extremely high standard of craftsmanship. Initially, bowls are thrown with walls at least twice their final thickness. Accumulated slip is removed with steel ribs inside and out and then Annen uses two hand-held gas burners to dry the piece until leatherhard. The burners are held opposite each other, one inside and one outside, and the wheel revolves. A chuck is thrown with the same porcelain body and turned precisely to match the diameter of the bowl's rim. Inverting the bowl onto the chuck, Annen gently taps it as the wheel rotates until it is properly centred and trimming can commence. Sharpened metal strip tools are used to shave away successive layers from the outer surface of the bowl. Then the bowl is placed upright in another chuck so that the inside of the bowl can be worked on with sharp, kidney-shaped steel tools, thinning the wall still further. The abrasive action of the clay makes it essential that tools are sharpened regularly as the work proceeds. The bowl is inverted once again for the footring to be opened up and, with care, shaped approximately but left thick enough to withstand the stress of further hand-ling. Annen checks the greatly reduced thickness of walls and base by shining a torch through them. At this stage they are little more than 1 mm thick. The rim is then refined with the same steel tools prior to decorating the outer surface of the bowl.

Annen re-centres the bowl upside down on the wheel to paint latex resist onto and around the foot and a little way up the side from the base. He holds the bowl by the resist protected foot while he squirts narrow lines of latex diago-nally across the form, working from the foot towards the rim, and force dries the latex with his gas burner. The emerging design is constantly checked and assessed. When satisfied, Annen takes a large Chinese brush to apply separ-

ate, sweeping strokes of porcelain slip over the latex, using the gas burner to dry the slip instantly. The lines of latex are then peeled away and, with a fine nozzle, he trails lines of slip selectively across the form and immediately dries them with the burner flame.

The extreme fragility of these bowls requires them to be fired upside down in a chuck made to fit from the same porcelain body. Annen makes his chucks with as much care as he gives to the bowls so that they can correctly support them in the kiln. Alumina is mixed with water and painted around the rim of the chuck to ensure that the bowl will be easy to release on removal from the kiln. The pieces are once-fired in a gas kiln to a maximum of 1260°C under a reducing atmosphere with spectacularly translucent results (see photograph below).

Porcelain bowl with extremely thin, translucent walls, by Arnold Annen, 1993. This piece was wheel-thrown and turned. Decoration was produced by using latex resist brushed over and trailed with porcelain slip. Unglazed. 17.5 cm high × 26.5 cm diameter.
Photograph by Reto Bernhardt.

Arnold Annen trimming a wheel-thrown bowl with sharp tools in order to reduce the wall thickness to just 1 mm.

Arnold Annen decorating a porcelain bowl with brushed slip over latex resist.

Arnold Annen trailing porcelain slip on a latex-resisted bowl.

Arnold Annen removing latex resist after decorating a porcelain bowl with brushed and trailed slip.

Annen uses a porcelain body from Limoges (TM 10) which is a popular choice among several of the European potters represented in this book. It takes him four days of concentrated effort to complete each piece together with its supporting chuck. Due to the extreme thinness of his bowls it is impossible to rectify any mistakes and even the slightest air bubble will ruin the work. Everything must be done at exactly the right stage and this demands absolute concentration throughout the whole process. He fires his unglazed bowls in a gas kiln under reducing conditions in order to obtain a cold, white colour as the body would

Left Flared, cylindrical vessel form, slipcast in two layers, by Jeroen Bechtold, 1993. The outer layer has been partially removed to reveal greater translucency. 34 cm high. In order to distinguish between the two white layers, Bechtold mixes organic colouring compounds (food colouring) with the second layer.
Photograph by R. Gerritsen

Below Eggshell porcelain vessel form slipcast in layers with decorative surface carved away to increase translucency, 21 cm high and 32 cm wide, by Jeroen Bechtold, 1992.
Photograph by R. Gerritsen.

Above Wheel-thrown 'supporters' made from the same porcelain body as the bowls they will support, upside down, during the high temperature firing, by Arne Åse.

Below Unglazed, translucent porcelain bowl, 38 cm diameter, fired in reduction to 1250°C by Arne Åse. The decorative surface detail is produced by painting a shellac resist pattern and then sponging away the unprotected areas of the design.

Above Unglazed, translucent porcelain bowl, 20 cm diameter, fired in reduction to 1250°C by Arne Åse. The decorative surface detail is produced by painting a shellac resist pattern and then sponging away the unprotected areas of the design.

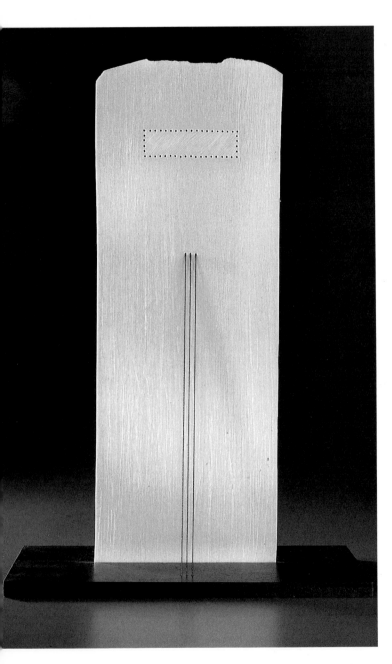

Porcelain slab form, unglazed, pierced, fired in reduction to 1280°C, and mounted on a painted, wood base, 54 cm high, by Horst Göbbels. *Photograph by C. Struck.*

have a rather warmer tint when oxidised. He built his kiln well-insulated with ceramic fibre and controlled by computer so that he could fire quickly, taking only one and a half hours between 900°C and 1250°C and, thus, avoid risking deformation.

Translucency can have a bewitching effect on the observer and many other potters also make use of this exceptional quality, although it does require directional lighting if it is to be fully exploited. **Jeroen Bechtold** (Holland), for example, carves away parts of the outside in varying layers from some of his pieces. Multiple glazes are applied and fired in oxidising conditions (see photograph on page 26). Again, it is necessary for light to be shining into the pieces from directly overhead if they are to be properly appreciated. **Arne Åse** (Norway) uses a different method to vary the thickness and thus the degree of translucency of his porcelain plates and bowl forms. He paints a design onto the raw pot with a shellac solution and allows it to dry before thinning the wall by carefully sponging away unprotected areas. His sensitive brushwork with the shellac resist helps him to achieve a richly textured surface whose delicate, translucent quality is revealed by the passage of light through the piece (see photograph on page 27).

Horst Göbbels (Germany) also exploits the full potential of translucent porcelain and gives extra emphasis to its exquisite refinement by incorporating precisely pierced holes in some of his sculptural objects. Thinly rolled sheets of porcelain stand unwaveringly straight alone or in formal ranks behind one another, minimally incised or pierced with strictly controlled designs. In some cases, additional linear elements are provided by coloured strings or wires which pass through the slab and appear to act as guy ropes holding the piece upright. The quiet, understated purity of these pieces achieves a sense of perfection that would be destroyed by unnecessary ornamentation.

Smoothness, whiteness and precision

One of the greatest attractions of the medium for those potters who choose to work in porcelain is its smooth grain and dense body. This invites a degree of precision in design and execution that would be difficult to achieve in a more granular clay. Clear, sharp profiles, positive shapes, crisply defined patterns and fine linear drawing seem to be completely appropriate to porcelain. Of course, strict control of the material, tools and processes is absolutely necessary by those who would work in this way and it will not suit any craftsman who prefers potting more freely and leaving more to chance. Often, it is a matter of personality. Ceramics, as in any other art form, reveals something of its maker's feelings and character. I must confess that much of the appeal of porcelain to me in my own work is the opportunity that it allows for preciseness. I like to be in control, to make things exact so that they fit as close as possible to a personal concept of perfection. Of course, I recognise that my ideal will not necessarily be the same as another would choose but I find great difficulty in working any other way. I can enjoy and admire asymmetry in the work of others but I am always searching to establish some kind of visual

balance in my own. I feel sure that any conscious attempt to adjust my attitude or approach would appear contrived and fail dismally. This does not mean that precise forms lack sensitivity. Expressive qualities are not the sole prerogative of wild abandon!

The vessels by **Anne Leclercq** (Belgium) are beautifully controlled in the throwing and turning. This precision is matched by the equally exact placement of lines inlaid with slips with which she decorates the surface. Thin lines around the inner and outer edges of the top of her flanged pot, illustrated overleaf, are totally in character with the

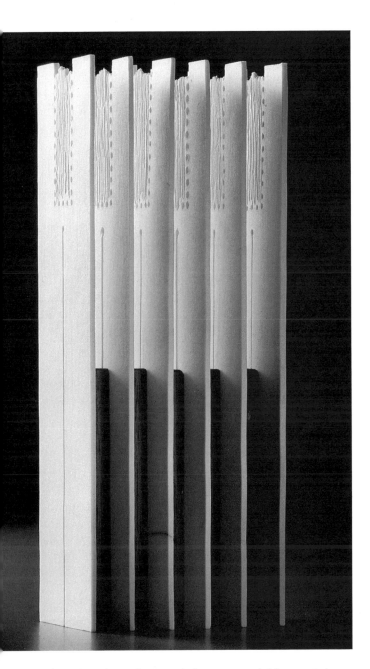

Above   Porcelain sculpture made from six incised slabs mounted together. This piece has been fired in a reducing atmosphere to 1280°C, 36 cm high, by Horst Göbbels.
Photograph by C. Struck.

Above right   Unglazed porcelain vase, thrown and turned, incised and inlaid with stained slips (pink and black), fired to 1280°C and then polished with silicon carbide paper, 11 cm diameter, by Anne Leclercq, 1990. *Photograph by Peter Bors.*

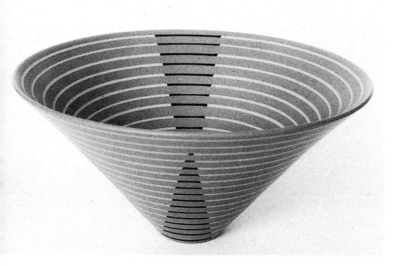

Bottom Unglazed, blue (cobalt oxide) porcelain bowl, thrown and turned, incised and inlaid with pink and black lines of stained slips to define a triangular section. This piece was bisque fired and then polished before refiring to 1280°C and then re-polishing, 13 cm diameter, by Anne Leclercq, 1991.
Photograph by P. Goossens.

Top Unglazed, white porcelain bowl with incised and inlaid slips in grey and pink, 15 cm diameter, by Anne Leclercq, 1990.
Photograph by Peter Bors.

severity of the form beneath. These lines, together with similar bands around the base, mark the boundaries of the piece. Her flared bowl also has narrow inlaid bands that define positive changes in the profile but they also confine shorter, coloured strips which appear to float freely between them.

A similar degree of control is evident in the vessel forms by **Johan Broekema** (Holland). Strongly defined horizontal bands, alternately light and dark, draw attention to the circular section of his wheel-thrown pieces. Using the wheel exclusively, he aims explicitly for ultimate perfection in his geometrical vessel shapes and, with a judicious use of glaze, bands them with contrasting lines in black and white to achieve a harmony between form and glaze. His work exhibits the same precise mastery of form when he uses other glazes like the traditional celadons, tenmokus, oilspots, or copper reds on his vessels and which often have narrow lines encircling them at strategic points to mark directional changes of profile. Geometric designs require exact placement of each element if they are to succeed. This degree of control does present the risk of producing a rather cold, clinical feeling which will not be attractive to everyone. However, such an approach is likely to be extremely successful when both form and surface treatment are composed in complete harmony. (Broekema's glaze recipes are listed on pages 188–9.)

Most potters will agree with **Caroline Whyman** (UK) when she says that, 'form, for me, is the most fundamental consideration for my ceramics. If the form is weak, I don't think that it can be redeemed by decoration. Finish is my next obsession, that is why I use porcelain because for me, it demands care and attention to detail. Nuance is what I look for in form, and subtlety.' She often uses grid patterns in her decoration and can draw them, without measuring beforehand, by banding guidelines (vertical and horizontal) on to the pots with a blue or red stain used in colouring food. This shows up well on raw porcelain for any kind of decorating and it burns away in the bisque firing. 'It's great for trying out various ideas directly on the forms.'

Whyman uses a series of tools with tiny loops for carving into porcelain preparatory to inlaying coloured slips. She also uses porcelain stamps to impress dots for inlay rather than drill bits because it is much quicker. Other stamps have been made with carved designs to impress into the clay. Her favoured slip is made from the porcelain body with the addition of one per cent cobalt carbonate which is cheaper and produces less speckling than the oxide. This is a simple recipe but she always adds a defloc-culant so that she has the advantage of a fluid slip without excess water wetting the leatherhard porcelain too much as she works. 'This is especially important on plates with lots of decoration because they would just 'pancake' from the effect of so much slip!' To save time, she applies the slip over the whole surface and lets it dry to a *hard* leatherhard condition before turning it away with a flexible metal 'kidney' tool. She lines her wheel tray with plastic sheet to catch and save the trimmings to be used to make more coloured slip. This precaution also prevents her wheel tray

Lidded vessel form with precisely placed bands of black and white giving further emphasis to the shape and sharply defined profile, 10 cm high, by Johan Broekema, 1993.

Top left Porcelain bowl, with high foot, wheel-thrown and turned to create a very positive profile and banded with sharply defined black and white lines, 13 cm diameter, by Johan Broekema, 1993.

Lidded box, porcelain, thrown and turned, painted with bands of colour to accentuate the form, 13 cm diameter, by Johan Broekema, 1993.
Photograph by Frankot.

from becoming contaminated. 'Occasionally, smudging occurs even when the pieces are quite dry, but I can deal with that more easily with *wet and dry* silicon carbide paper after bisque firing.'

Grids have always fascinated Whyman, 'they are *so* simple but offer *infinite* possibilities and I quickly found a connection between grid patterns and woven textiles. You either place something on the grid or below it; you either *add* decoration to the grid or leave it blank.' Much of her inspiration comes from geometric textiles and also from basket weaving, especially those from early civilisations. Similar patterns appear, she says, due to a basic grid framework that can be seen in work from South America, native North America, Maori carvings, African textiles, early Greek work, Indian/Asian weaving and Japanese textiles.

Another area of influence identified by Whyman is philosophy and, in particular, Eastern philosophy. 'I study a Chinese form of meditation and philosophy called *Qi ging*, and I find that I have used symbols, often universal, like triangles, dots and squares when I review my work over 20 years or so.'

She rarely uses images from nature and prefers the abstract to the concrete. 'Dots in grids were a symbol of the universe for the Chinese. These can be seen as spiralled dots on their jade *bi* or *pi* as they used to be called. I think that I could continue working with these symbols indefinitely, trying to create harmony and balance. The space in and around the design plays a vital role in the dynamic of the overall appearance. When I feel that a design *really* works it is because there is a dynamic tension between the decorated and undecorated area.

The physical properties of porcelain in its plastic and leatherhard state does, undoubtedly, have a profound effect on the approach to working with it for many potters. It seems to encourage them to work with a high degree of precision – crisp, uncluttered profiles, sharply turned with a

Porcelain bowl, wheel-thrown and turned, incised and inlaid with blue slip, 26 cm diameter, by Caroline Whyman, 1993.

Right Porcelain plate, 'Eternal Triangle' series, wheel-thrown, incised and inlaid with blue stained slip and then sprayed with blue and turquoise, barium/lithium based glazes, 27.5 cm diameter, by Caroline Whyman, 1993. This piece was made in the 'Audrey Blackman' porcelain (see recipe on page 16).

Opposite Porcelain plate, incised and inlaid with blue stained slip under a barium/lithium-based turquoise glaze, 29 cm diameter, by Caroline Whyman, 1993. This method of decorating the surface allows precise placement of all elements of the design.

positive and critical attention to detail. Often for those who work in this way, it is a reflection of their own personality.

Neatness in one's character need not be inhibiting although it contributes towards an ordered attitude to the material and to an individual's desire to remain fully in control of the form and its surface treatment. Clearly, there will be others whose nature will not permit them to work within such confines and they will approach porcelain making with greater freedom, as can be seen in later chapters of this book.

The extremely fine grain, whiteness and density of porcelain invites precise treatment in a way that would be utterly alien to coarser clay bodies. Cutting into the surface of sandy textured clays gives the potter a completely different feeling. My own work is mainly in porcelain but I find that my attitude immediately becomes looser and more vigorous when working in even a fairly smooth stoneware. Likewise, the work will appear more rugged than anything produced in porcelain.

FORM AND FORMING PROCESSES

Throwing and turning porcelain

It is a delight to watch any accomplished craftsman at work and to observe a skilled potter throwing on the wheel is particularly fascinating. The seemingly effortless rise and fall of the spinning lump of clay as it is coaxed towards the still centre and then opened up and raised so fluently. The stretching and swelling of the wet clay walls as they respond to the pressure of the potter's fingers to grow as if organic, magically into a new hollow form. This becomes a natural, intuitive process of making and one in which a feeling for the soft, plastic material flows through the potter's fingers as a sensitive expression of him or herself.

Porcelain is not the easiest of bodies with which to throw but it does have its special attraction. It does demand an acute sensitivity towards its condition at all stages of working. It can suddenly collapse if too much water is absorbed while throwing or if the thickness of the

Cup and Saucer, porcelain, 6.5 cm × 6 cm, by Susanna Fagermo, 1993. The cup has a transparent glaze fired to 1400°C with cobalt chloride and vanadium pentoxide decal fired to 1280°C. The saucer has an opaque glaze fired to 1400°C in reduction with vanadium pentoxide decal fired to 1280°C.

walls is irregular. Some potters illustrated in this book prefer to use slip rather than water as a lubricant. However, there is an element of risk attached to this practice if one allows slip to build up on the surface. It is wise to remove any surplus slip with a steel kidney or other tool from time to time during the throwing process.

An experienced thrower can produce large numbers of pots much more quickly than anyone who builds with slabs or coils. The wheel allowed me to make enough pieces to explore a variety of surface treatments during the period when I was a full-time teacher without the opportunity to devote long sessions to working on my own. Following several years developing thrown forms in earthenware and stoneware bodies my conversion to working almost exclusively with porcelain took place in the early 1970s when one of my students expressed a desire to formulate a porcelain body for a special project. I discovered a satisfying affinity with the nature of porcelain despite difficulties experienced with throwing it initially. Its smooth character and whiteness first appealed and then, as my ability to control it improved to the point where I could throw thinly enough to achieve a delicate translucency, I was completely seduced by it.

I have always enjoyed throwing with porcelain that has been properly prepared and is of even consistency, but I am less happy with material which has been reconstituted from previously used porcelain trimmings. I do not have access to a good de-airing pugmill and reclaiming 'old' porcelain effectively takes such an inordinate amount of precious time that I frequently mix it with stoneware bodies or use it for handbuilding where the danger of air bubbles appearing in thinly thrown walls does not apply.

Careful preparation of the plastic porcelain body is essential before commencing to throw. Unless all air bubbles are eliminated and an even texture achieved, porcelain is much more difficult to throw fluently and efficiently than stoneware or earthenware clays which have similar deficiencies. This is because the more open texture and larger particle size of coarser clays provides them with greater wet strength. In the right condition, however, porcelain is a delight to throw. The clay creams smoothly, sensuously through the fingers in a way that can be best appreciated after a period of throwing with stoneware material. This is because the open, sandy texture of most stoneware bodies feels decidedly gritty in comparison with porcelain. Porcelain potters are aware that their material is, undoubtedly, far less tolerant of insensitive treatment at any stage of throwing than coarser clays. Certainly with porcelain a deeper level of concentration is necessary. The thrower must be able to adjust pressure, movement and speed intuitively as the wheel revolves and should try to acquire a particular sensitivity to the changing condition of the clay. Porcelain can quickly become overworked and 'tired' and this makes it prone to collapse without warning. Some porcelain potters allow for the inevitable absorption of water during throwing by working with the clay in a slightly stiffer condition from the beginning because, unless they are kept sufficiently lubricated with water to prevent from them suddenly drying, the point may be reached where hands will stick to the clay and pull the piece out of shape.

When throwing, porcelain bodies can produce a good deal of slurry which should not be allowed to build up too thickly on a pot. It can be removed with a throwing rib or a modelling tool while the wheel is turning. Similarly, excess water must not be left to accumulate and pool inside as this can weaken the base and cause uneven drying. It is wise to apply sufficient pressure on the inside of the base to align the clay particles and reduce the risk of cracking. The way in which porcelain pots are released from the wheel can affect them later. Cutting through the base with an extra thin, stranded wire on a slowly revolving wheel helps to equalise the stress.

Right Miniature porcelain pots (maximum height 3.5 cm) thrown on a full size potter's wheel by Andrea Fabrega (USA).

Right 'Conical Vessel with Handles', by Andrea Hylands, 1993. Bone china, slipcast and assembled, decorated with airbrushed colours and fired to 1240°C in an electric kiln.

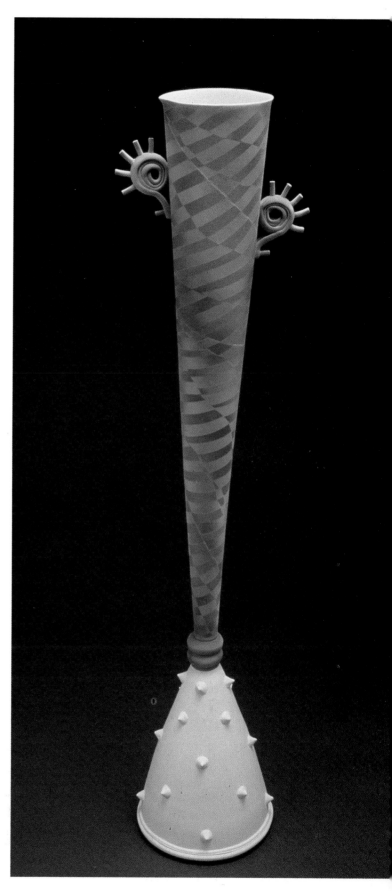

Vessel form, wheel-thrown porcelain, by Fritz Rossmann (Germany), 1993. With part kaolin engobe. 23 cm diameter. Salt glaze fired to 1250°C. This piece was thrown and then 'rolled on the ground or on a table' to produce the unusual texture which is given further emphasis by salt glazing.
Photograph by Baumann Fotostudio.

Caroline Whyman (UK) uses the 'Audrey Blackman' porcelain body referred to on page 16 but she has experienced an unusual number of problems with cracks forming in the base, both 'S' cracks and others in parallel series. She combats these faults by compressing the bases with a rib as she throws, and allows the pots to dry slowly and evenly. She says that she

always lets all my work equalise in dampness, before I do any turning, by wrapping it up in polythene sheet. This slows down the whole making process but ensures less cracks either in the base or the rims if I turn them when the tops are dryish and the bases damp. I throw by using slip instead of water, sometimes adding a minute amount of Fairy Liquid (dishwashing detergent soap) which makes a wetter lubricant and allows me to throw for longer. I also stretch the pots from the inside using wooden spoons modified to a Japanese egote shape. Turning and trimming is always done with very sharp metal tools and I take great pleasure in sharpening them on an oil stone each time I use them.

Two Jugs, 10 cm × 8cm and 14 cm × 7 cm, by Prue Venables (Australia), 1993. Wheel-thrown and altered porcelain. The bases of these pieces were removed when they had stiffened slightly and the sides pushed into the new shapes away from the circular section. New bases are attached when they have stiffened further. 'The intention is to introduce a sprung tension to the forms while retaining the softness of the throwing'.

'From the Sea', porcelain form, handbuilt with impressed texture inlaid with ceramic stains, unglazed but polished, fired to 1320°C in reduction, 30 cm high, by Erik Pløen, 1993.
Photograph by Jan Enoksen.

Some potters use the facility of the wheel only to make shapes which are then altered away from the circular cross-section or cut and reassemble them into new forms. Often, this leaves little evidence of the throwing process visible in the finished piece. The Australian potter, **Prue Venables**, enjoys making small, functional vessels which she finds provides her with constant challenges and excitement. All her work is thrown and turned. Much of her latest work has developed through an interest in altering simple thrown shapes. Their bases are removed and the side walls bent into new shapes. New bases are added when the forms have stiffened. She tries to introduce a 'sprung tension' to the piece while retaining the softness of the throwing. The

'Madame No No', porcelain sculpture, assembled entirely from wheel-thrown sections which are then altered and carved to complete the image, 20.5 cm high, by Dalit Tayar (Israel), 1993.
Photograph by Wolf Böwig.

Right Porcelain dish, decorated with latex resist pattern and copper red, fired to cone 10 (1300°C) in a ceramic fibre kiln with a reducing atmosphere, 35 cm × 10 cm, by Alistair Whyte, 1993.
Photograph by Avon Colour Studio.

Cups and saucers, wheel-thrown porcelain, 15 cm × 8 cm, by Prue Venables (Australia), 1993.

bending is often severe enough to cause cracking if the timing is not accurately judged. She finds that porcelain tolerates such movement only when precisely ready. If this pressure is applied too early in the drying it can collapse, while adjustments made to the form too late leads to cracking.

When **Alistair Whyte** (Australia) went to study in Japan soon after completing his ceramics diploma at the Bendigo Institute in Victoria, he had to make considerable adjustments to his throwing technique. Writing about his experiences in *Pottery in Australia* (Vol. 27, No. 4), he explained that all throwing of porcelain, apart from extremely large pots, is done off the hump. Many of the wheels used in Kyoto are fixed speed wheels and so the work is taken off the wheel while it is still spinning, and potters sit cross-legged in front of their wheels. The direction of the wheel spin is also opposite to Western potters, i.e. clockwise. Having initially learned to throw in Australia, most of these habits were too radical for me to change in a hurry, so I chose compromise and throw my own way using Japanese throwing techniques.

He goes on to emphasise the importance of making specific tools for a particular function in the throwing process.

When making a set of tools for, say, a saucer, the first tool made is the *tonbo* (or dragonfly) measure. This is made of bamboo and measures the inside depth and width of what is being made. It is to this measure that the throwing ribs are made. There are usually two, these being the *dango* (which is made from fine grained, softer wood) and the *hera* (usually made from *sakura* or *nashi* i.e. cherry or pear) which is the finishing rib. The *sanfo* is the throwing rib, being about the thickness of a finger, and is used to draw the clay up to the correct height and thickness. The *hera* is carved back to a fine edge and is purely a final shaping and finishing tool.

Making a new set of tools for each item proved to be an excellent learning experience for Whyte. It was also an essential practice because his master's tools were designed for throwing with the wheel spinning in the opposite direction.

Slipcasting

Slipcasting multiples is the method of production mostly associated with industry but it is also used with great success by studio potters, in particular those who choose to work with those white clay bodies which are lacking in plasticity. The prime concern of such potters is less likely to be mass production than the opportunity to prepare basic forms for further treatment such as by carving, piercing, individually decorating or altering in some other way. Porcelain lends itself as well to this process as does any fine-particled clay but it is especially appropriate for working with its close relation, bone china.

Bone china is renowned for its supreme whiteness and translucency. It differs from so-called 'true' porcelain both

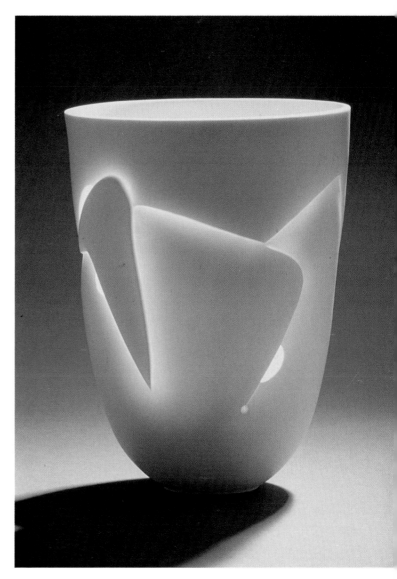

Vessel form in bone china, slipcast, carved and altered, 20 cm high, by Angela Verdon, 1992.

Bowl in bone china, slipcast, carved and altered, 20 cm diameter, by Angela Verdon, 1992.

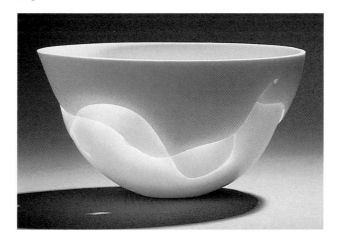

in its composition, which includes approximately 50 per cent bone ash (calcium phosphate produced from calcined cattle bones), and in its relationship with glaze. Whereas, normally, the porcelain body and glaze fuse together as one at high temperatures, bone china is fired to maturity in the bisque firing around 1250°C and a 'skin' of glaze is fired on at a much lower temperature. Bone china first appeared in England towards the end of the 18th century. It was the result of experiments attempting to match the translucent properties and refinement of Chinese porcelains which had captivated and defeated European potters for many years. Its manufacture was confined almost exclusively to England and factories in Stoke-on-Trent and elsewhere made great quantities of wares in this material.

Sandra Black (Australia) piercing bone china bowl forms with an electric drill, 1989.

Industrially-produced English bone china remains in popular demand all over the world but it is a medium that presents the studio potter with particular problems. Due to the necessarily high proportion of bone ash in a typical bone china body, it lacks the plasticity of porcelain and it is, therefore, mainly slipcast in plaster moulds. Models for casting moulds can be made in clay but plaster makes better original models. Solid lumps of plaster can be turned on a horizontal lathe to give a perfectly smooth surface or rectangular shapes can be cast between sheets of glass. Facets, twists and other details are introduced by hand carving or planing the plaster model. Careful attention must be paid to the profile when modelling for a one-piece mould to ensure it will release the eventual slipcast form. Multi-part moulds can also be used but seams are difficult to conceal unless the mould can be designed so that the seam runs along the edge of the model or where positive changes of direction occur. This is because seams will show up as raised lines on cast bone china after firing no matter how well they have been fettled away before placing in the kiln. Newly made moulds should be allowed to dry naturally because they can crack if exposed to excessive heat.

A few potters, notably Glenys Barton and Jacqueline Poncelet in England during the 1970s, attempted to explore the potential of slipcast bone china for individual work. In the following decades others, attracted by its response to light, were persuaded to experiment and develop their own answers to the inherent practical problems encountered. The scale of the work tended to be small, mainly slipcast vessels of various simple shapes made in one piece dropout moulds. **Angela Verdon** (UK) began working with bone china in the 1970s and over the years she has skilfully worked in this medium, having devised her own, somewhat time-consuming methods in order to creatively exploit its translucent properties. Her extremely thin, slipcast vessels are often pierced with intricate patterns of tracery so that they resemble lace. Occasionally, different colours of bone china slip were cast in layers through which she then carved her designs. Later work is less geometrically treated and the carving has assumed a more organic, linear character with patterns that flow around simple bowl shapes. When illuminated from above, light passes easily through the piece and gives extra brilliant emphasis to these sinuous lines so that the piece takes on a quilted appearance. Although Verdon is still very much concerned with luminosity and purity in her work, she now executes most of it in a slipcast porcelain body from Limoges and her current developments with this are more fully described on page 109.

The first contact that **Sandra Black** (Australia) had with bone china was at Canberra School of Art in 1983. She worked, initially, with a casting body fired to 1280°C but changed to using another which required a lower temperature in 1984 because it offered a better response to colour and the advantage of cheaper fuel costs. Later, having resolved problems previously experienced with colour, she returned to using the higher firing bone china. She prepares her casting slip with great care and describes the procedure as follows:

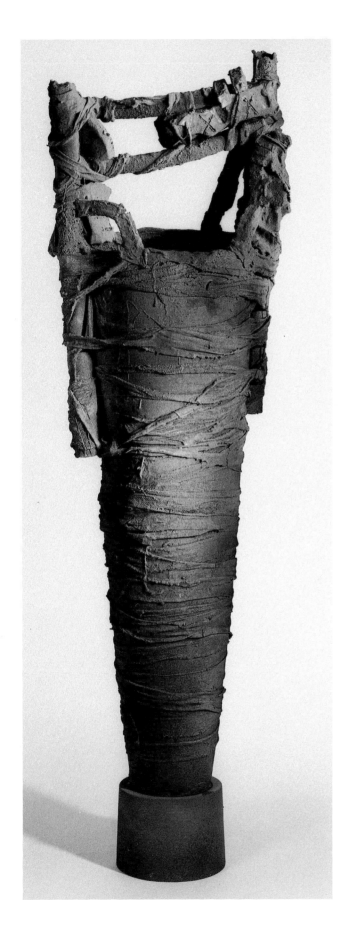

1. Measure the water at 600 ml to every kilo of dry material.
2. Add deflocculent to water. Dispex, sodium silicate or soda ash are used singly, or in combination.
3. Mix dry ingredients together, add to the water and stir using a power drill with a paint mixer attachment to ensure even dispersal. At this point a little more deflocculent may be added to increase fluidity if the slip is too thick. Care is essential because if there is too much deflocculent it will have the reverse effect.
4. The slip is then sieved and, if required, ball milled for 2–6 hours.
5. The slip is then tested by casting a small mould. Its condition is correct if it fulfills the following two parameters:

(a) casting time between 5–10 minutes = 2–4 mm in thickness.

(b) it should drain cleanly away without shaking the mould.

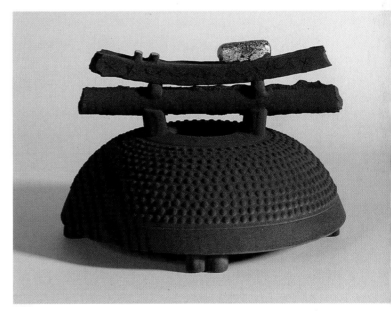

Teapot, 'Thai Memories', made in black bone china with applied gold leaf by Sandra Black, 1991. The bone china slip is stained with iron chromate 7%, black iron oxide 7% and cobalt carbonate 3.5% and, as these are strong fluxes, the normal firing temperature is lowered to cone 4–cone 5 depending on the firing schedule.
Photograph by Victor France.

Left 'Wrapped Vessel Form' in black bone china, 70 cm high, by Sandra Black, 1990.
Photograph by Victor France.

The slip is stored in an airtight container and then left to settle for 24 hours before use. It must be thoroughly stirred (being careful not to trap air bubbles which causes pinholes to develop) before each cast is taken.

Ready-made slips can be obtained from pottery suppliers for potters who find their preparation tedious. **Sasha Wardell** (UK and France) is one who feels that the material is difficult enough to cast and fire and she welcomes the opportunity to use prepared slips that help to simplify the process of working with bone china. She still finds it necessary to pass the slip through a 60s mesh sieve and to adjust its fluidity with a few drops of sodium Dispex deflocculant. Her pieces are cast for 1–2 minutes before draining the mould. Spare clay is then cut away and the cast left to

White 'wrapped vessel form' in bone china, 20 cm high, by Sandra Black, 1986. Muslin, nets and other textile fabrics soaked in slip can be wrapped or draped around clay forms and fired to retain its appearance. The organic fibres burn away to leave the fragile 'skin' of fired slip in place.
Photograph by Victor France.

Below   Three stoppered vases in slipcast bone china decorated with airbrushed ceramic stains, 15 cm and 21 cm high, by Sasha Wardell, 1990.

stiffen overnight (in order to reduce the risk of distortion) before removing it from the mould.

Normally, it is important to ensure that the mould is clean and dry for casting but, if it is so very dry that the cast releases while draining excess slip, then it can be dampened slightly beforehand. In any case, casts will release at different rates according to the dryness of the mould and the atmospheric conditions at the time. On no account should attempts be made to dry the cast too quickly. Sandra Black stresses the need for patience at this stage because bone china has a notorious 'memory'. Sasha Wardell also speaks of this problem which she describes as the 'idiosyncratic nature of bone china' not only in coming to terms with its high shrinkage rate but also with its tendency to warp alarmingly. Wardell finds this 'both intriguing and frustrating' at the same time. She referred me to an article she wrote for *Ceramic Review* Vol. 111 (1988) in which she described this memory manifesting itself when a cast has been knocked or dented in the green state. This will be 'remembered', despite any attempt to repair the damage, and revert to its distorted form in the high firing. This is a feature of other thinly potted porcelain bodies but its effects are more exaggerated in bone china. It is a characteristic which Wardell believes 'could be exploited and

Pair of jugs, with blue/pink/white or grey/black/white airbrushed decoration, in slipcast bone china, 12.5 cm high, by Sasha Wardell, 1992.

Teapot with cups and saucers in slipcast bone china, with airbrushed ceramic stains under a clear glaze, teapot 19 cm high, cups 8 cm high, by Sasha Wardell 1988.
Photograph by Hedges Wright.

Wide-based vase in slipcast bone china, made from two sections, with airbrushed decoration in yellows/orange/blue-grey/white, 19 cm high, by Sasha Wardell, 1988.

therefore open up a whole new way of working with china, if the "surprise" element is desired'. However, she prefers to remain more fully in control in order to secure reliable results.

Sasha Wardell's thinly cast forms are fired three times with, firstly, a 'soft' firing to 1000°C after which the work is sanded with fine grade *wet 'n dry* paper. Originally, she omitted this preliminary stage but too many pieces were lost when being handled and cleaned up while still in the raw state. The next firing is taken to 1260°C and soaked at that temperature for one and a half hours. This allows the body to mature and achieve perfect whiteness and translucency before decoration is applied. Finally, the work is fired to 1080°C to fix the coloured stains.

Sandra Black, on the other hand, uses an even lower bisque firing to only 750°C before sanding the carved surface decoration of her particular bone china pieces. If they are taken to a temperature above 800°C the bisque ware becomes too hard. She has fired bone china in both electric and gas kilns but warns that a heavy reducing atmosphere can cause grey areas to appear. However, further firing in oxidation overcomes this problem. She has found that bone china will withstand rapid temperature changes in the initial part of the firing cycle and in the latter stages of cooling. 'I have fired up to 720°C in one and a half hours for lustres and then opened the kiln at 600°C while cooling. One piece was fired three times in one day without cracking.' Such work is on a very small scale so pieces will accept these thermal stresses more easily. Her larger forms with

various draped elements have also survived fast glaze firings to 1260°C in $3\frac{1}{2}$ to $4\frac{1}{2}$ hours without cracking.

Among Sandra Black's more impressive pieces are a number of tall vessels wrapped in textile bandages soaked in slip. The taller pieces, mounted on thrown porcelain bases, have an air of mystery and appear almost threatening. Coloured slips are airbrushed on to these forms while they are leatherhard and then fired to cones 7–8. Other pieces are assembled from slipcast elements and airbrushed with a black slip at the bisque stage and then given a fast firing to cones 7–8 in six hours.

Recipes

Sandra Black relies on two different recipes for making her bone china casting slips. The first of these was developed by Dr Owen Rye at Canberra School of Art. It is normally fired to cones 8–9 and consists of the following materials:

(B6 Body)			
Eckalite No. 1 kaolin	30	parts by weight	
Bone ash (natural)	40	"	"	"
Potash feldspar	22.8	"	"	"
Silica	2.2	"	"	"

These ingredients are mixed with 600 ml of water together with 2 g Dispex and 1 g sodium silicate to each kilogram of dry material. In making her black stained bone

Large based vase, with delicate blues/pinks/white airbrushed decoration, in slipcast bone china made from two sections joined together, 21 cm high, by Sasha Wardell, 1990.

Three Vessel Forms, tallest vase 25 cm high, by Anne Hogg, 1993. Wheel-thrown bone china with carved decoration. The black spots in two of the pieces are from rust particles kneaded into the body in order to relieve the extreme whiteness. Fired in an electric kiln to 1270°C.

Teapot with overhead handle, porcelain with dry ash glaze fired to cone 10 with salt, 28 cm high, by Neil Moss (USA), 1993. *Photograph by Brian Goodman.*

china slip she adds 7 per cent iron chromate, 7 per cent black iron oxide and 3.5 per cent cobalt carbonate to the mixture. However, it should be noted that these oxides act as powerful fluxes so the firing temperature may need to be lowered to around cones 4–5 according to the firing pattern adopted. As with all ceramic materials, great care should be exercised during their preparation and use. Danger from ingested dust and toxic elements can be avoided by wearing protective clothing such as masks and rubber gloves.

The second slip is a recipe devised by Mike Kusnik at the Western Australia Institute of Technology in Perth. It is fired to cones 6–7.

Cresta BB kaolin	40 parts by weight			mixed with water and deflocculents in the same proportions as above.
Bone ash (natural)	40	"	"	"
Nepheline syenite	20	"	"	"

Casting slip can be recycled but care should be taken to avoid contaminating the new batch. Sandra Black suggests adding no more than 20 per cent scrap to any new mix of slip and recommends including 0.1 per cent barium car-

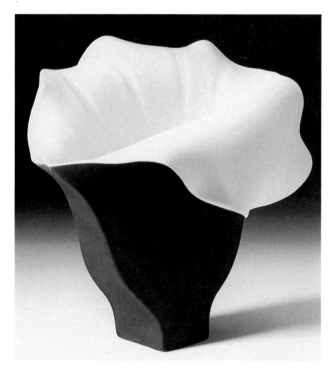

Slipcast and altered bone china vessel inspired by natural form, 20 cm high, Angela Mellor, 1990. Fired in an electric kiln to 1240°C, the form has been encouraged to deform gradually during the firing by reshaping part of the rim.
Photograph by James Austin.

bonate in order to neutralise sulphates which can cause peeling faults.

Bone china is generally acknowledged to be very difficult, if not impossible, to throw because it lacks plasticity due to the low percentage of clay in the body. However, **Anne Hogg** (UK) has been using a throwable bone china for several years. It is prepared to a recipe developed by her husband, Chris. They live and work in a quiet Cornish village close to some of the finest china clay deposits in the world. The recipe for this plastic body is based on traditional ingredients as follows:

Bone ash	50
Super Standard Porcelain china clay* (kaolin)	25
MF4 flux**	25
Westone-H white bentonite	2.5%
	added to the above.

Anne Hogg has found no real disadvantage throwing with this bone china body. Experience has taught her how best to come to terms with its individual character and so to anticipate the results. She has found that thrown shapes which are tall and narrow survive better than those which are more open. Shorter, wider pots having a V-shaped section are less likely to slump or warp in the kiln than those having a U-shaped profile. Throwing, turning, trimming, carving and reshaping in the pre-bisque state can be carried out in much the same way as with a standard porcelain. She kneads the plastic china body in a spiral motion before making it into a very round ball and *placing* it on a batt on the wheel. Centring is done quickly with hands and clay well lubricated with water because the clay must not be allowed to drag or spirals will appear in the fired pot. Sudden movements are to be avoided. Drying must be slow and gradual. The bisque firing is only to 840°C so that the pieces can be polished smooth with wet 'n dry silicon carbide paper ('any higher makes sanding hard work').

Firing is conducted in either gas or electric kilns to 1270°C in about ten hours. The temperature rise between 1170°C and 1270°C is carefully monitored to take an hour (to minimise the risk of distortion) because it is at this stage

*This special china clay, produced by English China Clays, is strong and plastic with a low iron content. It is distributed by Whitfield and Son, 23 Albert Street, Newcastle, Staffordshire, England. This company also markets the Westone-H white bentonite.

**The commercially prepared MF4 flux could be substituted by either Cornish stone or a combination of 15 per cent soda feldspar and 10 per cent quartz.

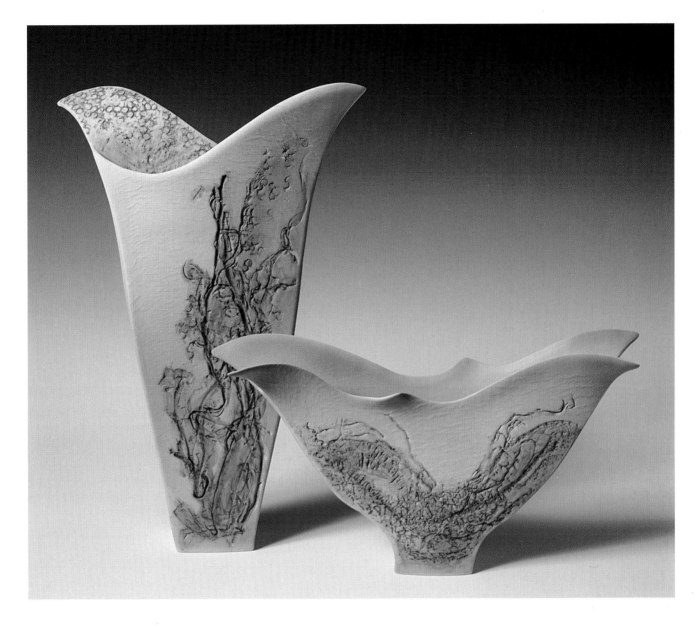

Slab-built porcelain vases with impressed decoration and ceramic
stains fired in an electric kiln to 1240°C, 27 cm and 14 cm high, by
Angela Mellor.

that 20 per cent shrinkage occurs. Kiln shelves coated with
Molochite (a china clay grog made by English China Clays)
allow the pot bases to shrink and move without snagging.
The kiln is held at the top temperature for a soaking period
of half an hour to improve the translucency of the china but
the pieces can suddenly melt and collapse like glass if that
temperature is exceeded.

Having been given a small sample of this bone china
body with which to experiment, I discovered that it is
creamily smooth while throwing. Small shapes can be
made with very thin walls if the approach to throwing is

direct and uncomplicated. I found that larger forms needed
to be left with rather more thickness but any excess material can be pared away by turning later.

It was the ultimate whiteness, thinness and translucency
of bone china that attracted **Angela Mellor** (UK) to
experiment with slipcast forms based on similar shapes that
she had previously produced by slab building with porcelain. She finds that the

tactile quality of bone china is very appealing and its
marble-like surface has a warm sensuality about it. Slip
casting bone china allows me to make ultra thin shapes
which are extremely translucent, pure and so white that
ordinary porcelain seems almost grey in comparison.
The supreme whiteness makes colours so much more
vibrant.

A part of Ole Lislerud's studio showing some large porcelain panels, inscribed with the Norwegian Constitution, waiting to be made up into a section of the architectural piece commissioned for the new Supreme Court Building in Oslo. The final work consists of two columns 32 metres high by 4 metres wide covered with thin porcelain slabs with a total area of 250 square metres. 1993.

She prefers to make asymmetric forms and does not use 'setters' to support the pieces in the kiln because she encourages the forms to 'move', to become more fluid during the firing and thus closer in character to the organic forms of nature that inspire much of her work. Alumina is packed inside her pots and around the base to prevent them sticking to the shelf.

Architectural applications of porcelain

The large sculptural works of **Ole Lislerud** (Norway) provide convincing evidence of the confident expertise with which modern studio potters have exorcised those peculiar problems, real or imagined, in handling porcelain. To be able to make, manipulate, decorate and successfully fire a flat sheet of porcelain no more than 3 mm thick and with a surface area up to one metre long by 80 cm wide is no mean feat. But to complete an architectural commission for the Supreme Court building in Oslo, which entailed the production of 250 square metres of equally thin porcelain slabs inscribed with the full text of the Norwegian Constitution, is a remarkable achievement. Lislerud was awarded this commission when he won an open competition for the

work in 1992. His winning design consisted of two tall columns each 32 metres high by four metres wide and curved as a section of a circle. The columns are covered with porcelain slabs, 300 mm × 650 mm × 3 mm, upon which he displays calligraphic inscriptions using a technique he has developed similar to making a lithographic print.

Ole Lislerud was born in South Africa in 1950 and educated in Norway where, initially, he studied Languages and Law at Oslo University prior to obtaining a masters degree in Fine Art at the National Academy of Art and Design in

Left A model of the 'Portal Avenue' architectural commission carried out by Ole Lislerud for the new Supreme Court Building in Oslo, Norway, 1993.

A rectangular piece of plasterboard edged with wooden battens acting as retaining walls is tilted to ensure an even flow of porcelain slip poured by Ole Lislerud to make one of his large panels.

Oslo where he now teaches. He explains the inspiration for his work as arising from his study of archaic forms and symbolism. His continuous search for appropriate aesthetic criteria to interpret and express his response to this interest led him to experiment with tablets or slabs and composite forms built up into columns and portals. Combining sculptural and graphic elements together in his search for artistic expression fascinates him. He feels that manipulating the smooth porcelain surface with lines and marks like calligraphy is essential to the process of emphasising his symbolic intentions. He states that, 'despite the minimalistic form, there is constant experimentation regarding surface treatment which is expressive and spontaneous in character. Thus a tension is created between form and surface – between the archaic and the contemporary.'

Lislerud firmly believes in the importance of acquiring knowledge and understanding through systematic research. The methods used to make the components to construct his sculptural installations were developed during a ten-year period of intensive experiment. Casting plaster on polished marble produces extremely smooth boards 25 mm thick. These plasterboards are then used to cast porcelain by pouring slip on them from one position while they are inclined at a sufficient angle for the slip to flow evenly. The size of the plasterboards matches that of the shelves in Lislerud's kiln. The procedure of actually casting thin slabs of porcelain is the most difficult part of the whole process of manufacture because small mistakes can create big problems. The most common faults resulting from incorrect casting are: cracking, warping and distortion with corners curling to destroy the flatness. Tilting the plasterboard while pouring slip from the top edge helps to avoid subsequent cracking. Lislerud discovered that pouring slip in a more random way shows up the drying process as cracks appear along the joins and overlaps as the

Top left Ole Lislerud pours a thin layer of porcelain slip containing titanium dioxide on to a plasterboard previously coated with a black stained slip through which calligraphy has been inscribed. This results in a yellow linear inscription on a black ground. Many layers can be added in this way to build up a composition. 1993.

Centre Ole Lislerud unloading one of his large (100 cm × 80 cm) porcelain panels, fired to 1300°C, from the kiln. He can fire as many as three of these stacked on top of each other without warping. 1993.

Bottom left Ole Lislerud painting a heraldic device on a once-fired porcelain panel with a red glaze to be re-fired to 800°C. 1993.

Right 'Script', a monoprinted porcelain tile 300 mm × 600 mm × 3 mm, by Ole Lislerud, 1993. With the colour and texture built up from several layers of porcelain slips containing rutile, titanium, iron oxide, and black stains. This piece is fired in reduction to 1280°C but left unglazed.
Photograph by Lislerud.

porcelain dries rapidly in contact with the plaster. Hence the need to ensure an uninterrupted flow of slip to cover the board. Wooden battens are placed around the edges of the plasterboard to contain the slip to a depth of 3 mm. The battens are not fixed to the board because he finds that they will maintain their position without moving while the slip is poured. After ten minutes the slip has dried sufficiently for the battens to be removed. A thin-bladed knife slices between the batten and the porcelain and also under the slab to loosen it. 'If this is not done carefully it will definitely warp.' Ten minutes later the slab is pulled gently away from the plaster, first one end and then lifting from the other. The newly loosened slabs are then placed on paper-lined plasterboard (as used for ceilings and partitions in the building trade. 'Fantastic for drying porcelain and keeping it flat!) of the same size and left to dry.

When trying to speed the production of his porcelain slabs, Lislerud abandoned the normal drying procedure and found that he could transport the newly cast slabs directly into the kiln. By applying a thin coating of aluminium oxide dust to the leatherhard slabs before turning them over onto the 'builders' plasterboard' they would slide easily onto the kiln shelves. 'These slabs turned out to be completely flat and, because they were leatherhard and only 3 mm thick, none were broken when stacking and sliding into position.' On the other hand, completely dry slabs are sometimes 'so fragile that they can crack just by looking at them!'

By carving into the plaster slab before pouring slip, precise, surface relief marks and patterns are produced on the smooth porcelain. Another technique is to incise through a very thin layer of coloured porcelain (e.g. black) slip applied to the surface of the plaster. A different coloured slip (e.g. yellow) is then painted over those incised marks before the final thickness of porcelain is poured. The first layer of thin slip tends to stick partially to the plaster ('which can produce very interesting visual effects') when the slab is released while a thicker layer of slip gives a more even colour. Multiple layers with different colours can be applied and scraped through to form quite complex designs. Lislerud is able, also, to change the scale and character of his calligraphy by 'writing' with a slip trailer, drawing directly on to the plaster with either coloured slips or specially formulated glazes prior to casting the porcelain slab. These designs trailed on to plaster will release completely with the cast slip. If necessary, he will leave such compositions to dry and be cast hours or even days later.

Lislerud's porcelain is fired to 1280°C in a reducing atmosphere. He obtains the raw material from Porsgrund

Dale Zheutlin working with large porcelain slabs in her studio. She avoids distorting the slabs by working on top of boards covered with plastic and newspaper. 1993.
Photograph by Nick Saraco.

Porselaensfabrikk, the only porcelain factory in Norway and which fires this same body to 1400°C. Occasionally he has fired as many as three of his thin porcelain slabs on top of each other without suffering any loss through cracking or warping. However, warping can happen from time to time and his remedy is to refire the slabs with pieces of broken kiln shelf on top to act as weights and, combined with a higher temperature, they will flatten out. Where there is no glazed area on the slab, it can be fired upside down to accomplish the same end. Some of the slabs are subjected to a final firing of 800°C with low temperature glazes giving bright colours.

Large-scale wall sculptures in porcelain are by no means the sole prerogative of European ceramicists and at least one American, **Dale Zheutlin**, has completed a number of important architectural commissions in this medium. Designing for specific sites involves collaborating closely with architects, interior designers, art consultants and

'Archisites' porcelain wall sculpture 420 cm × 420 cm (14′ × 14′), by Dale Zheutlin, 1993. Decorated with coloured stains and glazes, commissioned by JMB Properties, New York. Fired in oxidation. *Photograph by Paul Warchol*

'Twin Spans', porcelain wall panel by Dale Zheutlin, 1991,
450 cm × 180 cm (15′ × 6′) (fired in oxidation). Commissioned
by the Delaware River and Bay Authority, Wilmington. The image
is abstracted from the Delaware River Bridge.
Photograph by Andrew Bordwin.

clients representing public agencies and large corporations.
However, she says that it is important for the artist to
retain creative control. She described her experiences in
this kind of work in an article for *Ceramics Monthly* (June
1993) and I am indebted to her and to the magazine for
allowing me to quote some of the salient features involved.
She was awarded a financial grant in 1986 and this allowed
her to experiment and develop the necessary technology
to accomplish the kind of large-scale projects that
interested her.

Handling oversized slabs before they are fired presents
a problem. They are difficult to turn without stretching
or bending, so I dry them on boards covered with plastic and newspaper. Working directly on the floor, I
change the top layer of newspaper every six hours. The
clay is weighed down with boards for the first 24 hours,
then air dried.

In order to avoid firing difficulties, Zheutlin found that it
was necessary to work out her design in segments to be
fired together on site.

I started with slabs $\frac{3}{8}$ inch thick and no more than
18 × 24 inches overall, because that was the maximum
size that could fit into my 28 inch, octagonal kiln. These
segments were fired on edge, four at a time, then
regrouped as wall units. I now have a top loader, rectangular electric kiln, which offers flexibility in experimentation and a degree of economy, plus it will fire
larger slabs.

As her work evolved, Zheutlin changed from concentrating on 'flat, planar surfaces without colour to more
dimensional construction with colour developed from a
variety of glazes and stains. I began to cut the slabs, then
put them back together by overlapping, tilting, inter-
secting and reassembling.

Experiments and glaze tests were conducted with the
help of an assistant to establish a palette of 32 colours.
Taking into account a five per cent shrinkage rate, the slabs
were rolled out and allowed to stiffen before laying them
on the floor in preparation for carving, incising, the appli-

'Twin Span', porcelain wall panel designed and made by Dale Zheutlin, 1991. Mounted in the headquarters building of the Delaware River and Bay Authority.
Photograph by Andrew Bordwin.

cation of stains and glazes, and to be cut into manageable sections. They were left covered and weighted until dry and then stored in vertical racks. 'After firing, the sections were assembled on armatures so that a template could be made to serve as a hanging guide. I always try to do a trial hanging in my studio, although this is not always possible for very large projects.'

One of Zheutlin's most exciting commissions was a 15 feet wide abstract interpretation of the Delaware River Bridge for the Delaware River and Bay Authority.

It did not begin auspiciously. I was happy to receive an invitation from the art consultant to submit a competitive proposal for a sculpture to hang on the wall at authority headquarters. But the committee of architects and engineers who had designed the Delaware River Bridge had expressed a preference for something representational, whereas I normally work in the abstract. The only way I would stand a chance for such a project

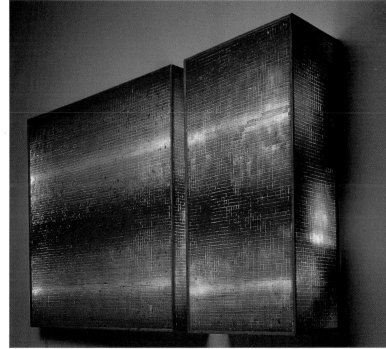

'Time Slice', translucent, inlaid porcelain mosaic panels with lights mounted behind, 120 cm × 60 cm × 240 cm approximately, by Curtis Benzle, 1980.
Photograph by Curtis Benzle.

55

'Night Landscape', porcelain panel with inlaid coloured porcelains mounted with silver on brass, fired to 1260°C in reduction, 55 cm × 30 cm, by Sony Manning (Australia), 1994.
Photograph by David McArthur.

'Weaving a Carpet' translucent porcelain tiles pierced and 'stitched' together to create a larger image, by Arne Åse.

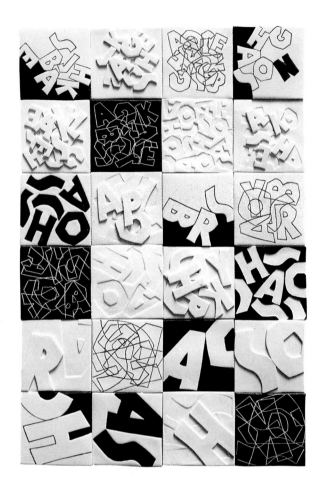

Black and white tile panel in porcelain and mounted on wood, 78cm × 58 cm, fired to 1250°C, by Mary White.

would be to make sketches (not slides) and a model of my concept, which I express-mailed to the art consultant. Imagine my shock to learn that my package had arrived the day *after* her initial presentation to the committee. Nevertheless, she was interested enough to show it at her second presentation and I was asked to meet with the committee to explain my proposal.

Following what she describes as 'a probing and stressful interview', Zheutlin was awarded the commission and was invited to view the bridge 'from the top down'. Donning a

hard hat and protective clothing she ascended to the small elevator 440 feet to the top of the south east tower. 'Its gently swaying motion was in rhythmic harmony with my shaking knees and euphoric head.'

She discovered that working for a public body was quite unlike anything she had previously experienced. 'It required a lengthy contract, $1 million in liability insurance and month by month documentation of my progress (including such details as how many pounds of clay I was using, and the firing schedules).' In addition, her proposal had been complicated by the fact that she was intending 'to work in a clearly unclaylike fashion'. Although she had submitted several options, the committee had chosen the most difficult and most sculptural of the models presented.

The sculpture needed to be understood from a distance of 100 feet by people entering the building but when seen at close quarters 'it had to be as precise and accurate as the bridge itself.' Zheutlin wanted to select a position as if in the middle of the twin spans of the bridge and she set about

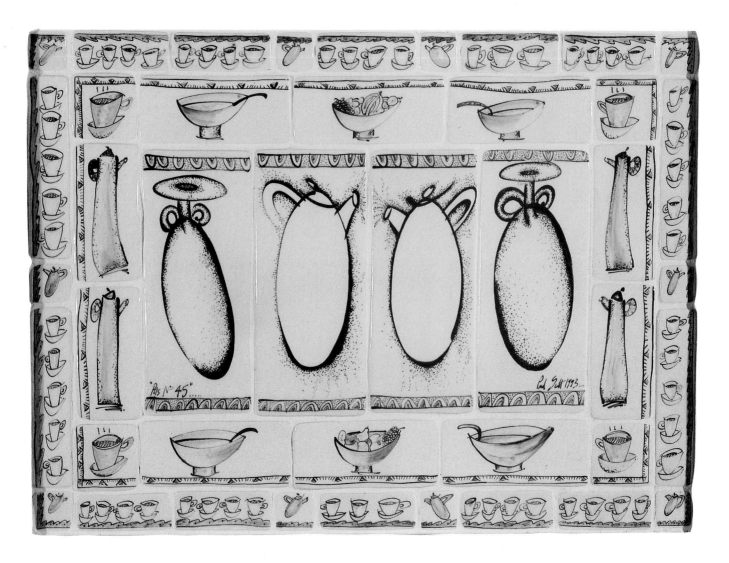

'Pots No:45', porcelain panel (60 cm × 40 cm) with pen and 'ceramic ink' wash and underglaze colours, fired to 1200°C, by Paul Scott, 1993.
Photograph by Andrew Morris.

preparing preliminary studies using archival photographs and then a computer to re-plot the image in perspective. 'Ultimately, it required five sculptural elements fitted together to create the dynamic tension of the bridge.'

The architects and engineers monitored Zheutlin's progress and she felt that she wanted 'to compliment their achievement with a wall sculpture that captured the blue light, the wind, the reflection off the water, the strength and beauty of the span, and my own unforgettable experience at the top of the tower'.

Smaller tiles have long been used to cover extremely large and often complex architectural structures but porcelain is a less familiar material for this purpose than either earthenware or stoneware. One of the most amazing uses of stoneware tiles is that of clothing the multiple arching roof of the Sydney Opera House. Porcelain is being increasingly used for more decorative purposes despite its inherent difficulties. **Paul Scott** (UK), for example, uses combinations of porcelain tiles to create panels and murals rather like a painter might use a white surface for drawing and painting. He prepares a mixture of ceramic stains suspended in water and proceeds to draw directly on to the porcelain bisque with a pen. This method produces fine linear drawings which he supplements with thin washes of similar ceramic 'inks'.

INSPIRATION IN THE DESIGN OF FORM

Sculptural objects

Potters have long exploited the marvellous versatility of porcelain for fashioning intricate, smoothly finished shapes from the whimsical to the more provocative and esoteric of three-dimensional expressions. **Carrol Swan** (New Zealand) has always worked with white clays but she enjoys the plasticity and extra fine smoothness of porcelain that allows her to pinch it into thin sheets or to build open mesh forms woven from rolls of clay. She made a series of grid-like basket pieces suggested by the kind of metal grids used to reinforce concrete in building construction. Her aim was to recreate an image of that encrusted metal in an open 'vessel' to which she could add 'precious objects, such as saggar fired eggs, rods

and spheres, in gleaming gold, platinum and copper, as a contrast between the old and rusting and the bright and new'. She began by actually coating a metallic mesh with porcelain slip but found that the metal slumped at about 1000°C and the slip had a tendency to chip off. The problem was solved by using extruded porcelain coils which could be easily bent and joined without cracking 'as long as you work quickly' and which became hard and strong at high mid-range temperatures. The unglazed grid baskets cradle slipcast spheres lustred in gold and platinum and whose 'polished' surfaces display curving linear patterns in

'Porcelain Basket', handbuilt from extruded, stained black porcelain, with spheres and rods marbled with gold and platinum lustres, fired in an electric kiln to 1180°C (final lustre glaze firing to 750°C), 15 cm high, 32 cm wide, 26 cm deep, by Carrol Swan, 1993.

reflecting the surrounding grid. Some pieces mimic other materials like paper and boiled sweets. These last were first produced in response to an invitation to participate in a Halloween exhibition. 'Paper' bags sprawl invitingly open spilling their contents across the table. The convincing 'sweets' are finished with underglaze and onglaze colours, enamels and lustres. Some are inlaid with body stains or are made of unglazed agateware.

Porcelain lends itself to working in such extremely fine detail that it has been used for modelling figures, animals, plants etc. for centuries. Victorian dolls often had porcelain heads so delicately modelled and coloured as to appear almost lifelike. Modern potters also have enjoyed this facility to imitate or recreate nature in porcelain. When increasing numbers began to rediscover porcelain in the second half of the 20th century, it seemed appropriate that they should work in small scale. This was due in part to the

Top left 'Minties', a 'bag of sweets', handbuilt, painted with underglazes and with onglaze enamels, by Carrol Swan, 1993. The 'bag' was fired to 1140°C bisque, painted with underglaze colours and then fired to 1020°C. The 'sweets' were fired to 1280°C and painted with onglaze enamels. Base size 10 cm × 23 cm.

Top right 'V Grid Basket', handbuilt with extruded porcelain coils stained black, by Carrol Swan. Fired in oxidation to 1180°C. The spheres and rods are lustre glazed with gold and platinum or with red crackle glaze fired to 750°C. 29 cm high, 33 cm wide.

Right Porcelain 'Head', 43 cm × 24 cm excluding the pedestal, by Gyorgy Fusz (Hungary), 1992. Made by preparing a plaster cast taken from a live model. The cast is then altered before plastic porcelain is pressed into it. The piece is fired, unglazed, to 1260°C in a wood burning kiln. *Photograph by Wolf Böwig.*

Teapot with lizard decoration, wheel-thrown porcelain with pieces of
porcelain added to the surface and then carved, turquoise celadon
glaze, 25.5 cm high, by Elaine Coleman, 1993.

perceived technical difficulties and partly in deference to it. The material was so different from the coarse, heavy-looking stonewares which had dominated the field of studio ceramics since the Second World War that it demanded a new approach. It could be easily pinched into paper-thin pieces and then manipulated and twisted into shapes that resembled natural forms whose delicate appearance belied their fired strength. From the 1960s onward natural forms like flowers, fungi, birds, fish, and a cavalcade of fantasy creatures have been produced in great numbers. Most are little more than shallow, decorative objects of no artistic significance destined to join the multitude of twee kitsch from previous generations.

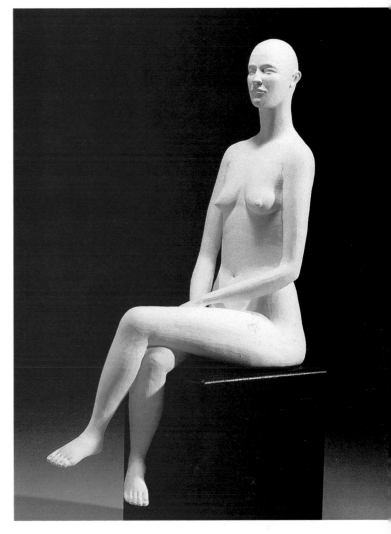

'Seated Woman', porcelain sculpture, assembled entirely from wheel-thrown sections which are then altered and carved to complete the form, 29 cm high excluding the pedestal, by Dalit Tayar (Israel), 1993. *Photograph by Wolf Böwig.*

Slab-built porcelain pot with impressed texture and green glaze, by Peter Beard.

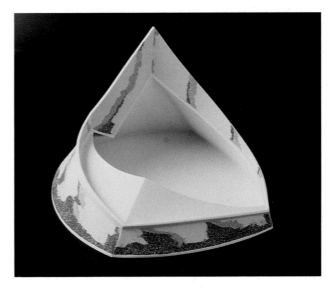

Sculptural Form, handbuilt from multi-coloured, laminated and inlaid porcelain slabs and fired to 1280°C in an electric kiln, approximately 25 cm within the square base, by Saskia Koster, 1991.

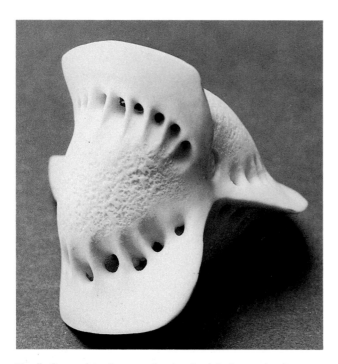

Handbuilt porcelain object, unglazed and polished, carved and pierced, fired to 1260°C in oxidation 10 cm long, by Maggie Barnes, 1991.
Private collection in Germany. Photograph by Maggie Barnes.

A number of distinguished English potters, attracted to porcelain by its fine working properties, proceeded to exploit it with imagination and distinctive flair. Foremost among them were Peter Simpson and Mary Rogers. Although their work was inspired by, or made reference to, organic forms, it rose far above the mere imitation of nature. Simpson's work in the mid-1970s evoked ripe fruits and seed pods with smooth spherical forms split apart to reveal interiors tightly packed with wafer-thin sheets. This contrast between simple exterior and crowded contents was an exploration not only of the aesthetics of form but also of the very nature of porcelain itself. Similarly, Mary Rogers pinch-built a series small bowls with walls so thin that they could be coaxed into folds and layers to orchestrate the quality of light passing through them rather like the petals of a poppy flower. They were as much a response to the plastic purity and translucency of the material and the process of making as they were a comment on the natural world. These expressions prompted many

'Bow Form', slab-built porcelain carved and pierced, with textured slip decoration, unglazed but polished, by Maggie Barnes, 1987.
Collection Wolf Böwig. Photograph by Wolf Böwig.

imitators, especially among students many of whom produced clusters of frilly, fungoid objects often lacking in understanding, sensitivity or purpose. Other potters chose to combine the contrasting character of heavily grogged stoneware bodies and that of porcelain within one object. Peter Beard (UK) developed a memorable series of pieces incorporating delicately pinched, conglomerate 'growths' of translucent, glazed porcelain erupting from geometrically-shaped black stoneware in a way that gave added emphasis to their respective natures.

Maggie Barnes (UK) worked initially in stoneware but, as her interest focused onto particular areas of the natural world which she found especially inspiring, she realised that only porcelain could provide the means that would enable her to express her feelings about them. 'The material both disciplines and rewards the maker, it is a demand-

Porcelain Bowl, by Maggie Barnes, 1989. Thrown, carved and pierced with the exterior surface covered with textured slip. Unglazed but polished. 12 cm diameter. Fired in an electric kiln to 1260°C. This piece was inspired by a prolonged study of dried, bracket fungus. *Photograph by Hans Friedrichs.*

'Marine Form', unglazed porcelain (polished), with textured slip decoration over the dome, fired to 1260°C in oxidation, 13 cm diameter, by Maggie Barnes.
Collection of Dr Wido Parczyk. Photograph by Maggie Barnes.

'Crater Bowl', handbuilt porcelain with textured slip, carved, 131 cm × 80 cm, by Maggie Barnes.

ing and seductive clay, responding better to coaxing than to a more forceful approach.'

Her fascination with natural objects began early in life.

Since a small child wandering around the beaches and waterways of East Coast with my father, who was a passionate fisherman, I have gathered from the natural world. The child's habit of collecting 'treasures' to hoard at home stayed with me, grew into adulthood with me, delights me still, and is the foundation from which creativity is fed to this day. I was fortunate to have a teacher in those formative years who encouraged me to explore the natural world of my childhood environment, to

'Crater Form', unglazed porcelain with slab base, textured with slip, and coiled, pinched and carved walls, 23 cm × 11 cm, fired to 1260°C in an electric kiln while cradled in a bed of silver sand to support the wide outer rim, by Maggie Barnes, 1992.
Photograph by Wolf Böwig.

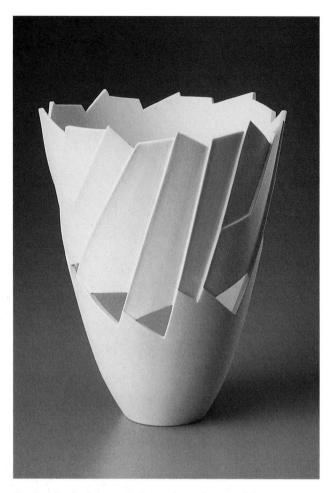

'Fan Bowl', wheel-thrown and carved porcelain vessel, fired in an electric kiln to 1260°C, unglazed and polished, 18 cm high by Rolf Bartz, 1988.

Barnes' explorations and these were made with two thinly rolled slabs of porcelain which were allowed to stiffen slightly in a curved mould and then joined at the rim to create a slim, hollow form. When leatherhard, the rims are reshaped with a scalpel to define the form and these edges are pared away with a stainless steel blade to thin them further. The main body of the piece is then carved and pierced on one or both sides and the openings gently cleaned up and smoothed with a very fine, damp brush. Sometimes the carving extends into and over the rims, altering the form and producing a less symmetrical shape. Pinching and/or paddling with a small wooden spoon helps to extend the narrow edge where the two rims meet before they are refined until they become wafer thin and translucent when fired. These pieces are textured by sponging and brushing thick slip onto selected areas, creating contrasting surfaces and adding tactile and visual interest. Following bisque firing, the pieces are polished with carborundum paper and the process repeated after the final firing. In these small sculptures that fit within the palm of one's hand, Barnes has managed to capture the *essence* of the found objects which inspired them.

Another, more recent development in Barnes' work is a series of pieces which she calls 'Crater Forms'. She describes these as a comment on the raw, more rugged beauty to be observed when elemental forces destroy with far greater energy than the more gradual and gentle process of decay. Because she was 'pushing porcelain to its extremes of tolerance' and encountering difficulties of splitting, cracking and, even, collapse, considerable technical problems had to be resolved before she was able to exercise some degree of control.

The bases of these pieces are made from slabs to which coils of clay are added forming the profiles and contours 'whilst allowing the natural movement of the piece to evolve'. Crumpled kitchen paper is used to pack inside the developing crater and to support the soft walls. Several pieces are tackled at the same time to permit the walls of each to stiffen while work continues on another. Carving around the edges of the 'craters' begins when the forms are leatherhard. The texture of the base form and the outer rim is built up with many layers of smooth and grogged porcelain slip by sponging and brushing. The unglazed porcelain contributes its own special qualities to the final effect.

The vocabulary of visual art often involves the organisation or adjustments in the relationship of opposites such as light to dark, rough to smooth, pattern to plain, colour to non-colour (i.e. to black, white or neutral tones), 'hot' to 'cold' colours, line to mass, positive to negative, open to

make drawings and to use words to record my findings. He remained my dear friend until he died and took pleasure in watching my obsession evolve until it found its natural expression in clay many years later. It has never been my intention to 'copy' nature but to somehow capture and express, through the medium of porcelain, some of that initial wonder and pleasure experienced with eyes and fingers when the 'found object' is first encountered. When someone says *it feels like a . . .* or *it reminds me of . . .* as they turn the porcelain piece in their hands, then I know that part of my own delight has been communicated and shared. It does not matter too much whether we are reminded of the same things or not; the fact that these are echoes of the natural sources which inspired the piece is enough. There is then a kind of dialogue between maker and those who encounter the work.

A series of 'Marine Forms' developed as a result of

Porcelain Form, decorated with black slip and gold lustre, 23 cm high × 24 cm wide × 8 cm deep, by Brigitte Enders (Australia), 1986. *Photograph by Klaus Moje.*

Three Cats made from individually thrown segments of porcelain and assembled by hand, approximately 17 cm high, glaze fired in reduction (gas kiln) to 1360°C, by Beate Kuhn, 1993.
Photograph by Peter Lane.

Porcelain Cat, handbuilt from individually thrown segments and fired in a reducing atmosphere to 1360°C, by Beate Kuhn, 1993.
Photograph by Bernd Gobbels.

closed, inner to outer, tall to short, wide to narrow, horizontal to vertical, etc., etc. We are usually more aware of these elements of design when viewing sculpture or two-dimensional art because 'function', in the sense of domestic application, is no longer part of the equation. On that basis, any three-dimensional sculptural object in ceramic should be judged to stand or fall on its own criteria because the *material* used in its manufacture has no bearing on its acceptance or rejection. However, the position of ceramic sculpture in the world of 'fine' as opposed to 'decorative' art, irrespective of scale or method of manufacture, is subject to continuing debate.

Beate Kuhn (Germany) is well-known for her imaginative sculptural vessel and animal forms constructed from multiple wheel-thrown sections which are assembled and fired to 1340°C in a gas kiln. She displays a mastery of technique that few can rival. As many as 50 separate pieces may be used to build one of her amusing cats but, despite the complexity of their construction, the artist has managed to capture the 'essence' of the animal with a touch of humour. Even the smallest features such as the eyes, ears and paws are wheel made. Sympathetic observation has enabled her to translate her feelings for the animal and for her chosen medium in a way that pays tribute to both. Although they are instantly recognisable, these objects are in no sense *realistic* models of cats. Apart from the natural softening effect of the glaze, no attempt has been made to disguise the individual segments which make up the form. Porcelain contributes a sumptuous quality to these very personal expressions that cannot be equalled by other clays.

Continuous exploration and re-examination of a recurring theme, whether it be of a particular form, an aspect of design, or an abstract concept is a fruitful exercise for anyone who responds to the necessary discipline involved. **Jeroen Bechtold** (Holland) is fascinated by vestiges of history that stimulate creative thought. He refers to the way his imagination is triggered by visits to museums where a simple cooking pot prompts questions about the hands that made it and the lives of those who used it. The tumbled, broken remains of once mighty buildings also promotes reverie. Bechtold likes to sit down by ruined castles and contemplate the decay of such symbols of

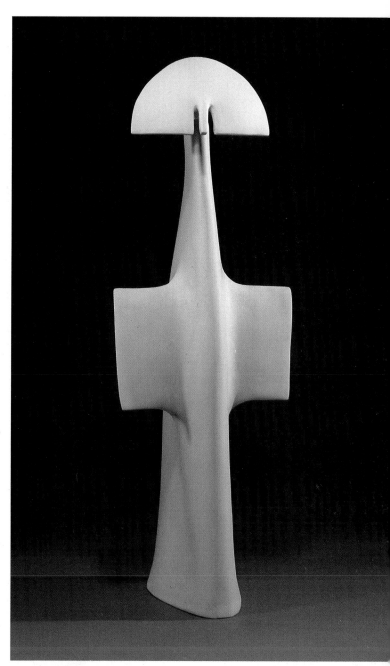

Porcelain sculpture by Ruth Duckworth.
Photograph by Wolf Böwig.

'Companions' porcelain sculpture, slab-built and painted with oxides, fired to 1250°C in oxidation and reduction, 39 cm to 65 cm high, by Fritz Rossmann, 1992–3.
Photograph by Baumann Fotostudio.

'82nd Reconstruction of the remains of the Holy Grail', (rear view) porcelain sculpture made from slipcast and press-moulded elements, with multiple glazes and firing under oxidising conditions. The interior of the form is covered with a 22 ct gold lustre. 48.5 cm × 48 cm, by Jeroen Bechtold, 1992.
Photograph by Rene Gerritsen

Front view of sculpture on p. 68.

sculpture, you can explain different things at the same time, like a Mozart opera where six people can sing different tunes and text, each and everyone of equal importance, but together in one sound. As you learn to listen to opera so you have to learn to "read" my grails, for explanations can be found in layers.'

Slipcasting is the main technique used by Bechtold because it allows him to easily control the wall thickness. He finds that casting is also best for the cut and assemble method he uses because the clay particles are not forced into alignment as they are when throwing and this reduces the risk of cracking. Originally, he graduated from art school intending to work as an industrial designer and was thus drawn to the casting process. He believes that 'it is better to be master of only one technique than to be average in many'.

power and wealth. 'Behind those walls, kings, princes, dukes and cardinals plotted, schemed and played their games. You can imagine their armies marching past. With the same eyes you can look at modern buildings of concrete and glass and wonder what will remain of our own civilisation.' He questions how much of the material wealth and power man values today actually remains when he dies?

A continuing body of work has been born of these musings. This is a series entitled 'The Reconstruction of the Holy Grail' of which each piece is individually numbered. He talks of reconstructing the remains of something that exists only in legend. The fact that people need what he calls 'myths' to be able to make sense of their existence intrigues him. He makes hollow forms having heavily textured walls, 'battered and weathered', with one side torn open to reveal the treasure of an inner purity. 'With a

'Time Well' series bone china sculpture (mounted on a thrown porcelain base), slipcast and assembled, with additions of slip impregnated fabric wrapped around the form and once fired to cone 7–8 to burn away the organic matter. This piece was airbrushed with coloured slips at the leatherhard stage, 75 cm high, by Sandra Black, 1990.

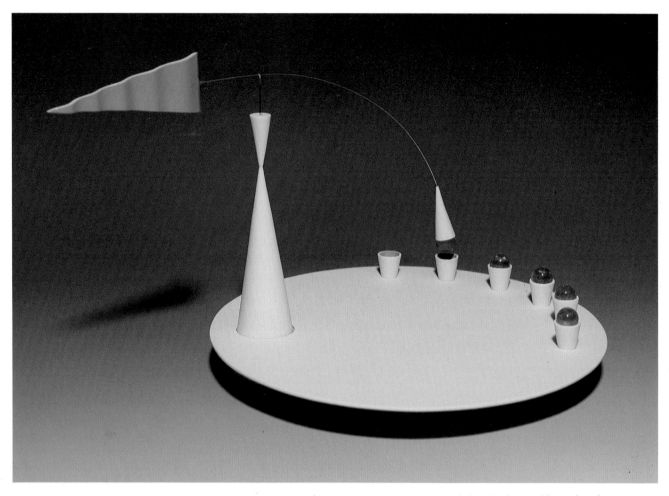

Bechtold begins by filling several moulds with porcelain slip which he leaves for half an hour or more, depending on the humidity in his studio. After draining the moulds the pots are left to dry naturally for a few hours. When he removes them from the moulds he selects one to become the main form which he cuts and folds open. 'This action helps to determine the final appearance.' Parts are cut away from the other casts and joined onto the first to increase its size and visual impact. 'In this way, I am able to free myself from the limitations of slipcasting.' Some of the remaining sections of clay are used as temporary 'architectural' supports to hold the opened form, 'usually, I open the pot so far that this is essential'. Similarly, further supports are required while in the kiln to prevent distortion. These must be made from the same material to equalise shrinkage. Smaller casts are made of figures and decorative elements

Porcelain sculpture, untitled, with steel wire, by Wil Broekema, 1990. This piece is made from handrolled slabs with the surface relief pressed into it by a cardboard stamp. The pieces are fired separately in an electric kiln to 1240°C and then assembled with an adhesive. cm × 4 cm × 24 cm.
Photograph by Dick Huizinga.

Porcelain Sculpture, untitled, with glass marbles and steel wire, 38 cm × 29 cm × 23 cm, by Wil Broekema, 1993. The porcelain is fired to 1240°C in an electric kiln before assembling this piece.
Photograph by Dick Huizinga.

which are sprigged on to the main form as the work proceeds. 'I always keep my eyes open for small objects or interesting reliefs which I can use as models for casts because I need a whole "library" of plaster moulds when working on a series of my grails.'

Final adjustments are carried out when the piece is leatherhard and able to stand without physical support and the inside is sanded until perfectly smooth. Then it is fired four or more times with successive layers of glaze ('I use glaze purely as a medium to apply pigments and stains'). The inside is coated with a clear glaze and often covered in a final firing with gold, platinum or mother of pearl lustres. Rather like a seashell whose rough exterior contrasts with its smooth inner face, these pieces evoke a feeling of precious quality, but with an added sense of mystery.

The emotional response to natural phenomenon or the human condition has been well-documented in my previous books. It will remain a constant source of inspiration for countless generations of potters but there are many others whose approach is more of an intellectual exercise which results in an abstract arrangement of shapes possessing no obvious points of reference. The Dutch potter, **Wil Broekema** (Holland), for example, works almost

Porcelain Sculpture, untitled, slab built from thin, handrolled sheets, and fired in an electric kiln to 1240°C, 30 cm × 25 cm × 6 cm, by Wil Broekema, 1986.
Photograph by John Stoel.

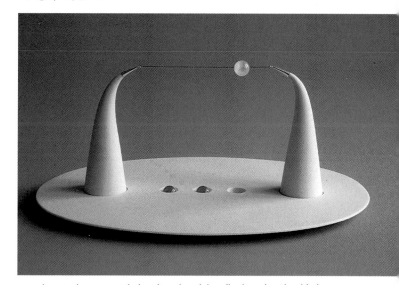

Porcelain Sculpture, untitled and unglazed, handbuilt and with added glass marbles, brass wire and tops to tapering columns, 35 cm × 25 cm × 13 cm, by Wil Broekema, 1993. The porcelain elements are fired to 1240°C in an electric kiln before assembling the work.
Photograph by Wil Broekema.

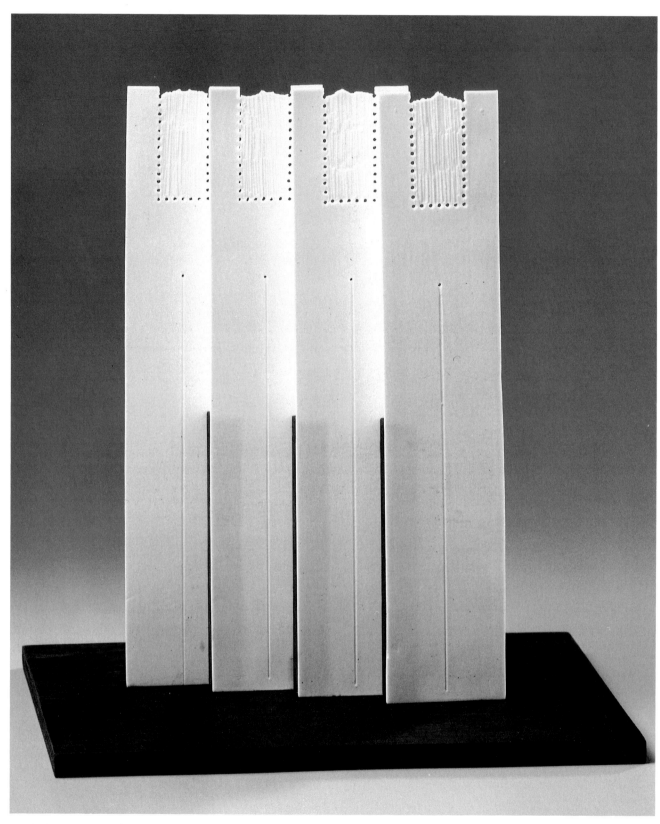

Porcelain Object, unglazed, made from thinly rolled slabs, pierced and
incised, 32 cm high, fired in reduction to 1280°C in a gas kiln, by
Horst Göbbels.
Photograph by Faahsen.

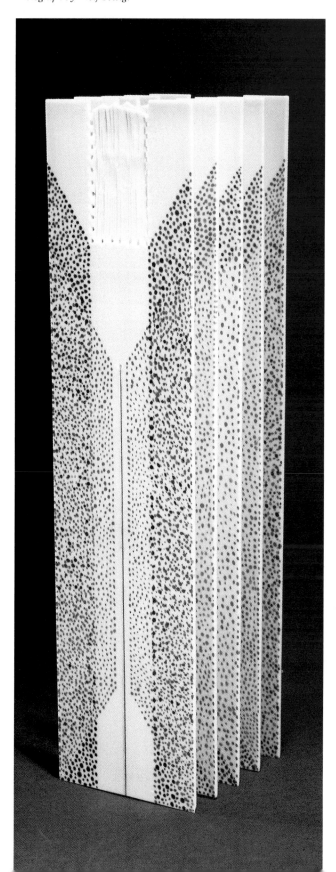

Porcelain Sculpture made from rolled slabs (Limoges porcelain body KPCL), perforated and painted to graphically define specific areas, fired in reduction to 1280°C in a gas kiln, by Horst Göbbels, 1992. This and similar works by Göbbels are often architectural symbols for towers, keeps, gates, pylons, etc. The perforations are intended to 'include the environment into the process of creating'.
Photograph by Wolf Böwig.

exclusively with precise geometric shapes made from thin, perfectly finished sheets of porcelain. A recurring theme is concerned with the subject of 'balance', physical, visual and aesthetic. Porcelain is the ideal material for her to use because, she says, it has a dense grain structure that allows her to make ultra thin sheets that are relatively strong and which become translucent when backlit. Linear elements, incised or in relief are drawn on the clay to complement the formal composition. The addition of wires and glass beads in some of Broekema's sculptures increases the impression of three-dimensional drawings in space. Feeling that some of her pieces seemed too severe she decided to introduce limited colour in an attempt to 'make them more dynamic' and light-hearted. Her paramount concern is to achieve 'harmony in form, composition and colour'.

Broekema rolls her slabs of porcelain by hand and cuts them into various geometric shapes. Surface reliefs are made by pressing cardboard 'stamps' into the thin sheets. Individual pieces that make up her sculptures fired separately to 1240°C and then assembled and joined together with adhesives. Coloured lines and other selected areas are glazed with a mixture of frit and body stains. Her finished pieces have an air of cool, reserved, understated elegance about them. This is a sensation also generated by the slab sculptures of Horst Göbbels who constructs his pieces with tall, rectangular sheets which stand alone or quietly ranked beside each other as objects for contemplation. Sometimes his slabs are pierced with holes regularly spaced to define selected areas. The spectator's attention becomes focused on the material, the form and the action of light in equal measure.

Ceramics is a wonderfully versatile medium but the nature of clay is such that the size of any form made and fired in one piece has to be quite small when compared to objects fashioned from wood or metal. Greater scale can only be achieved by making and assembling a number of separate components. The possibilities then become infinite. The process of making and handling, the need to ensure the clay is completely dry before firing and, finally, the capacity of the kiln all impose restrictions on scale. Therefore, the impact of much sculptural work in ceramics is diminished due to its small size. If we do not know the true scale of some of the porcelain assemblages by **Margaret Realica** (USA) and illustrated in this book, for example, we can imagine them to be several metres high. We are aided in this respect by seeing them as photographs rather than the objects themselves. They could, indeed, serve as maquettes for more substantial constructions. Realica was born in England but now lives and works in California. 'Deconstruction and reconstruction' is a recurring theme in much of her recent work. She draws on personal experiences in making these composite sculptures including images of bombed out buildings explored as a child. Giving an explanatory title to such works may help one to understand something of their origin and of the artist's intent. However, the objects are powerful enough to stand and be judged in their own right despite their small scale. She says that 'a piece of art should be able to stand alone, stripped of any verbal intervention. It should appeal to the eye, mind and spirit. Words should not be necessary.'

In Realica's 'Zone' series, angular structures pierce, define and dominate space with girder-like pieces of clay leaning against and supporting each other from opposing directions. Given no indication of actual size and seen only in illustration they assume magnificent proportions. Broader slabs set among the 'girders' suggest fragments of broken buildings precariously balanced between strong diagonals. These increase the feeling of violent destruction rather than gradual decay.

> My thinking and vision revolve around nature, the machine, the environment, human conditions, and experiences past and present. I work with the broken and the whole of these, the conflicts and incongruities, a world where the differences between the organic and the mechanical have broken down. The challenge is still within the theme of opposites (like) past and present, but working towards a harmony of the two and reaching for the unexpected.

Incredibly, every single piece of Realica's work in porcelain is initially thrown on the wheel. Even the slabs are made from thrown cylinders. These are allowed to set slightly and the walls are further compressed with a rubber kidney tool while the wheel rotates. When the cylinders have stiffened to the point where they are no longer sticky to touch but still fairly soft they are removed from the

Porcelain Sculpture, 'Zone Series', thrown, altered and assembled, 20.4 cm by 18.5 cm approximately, by Margaret Realica, 1991. The slabs used in constructing this piece were thrown as thin-walled cylinders before being cut open and rolled out. This method helps to prevent warping. Glazes are sprayed on and parts airbrushed with metallic lustre. The individual pieces are assembled and cemented together after the firing to 1260°–1300°C in an electric kiln.
Photograph by Robert Aude.

'T/Pot' porcelain sculpture, thrown, altered and assembled, 28.5 cm by 17.7 cm, by Margaret Realica, 1988. The slabs are made from finely thrown cylinders which are cut with a sharp surgical knife and opened out when they have stiffened slightly. The various elements of the sculpture are cemented together after the final firing (1260°C–1300°C).
Photograph by Robert Aude.

Porcelain Sculpture, 'Zone Series', thrown altered and assembled, 20.4 cm by 15 cm approximately, by Margaret Realica, 1990. The artist makes her slabs from cylinders thrown, using slip rather than water as a lubricant, which she cuts open and rolls out when slightly stiffened, in order to reduce the risk of warping. The pieces are fired separately and assembled after the final firing (electric kiln 1260°–1300°C) with adhesive.
Photograph by Robert Aude.

wheel, cut open with a surgical knife and rolled out flat. 'Rolling out thrown pieces produces finer slabs that warp much less and can hold their shape.' She finds that fewer stress cracks occur in slabs made this way and then combined with other thrown pieces. 'The procedure may seem a little lengthy but I find it actually saves time and it gives me a more polished, machined-like finish.' She feels that the action of pulling up the clay when throwing is more suited to the way she works rather than the heavier compression obtained by normal slab rolling.

In some of her porcelain sculptures, especially those based on the notional idea of teapots, Realica demonstrates the range of her technical skill by introducing convincing reproductions of machined metal objects like screws, threaded tubes and nut and bolts. The illusion is strengthened further by airbrushed metallic lustres. Her pieces are burnished with rubber when leatherhard and with a stone when dry. Bisque to 1060°C. Some parts are then glazed with either an opaque matt white or a bright white lithium glaze and fired in an electric kiln to between 1260° and 1300°C.

The porcelain sculptures of **Ruth Duckworth** (USA) cannot be easily classified. They grow out of a rich ceramic tradition but they stand alone being unlike other ceramic expressions from either the past or the present. Their subtlety and coolness owes something, perhaps, to her European background. Having fled Nazi Germany in 1936, she first studied sculpture, working mainly in wood and stone, in London. That previous experience as a sculptor was to stand her in good stead when she later made the transition into working with clay. In 1964 she moved to America to take up a teaching post at the University of Chicago and she has lived and worked in that city ever since. She managed to purchase an old factory building in 1982 and this was converted into a home with plenty of space for a large studio. This allowed her to work on a much larger scale. Several important architectural commissions soon followed and some of these have been illustrated in my previous books. However, it is her smaller pieces in unglazed white porcelain which, for the purposes of my current research, are worthy of particular attention. Some of these consist of an open topped, barrel-shaped form supporting a vertical slab which bisects the top and

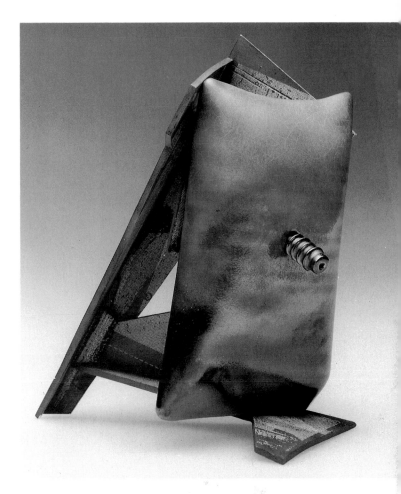

'Crated Teapot', porcelain sculpture, 16.5 cm by 12.5 cm approximately by Margaret Realica, 1993. Each part of this work was first thrown as thin-walled cylinders and then cut and rolled out when stiffened slightly. Elements are fired separately and assembled after glaze firing in an electric kiln. Glazes are sprayed and lustres airbrushed.
Photograph by Robert Aude.

cuts part way down into the vessel walls. Another small bowl has one side cut away as a semicircular section to reveal a bulbous form split vertically into two parts, each of which sprouts a horizontal wing with subtle changes of plane. This piece may suggest plant growth or bones (especially vertebrae or ball and socket joints) and it would succeed equally if executed in bronze or polished brass but the smooth white surface of porcelain responds particularly well to the soft modelling action of light falling across it. Duckworth manages to distil the very essence of morphological experience and sensation into these undemonstrative abstract sculptures.

A different kind of expressive action is demonstrated by the work of **Wilma Selten** (Holland). She responds to the plastic properties of porcelain itself in producing a series of pieces made from finger-grooved sheets which she cuts

'Electric Teapot', porcelain sculpture, 24 cm by 17.5 cm by 7.5 cm approximately, by Margaret Realica, 1993. The elements which make up this work are all made from thrown pieces. Even the slabs are cut from thinly thrown cylinders, rolled out, and press moulded onto a 'found' computer board. Sprayed glazes and airbrushed metallic lustres are applied. The various parts are assembled and cemented together following the final firing.
Photograph by Robert Aude

into strips and bends round spontaneously to link with others to create new forms.

Altering the physical properties of porcelain by mixing it with other materials has often provided a rich source of inspiration in itself. Stains and oxides are commonly used for coloured porcelain and grogs of various sizes are often added to strengthen the body for larger pieces or to supply textural interest, but mixing paper pulp 50/50 with the plastic clay offers exciting possibilities which several potters and sculptors are now exploiting. In Belgium, the sculptor, **Emile Desmedt**, uses 'porcelain paper' either on its own in smaller works or combined with other materials

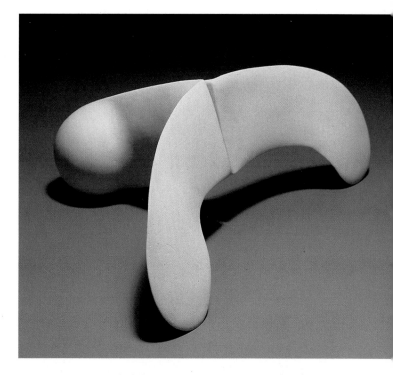

Porcelain sculpture (17 cm × 9 cm) by Ruth Duckworth, 1992.
Collection of Henry Rothschild. Photograph by Wolf Böwig.

Porcelain sculpture (10.5 cm × 29 cm × 19 cm) by Ruth Duckworth, 1993.
Photograph by Wolf Böwig.

Porcelain sculpture (17 cm × 20 cm) in three pieces by Ruth Duckworth, 1992.
Photograph by Wolf Böwig.

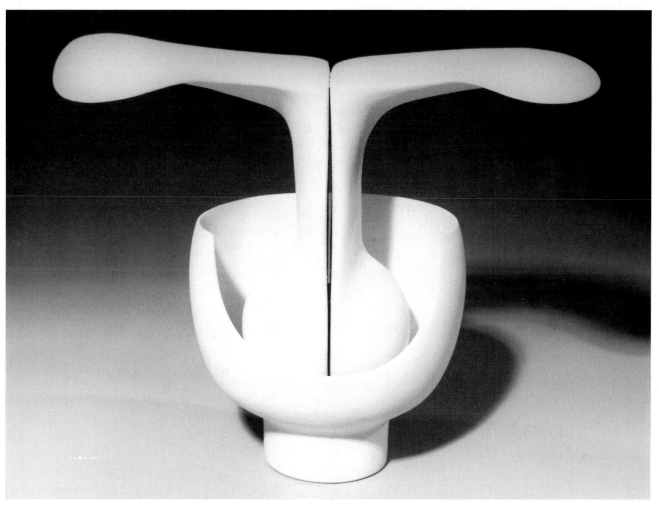

'Pink and Yellow Coiling', porcelain sculpture made from finger-grooved sheets sliced into straps and interlinked, by Wilma Selten Holland, 1992.

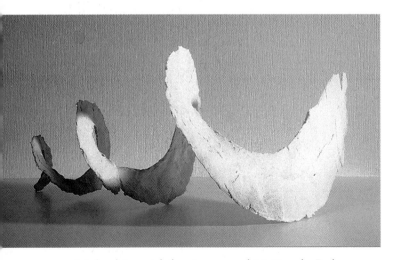

Spiral sculpture made from 'paper porcelain', 30 cm, by Emile Desjmedt, 1993. Porcelain slip is mixed with paper pulp to provide the basic material with which this piece was made.
Photograph by courtesy of Galerie La Main, Brussels.

in larger ones. His 'spiral' sculpture demonstrates the versatility of this adaption of the porcelain body.

Order and unpredictability come together in some of **Mary White's** sculptural work. In the early 1980s, she began to make organic forms in porcelain using the material rather like torn paper to be assembled in layers. Her ideas come from 'layers of rock on the seashore, shells, waves rippling over sand, and colours in the sea and sky. I like geometric forms which need skill in making and also freer organic forms which require imagination and even accident for their freshness. Sometimes, I can manage to combine these in one piece'. She returns again and again to the idea concept of 'craters'. She began making flanged bowls with cratered centres. These were followed by globe forms set into open-sided pyramids revealing craters which had coloured glass or mirrors at the bottom. 'Mystery fascinates me. I like to give people surprises. They see a simple shape, hold it in their hands and find something that involves them, perhaps a mirror that reflects their eye, or remove a lid from a box to find something unexpected inside.' The piece illustrated on page 81 is contained within a wooden box frame. The formality of the square frame draws attention to the irregular, cratered centre. We are invited to look into and past several separate, thin layers leading to the colour and reflections deep inside. A German quotation, beautifully lettered is visible beneath the top layer and encircling the crater. All her work is made from the well-known 'David Leach' porcelain body (which she colours with body stains to provide herself with a palette of almost 30 different shades) and fired to 1250°C in a small, top loading electric kiln.

Porcelain is an important constituent of the special body mixtures prepared by a number of ceramic sculptors who, rather than use porcelain alone, choose to combine it with white stonewares for one reason or another. Although this practice loses certain of those qualities we might reasonably expect to find in pure porcelain, its addition to other bodies can make a significant contribution to the character and appearance of a piece. **Mal Magson** (UK) has used porcelain in conjunction with 'T' material (a grogged white stoneware) or another white stoneware body which she colours with stains and oxides. The coloured clay and porcelain are laminated by repeatedly rolling and folding them together. Then the resulting agate slab is cut into slices and used to inlay patterns into other slabs of clay. Sometimes the agate becomes part of the wall so that the colours can be seen on both sides of the piece. 'Initially, I included porcelain in the mixture for its whiteness but that, for me, is the least interesting characteristic compared with the quality and nature of the surface it can produce. Vitrified

'Crater' sculpture made from thin sheets of unglazed porcelain in a wooden box frame, 26 cm × 26.3 cm, by Mary White, 1993. The centre of the crater is in coloured porcelain with a mirror mounted in the middle. The crater is inscribed with calligraphy, a quotation in German. Fired to 1250°C in an electric kiln.

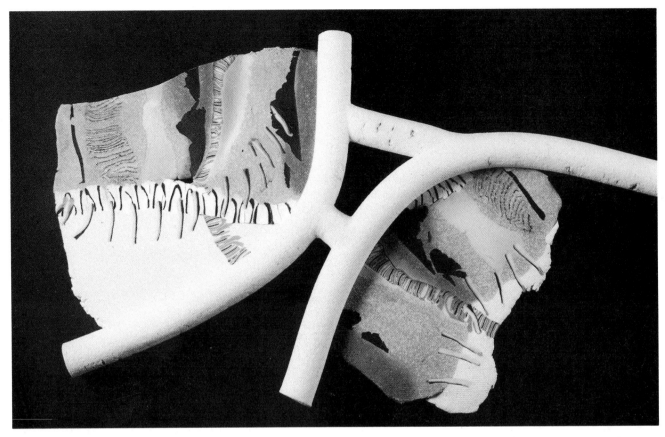

'Wall Piece', handbuilt in 'T' material with stoneware and porcelain inlay (elongated patches of porcelain is 'shadow' stained by copper contamination), 41 cm by 24 cm, fired to 1260°C, by Mal Magson, 1993.
Photograph by Andrew Morris.

porcelain has a slight sheen and a compact smoothness: a sensuous, tactile quality.' She says that she takes advantage of the way porcelain reacts when placed under, over or next to certain coloured clays to become 'suffused with shadows and dark haloes'. An extra depth is given to this suffusion of colour by the translucency of the porcelain which she finds especially appealing.

The most obvious and well-known problem experienced with the lamination of different clays i.e. splitting and separation, is manipulated and controlled by Magson to 'create a low relief across the surface of patterned areas similar to braille'. She has learnt which stains and oxides cause the greatest shrinkage to occur and which coloured bodies should not be placed next to one another to avoid splits and separation, although occasionally, splitting is encouraged to become part of the design.

Magson works on flat slabs using a roller to make a pattern surface or a laminated colour composition. These then become the basis for free-standing or press-moulded bowls. After drying thoroughly, the work is fired to a low bisque of 750°–800°C, so that it can be rubbed down with

'Wall Piece', handbuilt in stained stoneware and 'T' material with porcelain inlay, fired to 1260°C, 64 cm by 40 cm, by Mal Magson, 1993.
Photograph by Andrew Morris.

a fine grade of silicon carbide paper, followed by a final firing to between 1250°–1260°C according to the intensity or brightness of the colours required. 'The very special and characteristic qualities of porcelain are major elements in the aesthetic impact of my work.'

Porcelain is being increasingly used to make panels and wall sculptures some of which are quite substantial. Often, they are made up of a number of smaller elements for ease of handling and to avoid problems in drying and firing which can result in cracks appearing, but large panels can be made in one piece when the body recipe includes a proportion of bisqued porcelain ground into small particles as a grog to open up and to give support to the plastic material while working. Shrinkage and drying difficulties are thereby reduced.

Patchwork arrangements of flat porcelain tiles mounted on plywood cut to match the overall shape is the chosen method used by **Sylvia Hyman** (USA) to resolve some of her wall sculptures. Strong colours and positive patterns are organised by her so that they appear to overlap and counterchange and seem to be three-dimensional. To what extent these panels gain extra credence by virtue of being made from porcelain tiles rather than by direct painting in oils or acrylic on to board might be open to question but the artist has *chosen* to work in clay and to concentrate all her energies into controlling its behaviour. Hyman was trained originally as an art teacher specialising in painting and, like so many ceramicists who began working in other art disciplines, she found that 'clay was more enticing than paint' and she has remained with it ever since. The absence of a more formal training in ceramics encouraged her to discover how best to handle the medium as necessity demanded and, at the same time, she enjoyed the freedom to find her own means of expression. The more obviously organic nature of much of her earlier work in porcelain, some of which was illustrated in *Studio Porcelain*, arose out of the need to experiment with materials and techniques. Porcelain especially lent itself to a succession of sculptures inspired by 'spores and sperm and sexual selection' and which she called her *Sporophore and Sporophyll* series. These were composed of multiple sheets of thinly rolled porcelain mounted like wings on top of pedestals or bursting out of rounded, soft-looking forms in convoluted frills as if from a fruiting body. Some of her lively, tiled panels are made in white, unglazed porcelain reliefs with flowing ribbons of clay entangled with spiky growths casting complex shadows of varying depth. More recent work has given way to the exploration of new forms concerned with emotional aspects of human relationships and interpersonal communication. These consist of two or three separ-

'Patchwork' (Mixed Message Series), glazed porcelain tiles mounted on plywood, 41.5 cm × 47.5 cm, by Sylvia Hyman, 1989.
Photograph by John Cummings.

'Fading Memories' (Relationship Series), 45 cm × 37.5 cm × 26 cm, by Sylvia Hyman, 1992. Slab-built porcelain sculpture, bisque fired to cone 06 and then sanded smooth. Onglazes are sprayed directly on to unglazed areas over masks to produce the pattern before a final firing to 1200°C.
Photograph by John Cummings.

'Something in Common', slab-built porcelain sculpture sprayed with overglazes, 40 cm × 39.5 cm × 26.5 cm, fired to 1200°C in oxidation, by Sylvia Hyman, 1992.
Photograph by John Cummings.

Handbuilt porcelain with impressed textures inlaid with coloured ceramic stains, unglazed by polished, reduction fired to 1320°C, 20 cm high, by Erik Pløen, 1993.
Photograph by Jan Enoksen.

ate but related forms grouped together on a flat base. The outer profile of the major pieces describes a simple and complete entity while the inner ones are individually contoured to express an aspect of communication or, in some cases, non-communication between them.

Hyman's sculptures are handbuilt from slabs of porcelain, bisque fired to cone 06 (approx. 1000°C) and sanded until absolutely smooth. They are mostly left unglazed with only small areas of glaze for accents and fired again to cones 5–6 (approx. 1190°C–1215°C) before spraying onglaze enamels directly on to unglazed areas (with some parts masked to remain white) and refiring, finally, at low temperature.

Handbuilding is the method preferred by **Erik Pløen** (Norway) for his richly textured slab-sided forms. The distinctive surfaces of his porcelain objects are impressed and inlaid with ceramic stains of different colours to emphasise the texture. The pieces are left unglazed and fired to 1320°C before 'polishing' with silicon carbide paper. A reduction atmosphere is induced when the kiln temperature has reached 950°C and continued until the end of the firing. This process gives the porcelain an attractive, bone-like finish which is pleasant to touch. Pløen has not used glazes on his work for some time because he finds that the Limoges porcelain (HPB) is well-suited for his coloured textural pieces. He is not concerned with translucency and he improves the body further for sculptural work by adding five per cent Molochite (passed through an 80s mesh sieve) to prevent cracking and excessive shrinkage. This addition has no effect on the whiteness but he stresses the importance of firing it in a reduction atmosphere.

Pløen has two workshops, both by the sea. The main one is in Son, a small fishing village by Oslo Fiord while the other is on a skerry (a small island) in the North Sea, so nature has a great influence upon the way he thinks and works. Pebbles on the beach, rock strata with its cracks and cavities, and conglomerates of shells provided the stimulus which led to the pieces illustrated here. Sea creatures are also a rich source for ideas and it was a flounder, with its flattened form and strong pattern, that prompted the piece on page 37.

A combination of throwing and handbuilding is used by **Ingvil Havrevold** (Norway) to create her sculptural objects and, like her partner Pløen, she also adds textural interest to her work but in a different way. She applies layers of porcelain slip to enliven the surface which is then covered with a coloured glaze based on nepheline syenite. The pieces are fired in oxidation to 1280°C. The body used is exactly the same as Pløen's including the addition of Molochite. She can sometimes trace the source of a particu-

Vessel Form, handbuilt porcelain with impressed texture inlaid with
ceramic stains, unglazed but polished, fired to 1320°C in reduction, 30
cm high, by Erik Pløen, 1993.
Photograph by Jan Enoksen.

Porcelain Form, wheel-thrown and handbuilt, with impressed texture
inlaid with coloured nepheline syenite glazes and parts left unglazed,
fired to 1280°C in oxidation, 28 cm high, by Ingvil Havrevold, 1993.
Photograph by Jan Enoksen.

lar idea developed in clay but much of her work is intuitive. Like Pløen she too looks constantly to nature. 'I enjoy sitting on a rock looking out to sea, especially in a stormy wind with the sea and clouds in constant motion' (see illustration opposite). She also refers to the influence of landscapes and trees upon her thinking. 'In early spring, the birch has a fascinating lilac shimmer around the stem and branches' (see illustration on this page). 'I can remember the first photograph of the earth taken from space in 1968. It was very impressive and it has given me much inspiration'.

Unusual and exciting porcelain sculptural pieces, possessing elements of the kind of rhythmic geometry often found in natural forms, have been developed by **Peter Masters** (Australia). These pieces, which have no other function but to occupy space while delighting the eye, are executed with a high degree of mathematical precision that gives them a strong, tactile appeal. Despite the strict organisation necessary to achieve the precise placement of the individually applied clay balls or spikes, Masters works intuitively, relying solely upon the accuracy of his eye to judge the exact relationship of each to the others within the overall pattern. The spiral movements created with these additions energise the forms and call to mind similar patterns in nature such as cacti and sunflower seedheads without being in any sense imitative. He explains his concept of these forms as having a basic volume resembling, perhaps, a turnip or a bean, but he has 'attempted to transcend any association with recognisable species. Thus the environments in which these forms might exist may be earthly, but certainly not domesticated. However, a viewer may still feel that these forms are not of this world, and this is perfectly acceptable, because their origins could indeed be cosmic.'

The basic spheres and ovoids are either wheel-thrown (for smaller pieces than 50 cm (approx. 20 in.) in diameter) or coiled, to produce a domed 'onion' shape with thick walls that can be turned when leatherhard and refined to fit the precise curvature required for each piece. The spikes are made separately by rolling between forefinger and thumb, grading their sizes and spacing according to where they

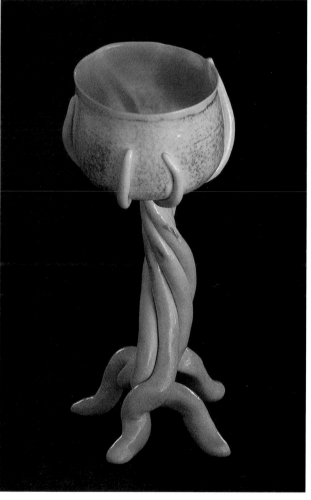

Porcelain Form, made from wheel-thrown and slab-built elements. 23 cm high, by Ingvil Havrevold, 1993. Texture is created by the application of slip in various ways. Coloured nepheline syenite-based glaze fired to 1280°C in an oxidising atmosphere.
Photograph by Jan Eriksen.

Goblet, wheel-thrown, with handbuilt stem, 22 cm high, by Peter Masters, 1989.

'Sphere Intrusion', handbuilt porcelain with white earthernware coils,
30 cm diameter, saltglazed, 1990, by Peter Masters.

are to be arranged on the main form, becoming smaller and more tightly packed towards the top and bottom. The repetition of so many small units produces an appearance of considerable complexity.

Masters has created many 'growth' forms incorporating patterned surfaces which have evolved intuitively. He has always been fascinated by the sea and sea life and by growth patterns in nature, and he is 'awed by gigantic vegetables like marrows and squash'. He describes the forms he makes as

consisting of a spherical shell with a relatively short, tapered extension referred to as the 'ovoid' (resembling perhaps the subterranean part of a turnip) and a singular projection, either extending into free space or rejoining the ovoid. Having only two contact points with the supporting surface, they are very dynamic, primary forms with visual rotational instability. They vary in size from about 20 cm to 60 cm (8 in. to 24 in.) in diameter. The ovoids have a high relief surface pattern of balls or spikes. Thus, there is a very active secondary

Bowl constructed in a complex open mesh pattern from extruded coils of porcelain, 47 cm × 40 cm, by Netty Van Den Heuvel, 1991.

'Protrusion' handbuilt porcelain sphere with earthenware spike (approximately 67 cm) by Peter Masters, 1990. The surface is enriched with individually applied pieces built up into a strong pattern resembling growth progressions developed in nature. Slips and oxides are sprayed on with an airbrush or an atomiser. The piece is salt glaze fired in a natural gas downdraught kiln. The atmosphere is oxidised to give brighter colours.

movement. With some patterns, incorporating holes or additional inserts in the balls or spikes, a tertiary movement takes place. The forms are high-fired and sodium vapour glazed giving them very luminous, and contrasting, matt surfaces with brightness or colour. The main hues are yellows, greens, blues, browns and pinks on a white porcelain ground.

The kiln is often cooled slowly to encourage crystallisation to take place in rutile slips and oxides.

Although he believed that nothing could be totally new, and had often suggested to his students that generating ideas for design was rather like taking water from an eternal source such as a mountain stream ('the same water but always fresh'), Masters had felt, initially, that his 'protrusions and intrusions' were in some way 'original'. However, he was 'not surprised to find several historical examples of pots including more contemporary work of noted ceramicists like France's Francine del Pierre and Emile Decoeur which employ similar use of pattern'. Further research led him to the mathematical work of Leonardo and others relating to numerical sequences to be found in nature.

Repeated linear elements form the basis of the amazingly complicated grid-like structures by **Netty Van den Heuvel** (Holland). Building constructions and the geometry of micro-organisms provide her with a constant

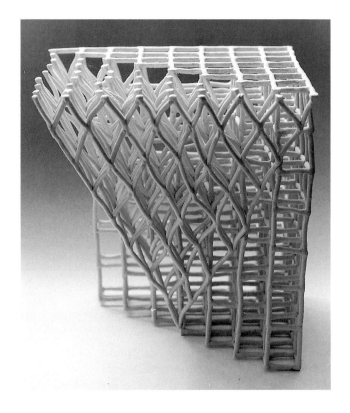

'Wall Ball', press-moulded sculpture in Limoges porcelain body (TM10) fired to 1260°C in a reducing atmosphere, 22 cm × 11 cm, by Netty Van Den Heuvel, 1991.

Porcelain sculpture 'Zonder Titel', constructed, layer by layer, from extruded coils of Limoges porcelain body (TM10) fired in reduction to 1260°C to obtain the colder bluish-white, 37 cm × 36 cm × 36 cm, by Netty Van Den Heuvel, 1992.

'Sailing Vessel' by Lara Scobie 1993, 58 cm × 27 cm × 20 cm. Handbuilt from layers of thinly rolled sheets of porcelain. The texture is enhanced by brushing oxides and underglaze stains over it and then sponging the surplus away to leave a residue in the depressions.

source of reference and fascination. She begins by preparing a drawn plan to work out a pattern for the grid. The three-dimensional form is built up with individual units or ribs of extruded porcelain attached to specific points to create a complex, but highly ordered, arrangement of connecting lines defining space. These pieces are made with Limoges porcelain body (LM10) and fired in reduction to 1260°C in order to obtain a bluish white colour.

The multiplication of units of similar shape but varying in size contribute to the imaginative porcelain sculptural objects by **Lara Scobie** (UK). Her forms are intricately constructed by building up complex layers of thinly rolled clay. Small strips are torn from thin sheets of porcelain and then pressed into an Indian printing block, of which she has a small collection, so that the resulting textured piece is incorporated into the design. Ropes and scrolls of clay are added to the assemblage, each unit helping to create a three-dimensional composition rich in texture, pattern and visual interest. These wonderfully evocative sculptures are bisque fired to 1000°C before oxides and underglaze stains are applied in broad washes of colour with a large brush. Sponging some of the colour away subsequently leaves deposits to pick out and give emphasis to the impressed textures. Several layers of colour are built up in this process. Finally, a large brush dipped into a transparent glaze is swept over the form and fired to 1300°C . Earlier pieces were subjected to a reduction atmosphere but she experienced increasing problems with cracking and warping

'Basket', by Lara Scobie 1993. Constructed by building up layers of thinly rolled porcelain. Texture is produced by pressing the clay into old Indian printing blocks. Colour is inlaid into the textures by brushing oxides and underglaze stains into it and then sponging away to leave a residue in the depressions.

which have been overcome to a large extent by changing to electric kiln firing. Scobie says that this has had an added bonus in that the porcelain retains its pure whiteness 'which gives it a lovely sparkle'.

Scobie's involvement with the material is somewhat unconventional but she was attracted to its use by its inherent fragility and its response to working in fine detail. Whilst she wanted to incorporate these qualities in her work she also felt a need to react against 'much of what is stands for'. Her ideas have evolved through the working processes.

> The suppleness and plasticity allows me to stretch and bend each tiny element, and to build up many layers of delicately patterned clay. The works are my interpretations of various objects both real and imaginary while incorporating relative symbols into the design to give the piece a unique identity and a true sense of worth and meaning.

The unique porcelain figures by **Richard Shaw** (USA) are skilfully assembled from slipcast elements that imitate a wide range of found objects. The transfer-printed, individ-

Top 'Steamship Jar', slipcast porcelain, 53 cm × 15 cm × 10 cm, by Richard Shaw, 1993.

Left 'Seated Figure with Grey Head', slipcast porcelain, 52.5 cm high, by Richard Shaw, 1985.

'House of Cards on a Brown Derby', slipcast porcelain with ceramic decals, 40 cm × 25.5 cm × 28 cm, by Richard Shaw, 1993.
Photograph by Lewis Watts.

ual parts which he uses to make up his forms are disturbingly realistic representations of familiar domestic items like jars, tins, books, chairs, twigs and other pieces of wood. He explains that

> ceramic decals offer several advantages which can't be obtained with hand decoration of a ceramic piece. Most obvious is the ability to make two or more copies of a particular design. Another advantage is the possibility of doing a drawing on paper, reproducing it through a printing process, and applying it to the work as a decal instead of drawing directly on the piece. Reproduction of photographs and found two-dimensional material can be obtained through the use of ceramic decals.

(See page 143 for further information on the preparation of ceramic decals.)

Vessel forms

Ceramicists frequently take a vessel form as their starting point to develop ideas. In some instances, the functional aspect of the form as a container remains, in others it may have completely disappeared. The teapot towers made by **Jane Smith** (UK) are sculptural, decorative *and* functional objects. They are partly thrown with handbuilt additions. The example illustrated shows four teapots stacked one upon another in ever decreasing size with spouts and hand-

Left   'Pasta Server with Two Spoons', porcelain with underglaze
decoration, by Dorothy Hafner (USA), 1984.
Photograph by S. Baker Vail.

Above   'Teapot Tower', four 'dragon' teapots, wheel-thrown
porcelain, carved and incised under a celadon glaze, mounted on a
carved plinth and stacked one upon another to a total height of 25 cm
with the largest being 19 cm wide, by Jane Smith, 1993.
Photograph by Andrew Morris.

pots equipped with spouts, handles and lids attached to a larger shape is merely the inception for the exploration and resolution of a new three-dimensional form. Their flat sides present broad areas for pattern or texture but Peach chooses to treat them boldly in geometric arrangements of colour outlined with narrow strips of white. The division of these flat areas is almost architectural in appearance with strong linear elements strategically placed at positive angles as if lending structural support to the piece. The colours are applied as underglazes and glazes by brushwork and then fired at a relatively low temperature in an electric kiln to cone 5 (around 1190°C).

The whiteness of porcelain holds attractions for those potters who do not necessarily wish to fire it to its traditional and more usual high-maturing temperature. Firing porcelain bodies in sawdust at relatively low temperatures well under 1000°C (after an initial bisque firing around 1040°C) appeals to some because certain colour effects and surface flashing from smoke and the reaction with metallic salts can be obtained. A fair amount is inevitably left to chance in this process and the ware is usually only decorative due to its comparative fragility. **Shellie Jacobson** (USA) makes sculptural vessel forms by handbuilding from slabs of porcelain and firing in a simple sawdust kiln. She tries to obtain the maximum effect from the simplest applications. She says that

for glazes, I use both raku and low fire recipes, especially ones with copper as they respond well to the reduction atmosphere in the sawdust fire. I also use a moderate solution of sulfates (about 5 g in half a cup of warm

Teapot and stand, semi-functional. 18 cm × 13 cm × 12 cm by Dianne Peach, 1993. Slipcast porcelain assembly with underglaze colours and glaze brushwork. Fired in an electric kiln to cone 5.
Photograph by Dianne Peach.

les aligned. The spouts are fashioned into the necks and heads of mythical dragons whose tails curl round to act as handles. The 'tower' is supported by a pierced and carved stand made from an inverted bowl. A pale blue celadon-type glaze gathers in the depressions and enhances the delicate modelling and impressed textures. Smith's delight in both her subject and in the use of porcelain shines through this piece and brings a smile to most observers.

The teapots by **Dianne Peach** (Australia) are very different in character. They are assembled from slipcast porcelain sections and she describes them as either semi-functional or non-functional. The notion of traditional tea-

Left 'Viking II' by Shellie Jacobson, 1993. Handbuilt porcelain body with glazes, stains and metal additions. Bisque and glaze fired to cone 04 and reduced in sawdust, 14.5 high.
Photograph by Philip W. Smith.

Above Ewer, handbuilt porcelain body with glazes, stains and metal additions, bisque and glaze fired to cone 04 and reduced in sawdust, 19.5 cm high, by Shellie Jacobson, 1993.
Photograph by Philip W. Smith.

water) which can be brushed or sprayed. My cone 04 firing temperature is the same for both bisque and glaze. This leaves the body open for the subsequent reduction fire, but still strong enough to withstand the thermal extremes of it.

A completely different approach to the *concept* of functionality as the starting point for creating forms in clay can be seen in the work by **David Jones** (UK). In this case, porcelain is merely a constituent part of the plastic body which can contain anything between 15 per cent and 50 per cent of Molochite (a porcelain grog) or 'T' material. Porcelain, as a clay body, he says has always held a special fascination for him

Raku fired porcelain bowls (1100°C) with lustres containing gold, silver and copper, by David Jones.

because it brings with it an aura of purity and refinement. This gives an axis on which to build and from which to rebel. My work has always been concerned with precision and the precious, or their opposites. Thus, a fine white body which will accept pure colours and lustres is very valuable. Originally, I was fascinated by a clay that would become translucent with heat, and I evolved a dialogue on the surface between a painted pattern and a revealed (thin) skin of translucent clay. I was dissatisfied with the (technically) superficial lustre on top of the glaze and was very excited by the opportunity to create in-glaze lustres using the raku process. I have slightly modified the body by using a mix of porcelain and molochite or 'T' material. The clay is still pyroplastic at the relatively low temperatures at which I now fire, and it is possible to deform the bowls by firing

them on their edge in order to hint at the transforming experience undergone by the pot in the kiln.

I have tried to establish a balance in my work between expressing a set of ideas in clay, i.e. comments on the material, and *the ceramic tradition*; that is the line from primitive utensils for everyday consumption of food and drink to objects for the court, for museums, or for the contemporary collector to whom function is not a necessary quality. The themes that I have used are very much centred on the Far Eastern ceramic tradition and the bowls that I make are a comment upon a Sung bowl or one from Arita. This has been mediated in recent years by a growing fascination with raku and, thereby, the vessels of the Japanese Tea Ceremony. In many respects, this tradition sets out to be the antithesis of court porcelain. It is a celebration of crude and spontaneous handling of clay, of directness and of accident. It is a naturalness that is highly refined. The attention given to the undulating rim and to the carving of the foot places this activity in exactly the same category as other court arts in demanding a highly educated audience to appreciate the nuances of the pots. In my raku work, although I start with a white porcellanous body (which is ideal for colour development) the unglazed areas of the pots end up black as a result of secondary reduction. Thus the colour of the body of a bowl is in complete contrast to that of a Ming bowl. It is important to me that this difference should be so dramatic.

Jones is now attempting to address another tradition through his work, that of industrially-made porcelain and bone china of the 18th and 19th centuries, while casting 'an oblique glance at the products of Wedgwood and Thomas'. He describes them as 'vessels associated with the "English Tea Ceremony". I use this phrase to deliberately echo the Japanese for it had a code of behaviour, equally as rigorous, regarding how the beverage should be served and consumed. Indeed, the arcane natures of both traditions as to the steeping of the leaves seem very similar in their pernicketiness.'

The 'Fin Pot' by **Eileen Lewenstein** (UK) illustrated on page 100, has more than a passing resemblance to the traditional teapot but the winged additions serve no other purpose than to extend the basic form of the spherical container and thus alter its character. For her 'Triptych' she has again taken a simple form, the cylinder, which is thrown and altered in an unusual way. Three cylindrical pots have been adjusted to a flattened oval section and then pressure is applied alternately inwards and outwards along vertical edges so that the pots complement and

relate to each other when they are placed in a line (see page 100).

Emmanuel Cooper (UK) also refers to vessel forms for continuing inspiration, in particular, a series of teapots, jugs, bowls, vases and lidded boxes, all of which are related to domestic function and to the traditional role of the potter as artisan. Cooper stresses the idea that a vessel should be an object of interest in its own right in addition to any purpose it may serve as a container. In discussing his work, he mentions 'anthropomorhic references' and his feelings for his jug forms and flared vases that 'seem to be

Above 'Deconstructed Tea Set', porcelain mixed with 'T' material, thrown and altered with slab additions and raku fired lustres (1100°C), by David Jones.

Right Teapot, 20 cm high, by Pam Korte (USA), 1993. Porcelain, thrown and handbuilt elements, with impressed decoration. Fired to 1280°C in an electric kiln.
Photograph by Ron Forth.

like people or animals. Some are tall and skinny, reminiscent of greyhounds or athletes while others are more sturdy and approachable, but all assert their own personality.' These pieces are partly handbuilt and assembled from several parts to break away from the complete domination of the wheel'. He uses glazes 'whether smooth and "wet" or with crusty, textured, dry surfaces in an attempt to form one seamless whole'. He is attracted to porcelain whether it is used alone or opened up with fine alumina hydrate because it allows him to produce a variety of intense colours that would not be possible in stoneware.

Top
'Triptych', three related pots, porcelain, thrown and altered, 20 cm high, fired in an electric kiln to 1250°C, by Eileen Lewenstein, 1988. *Collection of International Academy of Ceramics, Geneva.*

Left 'Fin Pot' vessel in the form of a teapot, thrown and handbuilt porcelain, with dark blue glaze fired to 1250°C in an electric kiln, by Eileen Lewenstein, 1990.

Porcelain vessels with undulating profiles, blue glaze fired to 1250°C in an electric kiln, tallest 40 cm, by Eileen Lewenstein, 1990.

Above 'Night Sky' (back) and 'Winter Sky' (front) by Emmanuel Cooper, 1993. Porcelain jug forms thrown in two sections and joined together. 'Night Sky' (28 cm high) has a dolomite glaze with painted oxide decoration, 'Winter Sky' (20.5 cm high) has zinc oxide/porcelain slip under a barium carbonate/zinc oxide with nickel oxide glaze. Fired in an electric kiln to 1260°C.

Opposite 'Folded Bowl', by Andrea Hylands, 1992. Bone china, slipcast and handbuilt, with airbrushed colour. 27 cm high × 31 cm wide. Fired in an electric kiln to 1240°C. The piece is 'wet and dry polished after firing to achieve a sheen'. This piece is one of a series in which lines and edges are of aesthetic and tactile importance.

Some of the most unusual and exciting work currently being produced in porcelain and bone china with reference to vessels is that by **Andrea Hylands** (Australia). She was born in Britain but studied at Latrobe University College in Northern Victoria where she obtained her BA (ceramics) degree and her present studio was established in 1984 at Chewton in central Victoria. The originality and high quality of her work was duly acknowledged in 1992 when she was the Joint Grand Prize winner at the 13th Biennale Internationale de Ceramique d'Art at Vallauris in France. Apart from its obvious visual relationship to vessels, Hylands' work is almost impossible to categorise. It can be analysed, of course, in terms of geometric shapes assembled in various proportions and combinations while their surfaces can be appreciated for their colours, patterns and textures, but, beyond that, her works have more eloquence than can be expressed merely in words. They seem to be of an unreality given concrete form.

Hylands describes the absolute whiteness of bone china as being 'ideal for the application of colour'. She combines both slipcasting and handbuilding in the construction of her pots but few clues remain to inform us of their origins or of the techniques used to arrive at the finished piece. Ceramic stains are mixed with frits or with porcelain and bone china slip and airbrushed to give a flat expanse of colour before bisque firing. Further colours are then applied over stencils in preparation for the final firing which is conducted in an electric kiln to around 1220°C with a half

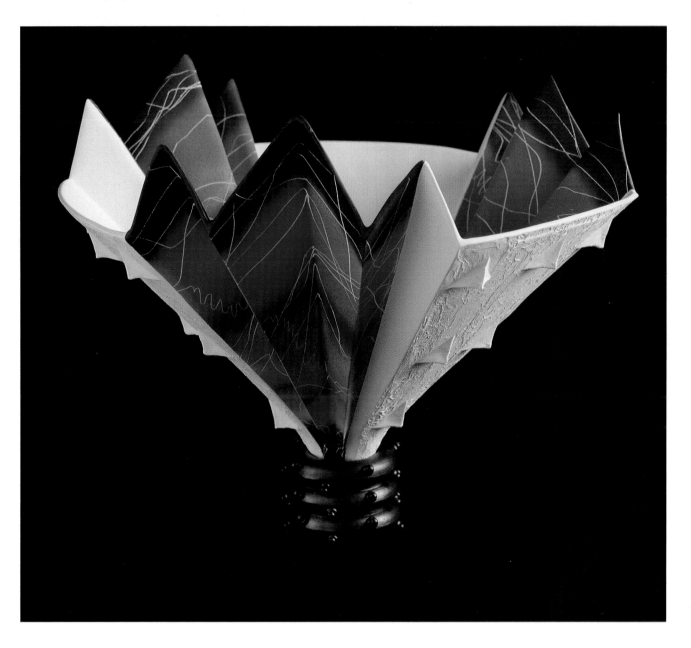

hour soak at the top temperature. Then the work is polished with silicon carbide paper, wet and dry, to achieve a surface sheen.

She explains that most of her work still relates to a vessel:

The vessel has an important physical function: that is one of containing. This function, owing to its familiarity, has a strong point of contact with an audience. The folded bowls are a series I am still continuing to make. Lines and edges are prominent qualities in my work and I allude to feeling and touching. The starting point for basic shapes depends on previous work. I do not jump around from shape to shape arbitrarily, but simply evolve and modify ideas for forms. I enjoy making them look as if they have not been made from clay.

The latest series is about reinterpreting the pot in an abstract way. These vessels are the products of an intricate process and they have been complicated and enriched with decoration and embellishment. Using distortion and deception places them between the ordinary and extraordinary, revealing some ambiguity of purpose. There is no overt symbolism in my pieces, but the familiar is turned into surprise, exaggerating the surreal aspect of a pot as opposed to a pot as a commonplace object. In the later series of abstract vessels, I have

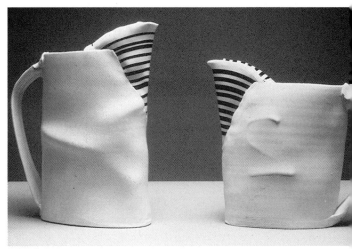

Above   Two porcelain jug forms with 'insert' spouts, by Sandy Simon (USA), 1986.

Left   'Cup on Pedestal', porcelain, slipcast and handbuilt, 32 cm high, fired in an electric kiln to 1240°C, by Andrea Hylands.

Right   'Vessel with Handles', by Andrea Hylands, 1992. Porcelain, slipcast and handbuilt. The first layer of colour is applied and bisque fired before stencils and airbrushed colours are used to complete the surface design. 52 cm high. Fired to 1240°C in an electric kiln.

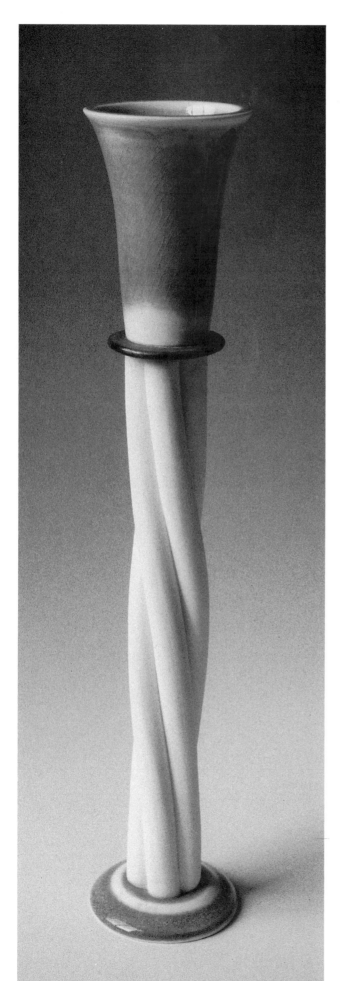

increased the scale of the work and some of my new forms are a metre high.

Maria Bofill (Spain) is another porcelain potter who uses distortion and exaggeration in her forms which claim only tenuous association with traditional vessels. Elevated cup shapes balance precariously on tall, undulating or twisted stems whose tiny bases seem barely capable of holding them still. She creates objects 'without function; it is a search fluctuating between the classical and the contemporary. I do not want to attain perfection: on the contrary, I love natural and living things.' She likes to make forms that appear to be in motion and she considers her pieces to be 'small, Mediterranean architectonic objects'. She is particularly interested in goblets, columns and capi-

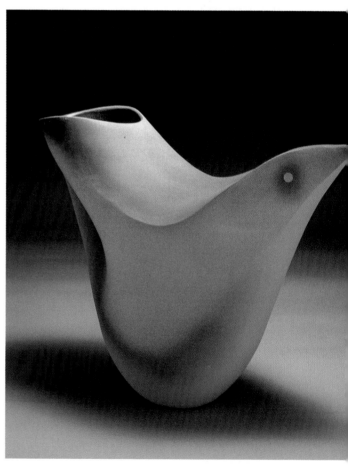

Porcelain jug in the form of a bird by Peter Lane, 25 cm high, 1991. Wheel-thrown and altered while still wet, airbrushed with underglaze stains on the bisque and fired to 1240°C in an electric kiln.

Left Goblet form with a tall stem of twisted coils, porcelain, 38 cm high, reduction fired to 1280°C in a gas kiln, by Maria Bofill, 1993.

Right Two tall 'goblet' forms, porcelain, wheel-thrown with handbuilt additions, 39 cm and 28.5 cm high, fired in reduction (gas kiln) to 1280°C, by Maria Bofill, 1993.

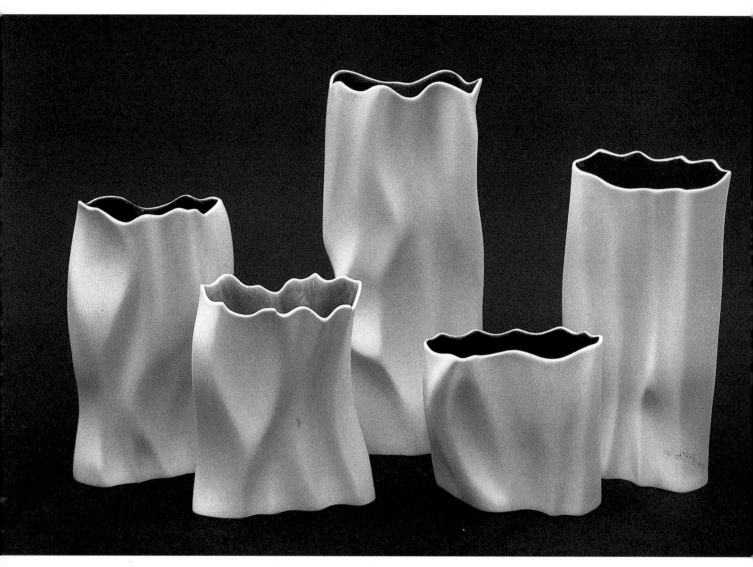

A group of slipcast porcelain vessels with carved rims, glazed inside but with polished exteriors by David Fink (USA), 1993. Tallest approximately 31 cm.

tals and often starts work with a clear idea of the form in mind but this may undergo modification during the creative process.

Bofill uses the wheel and, also, slabs to produce her pieces.

After an idea has taken shape, I make each of the various elements separately. I am always working on several pieces at the same time. Firing of these elements is also done separately and it is only after the second firing that I decide on the definitive shape of the piece. Mounting them is complicated. It is, in a way, the creation of an architectural structure: placing and removing the parts,

examining and combining the different elements until a satisfactory shape is achieved. This may be the original idea or not. Problems arising during the work with porcelain often give me new ideas for further pieces.

Glazed work is fired in a gas kiln and subjected to a reducing atmosphere to 1280°C , while those pieces which are decorated with engobes are fired in an electric kiln in oxidation to 1240°C.

Working to a particular theme concentrates the mind wonderfully. This may involve examining a certain form and trying to discover various options and nuances that give it fresh life and interest. Changing between techniques of making, decorating, glazing or firing may spark off new ideas or inspiration may be stimulated by the struggle to resolve problems of design or those judged to be inherent in the material itself. Certainly, it was an invitation to take part in an exhibition entitled '101 Jugs' that made me address myself freely to a vessel form that rarely figured in my repertoire. I approached the subject in a light-hearted way with function as only a minor consideration. Having decided to work in porcelain, I threw a tall V-shaped bowl about 30 cm (12 in.) high with walls no more than 4 mm ($\frac{1}{4}$ in.) thick. Realising that the piece was close to collapse towards the end of the throwing cycle, I encouraged opposing sides to fall inwards until they met in the middle while the clay was still very wet. Without adding any extra clay, the original piece was flattened slightly into an oval section and further adjustments were made to define the 'tail' and these act as a kind of handle. Meanwhile the 'beak' became the spout with the larger opening by the 'tail' giving easy access to the volume inside. Airbrushed ceramic stains were shaded to accent the 'bird' shape and add to the allusion. Although pure function was not uppermost in my mind, the pot actually works as a jug. It holds liquids and pours well with one hand under the 'tail' and the other beneath the 'throat'! (see illustration on page 106).

Natural rock formations, especially concretions like stalactites and stalagmites or sandstone and igneous rocks eroded by wind and water into convoluted shapes provide ample reference points for the work of **David Fink** (USA). He arrives at his forms by carving plaster models in an attempt to capture some of the sculptural qualities produced by natural forces of erosion over millions of years. The models are used to make plaster moulds for his slipcast porcelain. The rims are hand carved when the casts have stiffened to give greater individuality to repeated shapes. The interiors are glazed but the outer wall surfaces are polished after the final firing taken to cone 5 (almost 1200°C). Visual interest is increased when light falls across the white surface creating hard and soft shadows that articulate the form.

Nature provides much of the stimuli for the exotic vessels by **Curtis Benzle** (USA). His pieces are made up of multiple layers of coloured and patterned porcelain sheets laminated together and compressed while the clay is at the wet stage. In any one piece there may be up to six different layers.

The intended result is for the viewer to be confronted with a constantly changing imagery dependent on the available light. For me, this represents the reality of mentally processing the many elements of my environment simultaneously. For instance, when I gaze out of my studio window I see certain objects immediately brought into focus: trees, grass, flowers. As I continue to look, I bring into focus dew, mist, birds passing and a

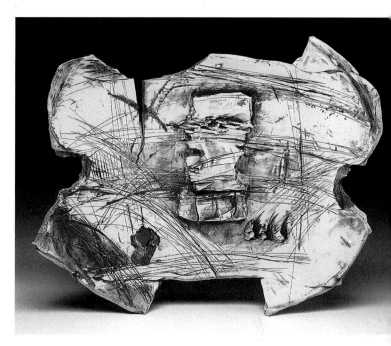

'Landscape', porcelain plate, handbuilt, incised and coloured with black ceramic stain, fired to 1280°C in reduction, 50 cm, by Ole Lislerud.

subtle shifting of light and shadow. To all this is added the remembered images relevant to the same scene: days of rain, snow, children playing, leaves changing and on and on. It is this 'layering' of imagery that encourages *my* layering of translucent porcelain surfaces.

After many years working exclusively with slipcast bone china, **Angela Verdon** (UK) decided that it was no longer acceptable to suffer the very large number of pieces that were lost in the making process. The loss rate had always been high, especially when she worked with paper-thin clay

but the desire, almost an obsession, to create forms which utilised and exploited the maximum amount of light, to create vessels so fragile and translucent as to be almost unbelievable overcame the disappointment. However, later, the restrictions of the medium proved too limiting for me and the work became sterile and mechanical. There seemed to be nowhere else I could go with bone china.

She had completed a series of extremely thin forms; some very thick black and white laminated pieces; she had also

'Passage', handbuilt porcelain, inlaid and incised, 20.5 cm × 45 cm × 10 cm, by Curtis Benzle, 1990.

want the medium to dictate the message and, hopefully, this is the state I am moving towards'. She feels that she is just beginning to understand and appreciate the differences between bone china and porcelain but is enjoying the opportunity to make much larger pieces. More of the actual work is carried out in the 'green' state and she has discovered a strength and plasticity that was lacking in the china (which she had always fired to a soft bisque 'before I had hardly touched it').

Verdon now draws marks and images directly on the clay cast and carves them out or around, leaving certain parts prominently raised and surrounded by very thin areas. 'I want to draw the eye in and towards an image by the light and colour in a subtle way to create a sense of calm stillness in the piece.' The concept of 'less is more' is what she strives to achieve in these works, to move away from what she feels is her almost obsessive attention to carving pierced detail and to 'really simplify'. Her current work in Limoges porcelain is first fired to 900°C and then thoroughly sanded smooth before refiring up to 1260°C in an oxidising atmosphere. A final polish during which she pays special attention to the raised areas of the surface relief completes the process.

Another potter who prefers to retain the white appear-

Slipcast and carved porcelain vessel, first bisque fired to 900°C and then further refined and sanded before firing up to 1260°C in oxidation, 34 cm × 26 cm, by Angela Verdon, 1993.

tried staining the body with rich, dark blues, greens and blacks and inlaid gold and silver but it was with 'considerable relief' that she obtained a residency in Cleveland that allowed her time to experiment widely for two years. (It was during this period that she won the Inax Prize which enabled her to work for three months in Japan.)

Verdon worked with many different clays and made countless tests with various materials while attempting to rediscover her true sense of purpose, without the attendant problems experienced with bone china, only to find that she came back to the realisation that light, purity, simplicity and all the other qualities that had captivated her in earlier work remained dominant. 'I realised that stoneware, "T" material, brightly coloured glazes, etc., were not for me.' She decided to switch her efforts to slipcasting with a more reliable porcelain body from Limoges in her search for greater spontaneity and freedom in her work without the labour-intensive involvement of bone china. 'I don't

Porcelain Bowl, trimmed and altered, with a matt feldspar glaze fired to cone 9 (1280°C) in an electric kiln, by Gwen Heffner, 1993.
Photograph by Ron Forth.

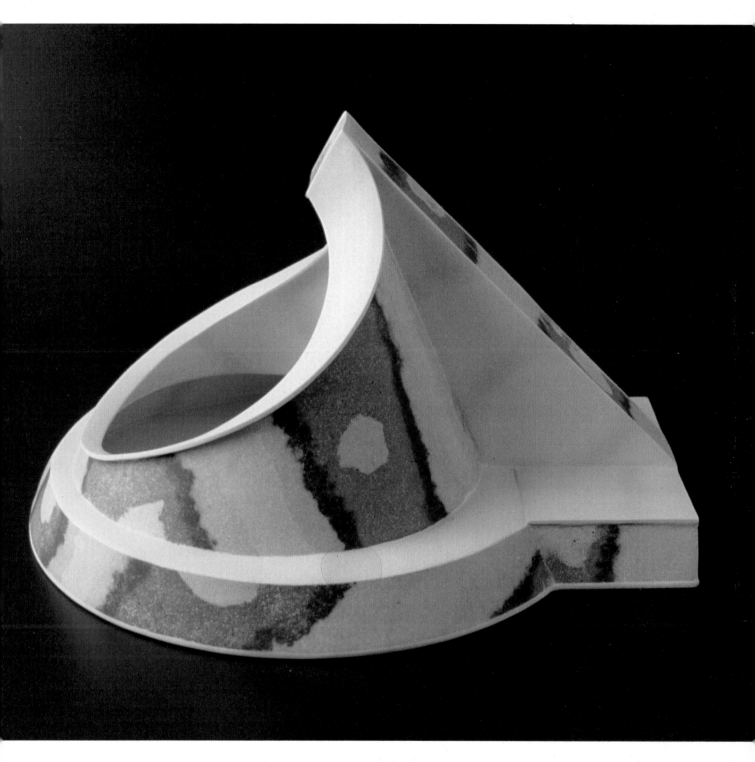

Porcelain Form, 33 cm × 28.5 cm, by Saskia Koster, 1990. Handbuilt
with slabs of laminated and inlaid, multi-coloured porcelain. Fired to
1280°C in an electric kiln. The artist plans her pieces first by making
them in paper and then deciding which colours and patterns are the
most appropriate to complement the form.

Lidded jar with richly coloured blue and red feldspathic glaze containing copper, cobalt, iron, and manganese, fired to cone 10 (1300°C) in reduction, by Christopher Sanders (Australia), 1993.
Photograph by Terence Bogue.

'Ripple Jar' with red feldspathic glaze containing iron and copper, fired to cone 10 (1300°C) in a reducing atmosphere, 32 cm high, by Christopher Sanders (Australia), 1993.
Photograph by Terence Bogue.

ance of porcelain or to use fairly matt glazes is **Gwen Heffner** (USA). All her vessel forms are wheel-thrown and turned while still quite wet. 'Since form is my main focus, I throw with an inside rib and a flexible metal outside rib to get a clean form without throwing rings.' She pushes her bowls into an oval form after trimming them 'thus creating the symmetry of the wheel and allowing an easy trim on a round pot'. She cuts into and alters the rims of her pieces with a fettling knife and then uses a sponge to wet and stroke the edges 'much in the way that one *pulls* a handle', coaxing them into new shapes. In order to overcome

uneven drying problems with altered rims and forms, she inverts them onto pieces of plastic 'bubble wrap' which protects them from damage while they dry more evenly.

One porcelain potter who became well-known for her strongly thrown, classical shapes (and whose work was included in two of my previous books, *Studio Ceramics* and *Ceramic Form*) but who felt an urgent need to pursue new directions in her vessel forms is **Catharine Hiersoux** (USA). She mentioned a moment when she was unpacking her kiln and discovered a beautiful, narrow necked vase, with a copper red glaze, that had become separated around

'Abyss', handbuilt, wood-fired porcelain, by Catharine Hiersoux, 1990.
Photograph by Richard Sargent.

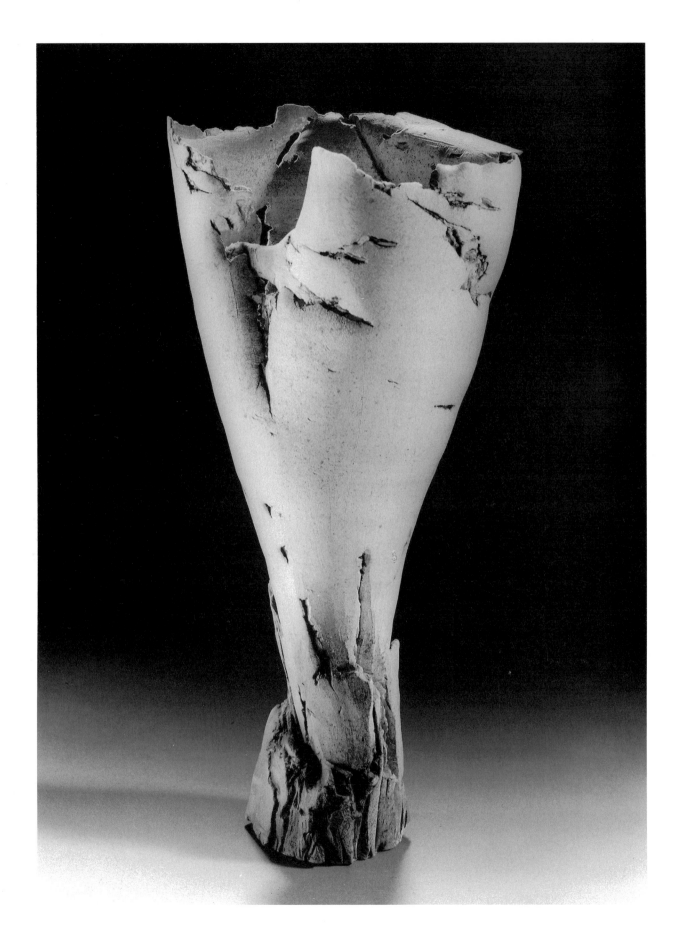

its widest point. When she lifted the top of the vase, the bottom remained 'open like a cracked eggshell.' This stimulated her into searching for new means of expression with looser forms. She knew then that she wanted to free the clay and herself from 'strict, formal bonds and to open up the forms, to push the translucency of the porcelain and work more with the inner space, both literally and metaphorically'. Loose, altered forms were placed on more clay which she sculpted, beat, shaved and pierced for freer movement between inside and outside. 'I wanted translucency, but needed structural support ... maybe the whole piece did not need to be that thin.' She began trying to establish a balance between translucent and opaque areas, between fragility and toughness (thin, high-fired porcelain is much stronger than any similar piece made in earthenware). 'There was a sense of either having endured time or of *being new growth*, an ambivalence that still exists. The challenge was for me to explore the dimensions.' She remains committed to the vessel as a point of departure in her exploration of form but is prepared to adapt to any future changes that may develop. She built a wood-burning kiln to fire these new pieces because she wanted to use a process that 'just "touched" the forms, enhancing, highlighting them ... these pieces were still of the earth but not just natural. There are lots of problems with wood firing ... it's not very predictable ... but the chance for magic is much greater.'

'Teapot', slipcast porcelain with painted decoration, 15 cm high × 27 cm × 7 cm, by Sandor Dobany (Hungary), 1992.
Photograph by Wolf Böwig.

Left 'A piece that works', handbuilt porcelain, wood-fired in an anagama type kiln, 40 cm high, by Catharine Hiersoux, 1990.
Photograph by Richard Sargent.

Porcelain vessel forms by Fritz Rossmann (Germany), 1993. Made by initially throwing shapes on the wheel and then rolling them on the ground in a spontaneous way. 20 cm and 27 cm diameter. Fired in salt glaze to 1250°C.
Photograph by Baumann Fotostudio.

SURFACE TREATMENTS FOR PORCELAIN

Painted decoration

The pure white porcelain body lends itself especially well to surface designs applied as stains, oxides, slips, glazes, lustres or enamels. Tools used may be paintbrushes of various sizes and shapes, sponges, rubber stamps, transfers, slip trailers, or spray guns and airbrushes. Colours can be overlaid and the piece fired and re-fired several times to different temperatures, and in all kinds of kiln atmospheres until the desired result is achieved. Resists and masks of paper, card, tapes, nets, latex and wax are often employed to widen the range of creative possibilities. Sources of both figurative and abstract imagery are infinite.

Arne Åse painting an inverted porcelain bowl with shellac resist and water soluble colourants. The shellac burns away in the firing.

Water-soluble colourants

One of the more unusual methods of applying colours to porcelain has been comprehensively explored by **Arne Åse** in Norway. His book, *Water Colour on Porcelain* (published in 1989 by the Norwegian University Press) deals with this in considerable detail. Rather than use the heavier pigments made from metallic oxides, Åse has conducted an enormous number of experiments with water-soluble colourants such as iron chloride, nickel chloride, ferrous sulphate, potassium dichromate and many others. He points out that most, if not all, of these materials are extremely poisonous and hazardous to health. They must be stored, handled and fired with great care. Åse compares the softer, gentler colours given by water-soluble metallic salts with effects achieved by using oxides and offers an analogy with watercolour and oil paints. Certainly, the spectrum of colours developed by him is unusually delicate and distinctive. He expresses the view that 'ceramics is a pictorial art, artists relate to the world of visible phenomena from which they draw their inspiration and which governs their main modes of expression'. He refers to the changing role of contemporary ceramics and believes that the subject reveals evidence of 'a completely new branch of the fine arts on the verge of breaking through in all parts of the Western world'. He feels, as do I and many others, that ceramic art bears no direct relationship with traditional criteria of usefulness and function. Its more important purpose in a contemporary setting is the communication of thoughts, feelings and impressions through visual means.

Arne Åse has specialised in studying the effects of water-soluble colourants when used on unglazed porcelain fired to 1280°C in a reduction atmosphere. Concentrating his efforts in this way he has managed to produce a reliable palette of stable colours mixed in various solutions and combinations. Shellac is often used as a resist medium on his painted porcelain bowls. Sometimes, colourants are dis-

Right
The finished porcelain bowl after once-firing in a reducing atmosphere, unglazed to 1250°C. This bowl was fired upside down on a porcelain ring to prevent any distortion. By Arne Åse, 1993.

Porcelain Plate, unglazed, 65 cm diameter, by Arne Åse, 1993.
Decorated by painting a shellac resist and washing away part of the
unresisted surface (the shellac burns away in the firing). Some parts
also painted with water soluble colourants. Fired to 1250°C in
reduction.

solved in glycerine or syrup to improve their workability.
Occasionally, he combines phosphoric acid with the
soluble salts or, possibly, a thickening agent may be added
to the mixture to be painted under or over other colours.
Solubles added to oxides extends the options even further
so that the subtlety and range of colour effects appear to be
infinite.

Using precious metals

Greg Daly (Australia) is another potter who has developed an unusual and expressive technique using colour. His current work is an exploration of light and illusion with images which 'are abstractions of landscape and objects I have experienced in and around my environment'. Wheel-thrown plates, dishes, bowls and spherical forms with richly glowing glazes have long been a feature of his ceramics. Porcelain is a material perfectly suited to accept the high gloss glazes he favours. Coloured glazes are used as the base or background for painted additions of lustres made from gold, cobalt, bismuth and zinc in different combinations. The addition of gold and silver leaf helps to enrich the surface imagery even further. Linear patterns

Above Lidded Pot, 15 cm × 12 cm, by Greg Daly, 1992. Porcelain, decorated with gold and silver leaf. Glaze fired to 1280°C. The leaf is then attached to the surface, prior to refiring (between 720°C–800°C), with a medium made from pine resin mixed with a light oil such as lavender or eucalyptus (approximately 10 g of resin to 50–70 mls of oil).

Porcelain Vase, 35 cm high, by Greg Daly, 1993. Wheel-thrown, with resist lustre decoration. Fired to cones 9–10 (1280°–1300°C) with a high gloss glaze and then subjected to further firings to apply lustres at 760°C. The surface was prepared with wax resist over which acid is painted to etch into the surface.

Right Porcelain Vase, with bright blue, glossy glaze and gold lustre decoration, 20 cm high, by Greg Daly, 1993.

are etched into the coloured areas making a silky matt surface that acts as a foil for the lustres. Daly aims in this way to create illusions of colour and light that flow over the surface (drawing the viewer) into the depth of the glaze. The intensity of tones and colours changes when viewed from different angles and light sources.

Daly has had considerable experience of working with precious metals on ceramics and he says that he finds the application of gold and silver leaf is relatively simple to accomplish. The best results are usually produced when used on a glossy glaze but leaf can also be applied to ceramics for 'black firing' or on to a satin matt surface for different effects and with varying degrees of success. It is important to use the correct medium to attach the leaf

Porcelain Platter, 80 cm diameter, by Greg Daly, 1991. Wheel-thrown, with resist lustre decoration. Fired to cone 9–10 (1280°–1300°C) with a high gloss glaze. Lustres are then applied over a hot wax resist and refired to 760°C one or more times. Finally, acid is painted over wax resists and allowed to etch into the surface.

leaf and, in the case of gold, that it should be as pure as possible '22 ct at least'. When dry, a piece of paper is held over the leaf and light pressure applied to ensure consolidation with the ceramic surface.

Metallic lustres and onglaze enamels

Daly sometimes makes up his metallic lustres in a similar way to those used in conjunction with gold or silver leaf and these can be painted on together with enamels if required after applying the leaf and the whole is then fixed in the same firing. In some instances the leaf is placed on top of a previously fired lustre. Firing temperatures vary to allow for the different softening points of glazes used. Earthenware glazes soften at lower temperatures than

because ordinary glues can leave scumming on the glaze or a layer between the glaze and the leaf which prevents proper fusion taking place. The medium he uses is made from pine resin melted with a light oil such as lavender or eucalyptus with approximately 10 g of resin to 50–70 ml of oil. This produces an oily, sticky medium that may also be used as a base for enamel painting. This medium is painted on to the surface to be decorated with the leaf which can then be manoeuvred into position quite easily to define a pattern. Daly recommends the use of high quality

Three Porcelain Vases with resisted lustre decoration painted over previously fired lustres, 10 cm diameter, by Greg Daly, 1993.

stoneware or porcelain but generally the lustre and leaf firings are conducted between 720°C – 800°C.

Daly prepares his lustres by melting 10 g of pine resin and then adds metallic salts in the form of nitrates or acetates. For a 'mother of pearl' effect, he adds 3 g of bismuth nitrate and 2 g of zinc acetate by constantly stirring 'until the mixture takes on a glossy appearance, slowly adding lavender or eucalyptus oils (pure turpentine can also be used with the oils). Other lustre colours can be made in a similar way. Gold, in combination with other metals can give reds, pinks, blues and copper colours.' The lustrous coloured surface of these ceramics develops as the resin is burnt away *reducing* the constituent salts to a metallic state. This local reduction can take place in an electric kiln without causing damage to the elements but good ventilation should be ensured by leaving spyholes open with the bungs out.

Another highly effective technique imaginatively used by Daly is that of etching glazes with acid. An acid-etched surface provides an excellent foil for the lustre surface or a glossy glaze. In this case, more than one glaze may be used. If a solid lustre is applied over them, it will block out the underlying colour but etching through this reveals varying colours with a satin matt surface. In the lustred bowl (illustrated on page 14) two different glazes have been used and gold and silver leaf applied as previously described. Resin-based lustres were then airbrushed over the surface followed by an enamel colour. When the bowl has been fired, latex, wax and/or tapes can be used as resists for the acid which is to be painted over the surface. Daly emphasises the attention he pays to safety when working with acids.

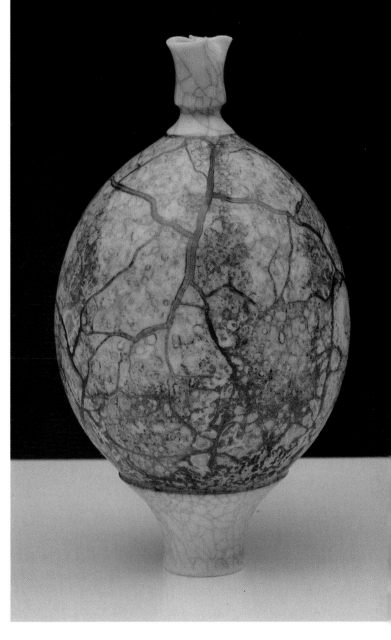

Porcelain pot, 11 cm high, by Geoffrey Swindell, 1989. Wheel-thrown, fired to 1250°C in an oxidising atmosphere (electric kiln) and then decorated with onglaze lustres, the surface of which has been marbled and broken by painting or spraying a medium selectively (paraffin or detergents will beak the surface of resin/oil based lustres) before the lustre has fully dried and prior to firing to 750°C in an electric kiln.

Rubber gloves should always be worn and the process must be carried out in a well-ventilated area. 'The straight hydrofluoric acid is not very safe for this work but another form has bifluoride as an active ingredient. This may take a little longer to etch the surface but it is a little safer to use.' The time needed for the acid to take effect depends upon

Globe form, 14 cm diameter, by Mary White, 1993. Porcelain, with a white, barium glaze, fired to 1250°C in an electric kiln and then decorated with calligraphy in black oxide and gold lustre and refired.

'Vanitas' container form, wheel-thrown porcelain with underglaze and high fired painted glazes and gold lustre, 21 cm diameter, by Olaf Stevens, 1990.

the hardness of the glaze and the requirements of the design. Hot water is used to wash the piece and remove any wax resist followed by further washing with liquid soap to neutralise the acid and prevent any scumming from spoiling the surface.

Acid etching of ceramic glazes creates a surface which is very smooth to the touch and quite unlike anything achieved by sand blasting. Daly has discovered that 'the combination of different coloured glazes and finishes with lustres, gold and silver leaf, enamels and etched surfaces can lead to surface decoration which has great depth, illusion, colour, pattern and design. The exploration of these techniques releases the imagination through its countless subtle variations.'

I have discussed the painted lustres of **Geoffrey Swindell** (UK) at some length in my previous books and, although his many commitments in other areas have greatly reduced the amount of time he is able to devote to his own creative ceramics, the answers he gave in response to my questions precisely echo those of so many ceramicists who choose to work in porcelain. Like Arne Åse, Swindell is not concerned with functional applications in the way that a teapot, for example, might be used for making and serving tea. 'But there are practical considerations like fired strength, stability and durability. However, the main function I aim for is that the "presence" of the form should affect the senses and give pleasure by its beauty as do many natural objects.' He admits that, for him, the nature of the materials used in his work have a profound effect on the finished image. Combined with the techniques and the concept they are 'inseparable' elements in any good work of art or craft. Swindell says that the whiteness of porcelain gives him a perfect ground as it does not interfere with the purity of applied colours. He likes to make 'well-engineered, precise forms — almost mechanical — and then soften the appearance with a more "organic" quality of surface' with glazes that are textured with marbled lustres. It is through this image of 'precision and looseness' that he attempts to communicate his interests in other objects that he collects, thus presenting a 'synthesis' of both man-made and natural qualities.

Swindell paints commercially-prepared lustres on to glazed pots and then breaks the surface tension of the medium with solvents such as paraffin or detergents brushed or sprayed selectively on to it. This action causes the lustres to retreat away from the solvent spot or line with a halo of concentrated colour around the edge. Further colours can be added and the piece might be fired several times with successive treatments until the visual texture and colour fully fits and complements the form.

Gold, silver and platinum lustres are very expensive

'Container with Circles', wheel-thrown porcelain, with yellow glaze and gold circles (23 ct gold), 25 cm diameter, by Olaf Stevens, 1993.

Porcelain Plate with high-fired painted glazes, and bees painted in gold lustre, 53 cm diameter, by Olaf Stevens, 1990.

'Horizons', porcelain bowl, 59.5 cm diameter × 17.5 cm high, by Pippin Drysdale, 1990. Wheel-thrown, painted with layered, prepared glaze stains on top of a white tin glaze using latex resist as a drawing agent in producing the design.

items in the potter's palette. Therefore, the traditional and more familiar use of precious metals in ceramics is to apply them sparingly as banding or outlining or to highlight details of the design. **Mary White** (Germany) makes good use of her training in calligraphy to paint gold lettering on some of her porcelain bowls and pots. Her calligraphic script is fluently executed encircling the forms as a fully integrated part of the design. **Olaf Stevens** (Holland) is more extravagant with the application of gold lustre. The inner surfaces of some of his simple bowl shapes are completely covered with shimmering gold. His bowls are all thrown with unusually thick walls but he refines their surfaces until they are perfectly smooth and ready for painting. These rather severe forms might easily appear dull but Stevens enlivens their surfaces with generous discs and ovals of gleaming gold, loosely placed, around their circumferences. The first colours are applied as underglazes on the bisque to be covered with a translucent yellow glaze. Onglaze enamels are painted before a third firing and, finally, the gold lustre and a fourth firing. This bold approach to decoration is very different to the elaborate, crowded ornamentation he has applied to other vessel forms of similar shape. A skull and crossbones symbol makes an incongruous appearance among a multitude of colourful flowers and insects jostling for space around the outside of one bowl while the inside glows with plain gold

lustre. The result fits uncomfortably close to becoming kitsch for, apart from its technical excellence, it bears little relation to mainstream studio ceramics at the time of writing. But Stevens' intentional note of discord is intended to shock, to draw attention to the transitory nature of human life. He quotes 'all is vanity' in describing this aspect of his work which closely follows a similar allegorical theme in 17th century Dutch painting.

Right 'Logging Series', porcelain plate, 60 cm diameter, by Pippin Drysdale, 1990. Wheel-thrown, painted with layered, prepared glaze stains on top of a white tin glaze using latex resist as a drawing agent in producing the design.

Porcelain Bowl, 'Russian Series', 20.5 cm diameter × 13 cm high, by Pippin Drysdale, 1993. Wheel-thrown, with painted coloured stains on top of a white (tin/zirconium) glaze fired to 1200°C in an electric kiln, followed by lustre firings to 780°C. The lustres are applied as an 'extra skin' on the fired stains to add richness to the colours.

Porcelain Bowl, 'Australian Outback Series', diameter 35 cm, by Marianne Cole. Wheel-thrown, with shiny black glaze fired to Orton cone 9 in an electric kiln, and then decorated with painted liquid bright gold lustre and coloured enamels and refired to cone 018. *Photograph by Michal Kluvanek.*

Freely painted brushwork in both lustres and underglaze stains is a strong feature of the work by **Pippin Drysdale** from Western Australia. She lives in Perth which she describes as 'the most isolated city in the world — surrounded by desert and the Indian Ocean'. This feeling of isolation is reflected in her artistic endeavours giving it a regional identity. She states that all her life she has been surrounded by wide open land and seascapes and she has always been fascinated by contrasts of light, colour, space, texture and spirituality. Her work is directly inspired by her experience of that environment. She is noted particularly for her large, painterly platters which incorporate each of those elements expressed in terms of colour. All her pieces are individually made and decorated in wheel-thrown porcelain, bisqued to 1000°C and then painted with stains mixed in equal parts with frit 4712. Bentonite from the USA (three per cent) is added and the mixture is put first through a 150s and then a 200s mesh sieve to ensure even dispersal. The stains are applied in layers, hand-painted, sprayed and dipped on top of a white glaze using latex resist as a drawing agent. The base glaze has a

wide firing range and contains tin oxide and zirconium silicate with zinc oxide and barium carbonate. This is fired to Orton cone 4 or 5 (1180°–1200°C) while lustres are often applied for the third, fourth and, sometimes, fifth firings to Orton cone 016 (780°C) on top of the previously painted and fired stains 'to add an extra skin which gives a rich dimension to the colours'.

Pippin Drysdale's painted designs are confident, bold and vigorously executed. Colours and shapes swirl over and around her pots as if in constant motion. She feels that the essence of her vessel forms is a 'solitary explanation of celebration' ... an embodiment of refreshed emotional response to my unique Western Australian environment, depicting subtle landforms and colours expressing light, skies, deserts, oceans and horizons'. She travelled extensively during the early 1990s to further widen her experience by working in a traditional Italian majolica factory and teaching in Britain, Siberia and the United States. This has provided her with new influences, 'from Russian icon paintings to the flamboyance of Italian carnivals', which are beginning to appear in her work.

The bowls, elaborately decorated with gold lustre and coloured enamels, by **Marianne Cole** (Australia) are inspired by aboriginal painting and the Australian Outback. She describes her work as 'an ongoing experiment with ideas derived from many sources, in particular, the vast ceramic legacy left to us from ancient cultures'. Extensive foreign travel has enabled her to see such works in their environmental and cultural contexts. Their 'physical presence exudes an aura reflecting each culture's passion for form and decoration' and these influences are in tune with her own 'unabashed zest for rich and complex surfaces'.

The painted decoration on top of a shiny, black glaze which has been fired to 1280°C in an electric kiln is undertaken in a dust-free room. It is a lengthy process, using commercial enamels and liquid bright gold. A special pen (a miniature version of a batik pen) is used to draw the network of fine gold lines. Gold 'thinners' can be added to allow the liquid gold to flow freely. 'It is a precise process requiring a steady hand, good light and good eyesight.' Although she has a *general* concept in mind when she begins decorating, the design actually develops on the bowl as she works.

Mary Rich (UK) prefers to cover her porcelain vessel forms with underglaze stains and coloured slips to provide

Porcelain Teapot, wheel-thrown, decorated with coloured glazes and gold lustre brushwork, by Mary Rich (UK), 1992. *Photograph by Jon Furley.*

Porcelain Bowl, 26.5 cm × 10.5 cm, by Mary Rich, 1993. Wheel-thrown and banded with purple slip under a barium carbonate glaze which has been fired in reducing conditions to cone 10. With painted decoration in liquid bright gold with purple and black lustre.
Photograph by Roger Slack.

Porcelain bowl, 38 cm × 7 cm, by Russell Coates, 1993. Wheel-thrown, with underglaze blue and enamelled design of square cross with paired cormorants and a geometric border surrounded by sealions swimming amongst seaweed.

a dark ground which is then fired with a clear, satin matt glaze prior to painting her intricate, decorative designs in gold lustre. Much of her work is small in scale from jewel-like, miniature bottles and bowls to cane-handled teapots, banded and crosshatched with fine gold lines to make complicated, geometric patterns. Similarly involved patterning features in the work of **Russell Coates** (UK). Having won a scholarship to study ceramics in Japan, he spent a fruitful period during the 1980s learning about the art of underglaze blue painting and enamelling on porcelain (Kutani ware). His work remains strongly influenced by that experience and it still demands very careful planning and rigorous preparation. Designs are worked out in detail on paper first and then transferred on to his dishes using tissue paper and charcoal. Colours are chosen as the work progresses.

Coates likes porcelain, especially for throwing. One of the bodies he uses is a natural porcelain from Japan similar to that first found at Arita where Imari ware is made. He says that the use of this clay 'tends to shift the emphasis away from translucency', a quality which has been so important in Western porcelain, due to its iron content. He bisque fires between 800°C and 1000°C and then outlines his patterns in underglaze blue which is eventually covered with a clear, white glaze and fired again to Orton cone 9 (1270°C) in a reducing atmosphere. (The plates and bowls are supported on setters in the gas kiln.) Further decoration is accomplished with five enamel colours, red, yellow, green, blue and purple, underpainted with black. Burnished gold may be included also and the final firing is taken to a temperature of 830°C. Stylised birds, animals, fish, dolphins or plants encircle the rims of his decorative plates surrounding an elaborate centrepiece reminiscent of Celtic designs. Describing his choice of subject matter for his painted designs, Coates says,

> Dolphins are liked by all and they introduce environmental and conservation themes. Creatures and plants look well painted in enamels which can be too hard and shiny for purely abstract or geometric patterns. In the last few years, I have been inspired by Cretan, Celtic, Anglo-Saxon and Mediaeval themes. Unfortunately, they take a long time to do.

Porcelain Bowl, 41 cm diameter × 8 cm high, by Russell Coates, 1993. Wheel-thrown, with underglaze blue and enamelled design rose window surrounded by fish and a geometric border. The underglaze pattern is covered with a clear/white glaze and fired in reduction to 1270°C before applying the enamel colours and refired to 870°C.

He explains that the lengthiest part of the making process is the enamelling on the fired glaze, at a point 'where the work of most potters has finished'.

Coates admits that enamelled porcelain may have a limited appeal. 'It seems that although many people have heard of Imari ware, few potters even know much about "Kakiemon" or "Dovetailed Colours" which are the roots of the tradition that I studied in Japan.' He feels it is unfortunate that 'the level of boredom bequeathed by Western transfer printed enamels is such that most potters lose interest at mention of the word'.

There is certainly an appreciative audience for highly patterned wares at the time of writing but such detailed painting requires careful, thorough planning and great discipline in its execution. **Peter Minko** is an Australian potter working in the Bendigo region of central Victoria who gains much of his inspiration from the wealth and variety of the natural flora in the surrounding bush. Con-

'Goldfields' porcelain vase, 18 cm high, by Peter Minko (Australia), 1993. Wheel-thrown and burnished at the leatherhard stage, bisque fired to 920°C and then painted with finely ground pigments made mainly from metallic oxides. Fired twice more to 1280°–1300°C to fuse the colours to the unglazed surface.

Porcelain Bowl, wheel-thrown and altered while still soft, with painted decoration, 20 cm diameter, by Kevin White, 1990.

'Goldfields 2', porcelain plate, 30.6 cm diameter, by Peter Minko (Australia), 1992. Wheel-thrown and burnished at the leatherhard stage. Bisque fired to 920°C and then individually handpainted with finely ground pigments (mainly metallic oxides). Two firings up to 1280°–1300°C in oxidation conditions fuse the colours with the unglazed porcelain surface. Gold lustre is applied in a further firing to 760°C.

Porcelain Bowl, wheel-thrown and altered while still soft, with painted decoration, 20 cm diameter, by Kevin White, 1990.

Porcelain Dish painted with underglaze blue (cobalt) fired to cone 11 and then onglaze enamel added and refired, 26.5 cm diameter, by Kevin White, 1989.

centrating on fairly simple vessel forms, he has been able to embellish them with an exotic range of richly coloured patterns. Each piece is wheel-thrown in a fine porcelain body and burnished at the leatherhard state to ensure the surface is smoothly compacted. Bisque fired to 920°C they are then individually painted with finely ground pigments (predominantly metallic oxides) and fired twice more to between 1280°–1300°C in oxidation to fuse the colours on the unglazed surface. Only the inside surfaces are glazed. Those pieces with gold lustre applied in parts are fired again to 760°C. Minko says that he chose to work with this particular porcelain and technique because it was the only way in which he could obtain the kind of finish to display his detailed painting with complete clarity. His fluent draughtsmanship is well-illustrated in the pieces on pages 132 and 133.

Brushwork

Kevin White is another Australian potter who makes decorative bowls and plates decorated with brushwork which is rather more abstract but still clearly based on plant growth. These pieces are obviously functional although not specifically utilitarian. He manipulates and alters wheel-thrown forms while they are still soft 'to impart structure and movement' and uses decoration to emphasise their dynamic aspects. In commenting on his objectives, White states 'whilst at rest the work seeks to act as the custodian of ceremony and through use to celebrate it'.

Porcelain Vessel with painted decoration by Paul Davis, 1989.

Shallow, porcelain bowl, 45 cm diameter, by Paul Davis, 1993.
Decorated with maiolica type glaze coloured with ceramic stains
painted over a sandy textured high fired glaze containing a large
mount of calcined alumina.

Porcelain Bowl, 45 cm diameter × 15 cm high, by Paul Davis, 1993.
Wheel-thrown with slab additions, with a very 'dry' glaze (1320°C
reduction fired) and painted with coloured maiolica type glazes and
refired to 1100°C.

Above Porcelain Vase, wheel-thrown in two parts, with slab additions, decorated with brushwork, by Paul Davis, 1989.

Top left Porcelain vessel, 45 cm diameter, by Paul Davis, 1993. Wheel-thrown with slab additions. The very 'dry' glaze (1320°C in reduction) has a high proportion of calcined alumina producing a sandy texture. Painted colours provided by ceramic stains in a maiolica type glaze and refired (1100°C).

Left Bottle Form, by Derek Clarkson. Wheel-thrown porcelain, with brushwork motif painted in a diagonal rhythm (this motif is repeated four times up the pot). Fired in reduction to 1300°C.

Right Porcelain Bottle, 30 cm × 18 cm, by Alistair Whyte, 1993. With leaf decoration in latex resist and copper pigment under a clear glaze. Reduction fired to produce the copper red colour.
Photograph by Avon Colour Studio.

136

Three incense burners, porcelain decorated with painted gold and silver decoration, approximately 12 cm × 12 cm, by Alistair Whyte, 1993.
Photograph by Avon Colour Studio.

Large Lidded Jar, wheel-thrown porcelain, with brush decoration, by John Takehara (USA), 1993.

Some earlier work by **Paul Davis** (Australia) also is freely decorated with brushwork motifs developed from plant design (see page 136) but it is his latest pieces that are more unusual in their treatment. He uses mainly an insulator porcelain made by a local manufacturer. This clay is not particularly white but it is milled to an extremely fine particle size. Most porcelain glazes fit this body well. (See the glaze recipes listed on page 187.) Excellent white clays are available in Australia, he says, but industry does not seem to have a need for translucent porcelain. Davis' brightly coloured pieces are produced by a fairly complex process. After a normal bisque firing they are coated with a glaze containing a large quantity of calcined alumina which develops a sandy texture on the surface when fired to cone 11 (1320°C) in a reduction kiln atmosphere. Then he reworks the surface with a majolica-type glaze stained with various colours that is refired to 1100°C. 'This method provides me with a chance to use a wide range of colours which would otherwise be difficult to achieve at 1320°C.'

Alistair Whyte (Australia) spent several years studying porcelain ceramics in Japan and he acknowledges that oriental influences remain strong in his work although he does not try to produce 'Japanese' pots. 'Apart from making use of learned techniques, I try to be true to my own feelings of design and decoration. I am strongly drawn to the use of blue and white on porcelain because I feel that it enhances the whiteness and purity of the material.' It was while he was in Japan that Whyte first began to use *gosu*, the natural cobalt blue colour to be found in

Kiyomizu sometsuke (blue and white ware), which is a familiar aspect of much of his own work. At the present time, he is slowly exploring the use of a variety of glazes and more and more colour but he would probably regard himself as 'something of a purist'. He talks of

the meditative aspect of designing and carving the tools in the making process and of the patience that has to be learnt from the time of making and drying to the final firing of the kiln. The sense of satisfaction when, having created an object of beauty in porcelain, the light shines through between your fingers.

As with so many of the potters I have met, **Gordon Cooke** (UK) uses porcelain for its whiteness and close grain, and the opportunities offered by this to work in very fine detail. His unusual method for manipulating surface texture was fully described in *Studio Porcelain* but his latest work is rather different in character and treatment. He aims to create a unity between form, surface and colour. He says that he is motivated by many things ('not least the necessity to pay the mortgage!') but he thinks that the endless

Two porcelain boxes, by Gordon Cooke, 1993. Handbuilt, carved and stamped surface with low fired glaze and lustres. Bisque fired to 1250°C before glazing and refiring to 1100°C and decorating with colour on top of the glaze. larger box is 10 cm × 13 cm.

Open Vessel, 14.9 cm × 12.8 cm, by Ursula Scheid, 1992. Porcelain with paper resist design in black slip applied by brush under a feldspar/barium glaze and fired to 1360°C in a gas kiln with a reducing atmosphere.
Photograph by Rolf Zwillsperger.

permutations that are possible in arrangements of texture, pattern and colours that appeals to him most of all. He especially likes the 'secretive nature of boxes and the element of surprise when the lid is lifted to reveal inner decoration'. His present work is influenced by African fabric patterns, natural form and the paintings of Gustav Klimt and Friedrich Hundertwasser. He is also fascinated by certain architectural details which he records constantly in drawings and photographs. His pots are fired to a high bisque at cone 8. An earthenware glaze fired to 1100°C is applied to those areas which he wants to shine. Onglaze lustres are painted on to this as well as on some unglazed sections adding extra visual interest.

Painting with coloured slips enables the ceramicist to define precise areas with completely flat and opaque colour. They can be matt or shiny according to their composition. Normally, the same body provides the base material for making the slip but small additions of flux to this will encourage greater fusion and give the surface a sheen. **Ursula Scheid** (Germany) uses slips on some of her porcelain vessels in conjunction with intricate, geometric designs made from arrangements of cut masking tape which encircles and complements the forms with positive vertical and diagonal elements. The precise placement of the masking tapes is worked out directly on each unique piece before coloured slips are applied by painting. It is a

Lidded Box, slab-built porcelain with tape, resist design in coloured slips under a matt glaze, fired to 1360°C in reduction by Ursula Scheid

Vessel form, porcelain with resist design in coloured slips under a matt glaze, by Ursula Scheid, 1992.

Vessel Form, 30 cm high, by Kristin Andreassen, 1991. Handbuilt porcelain, with multi-layered slip decoration, fired to 1260°C in reduction.
Photograph by Teigens Fotoatelier A.S.

'Autumn Landscape', porcelain vessel, handbuilt, decorated with layered slips of various colours, fired to 1260°C in reduction, 32 cm high, by Kristin Andreassen, 1990.

firmly into the shape of the mould. The top of the pot is covered with a polythene sheet for an hour or so to allow the pot to stiffen further before 'stretching' the walls outwards with the bowl of a large, old-fashioned, egg-shaped, kitchen spoon. The curvature of the spoon fits most shapes and is easy to hold. A cardboard paddle is then used to refine the outer surface of the form.

Since I make my pieces by handbuilding, there is no reason why my pieces should have perfect symmetry. As I work on the shape, I look for lines and directions in the surface which I can use to make changes in the form. I often start by creating an imbalance, and try to recreate a balance by altering other parts of the 'cylinder'. Working with wet clay, the material itself will tell me by collapsing when I have crossed the boundary because a shape that stands well while wet can also survive a high-firing temperature without collapsing.

Andreassen uses a wide variety of coloured porcelain and slips for her decorated surfaces. Many layers of coloured porcelain covering each other partially or totally comprise the patterns.

Usually the bottom layer is black because other colours are intensified by its presence. Since the black contains much cobalt oxide, it may shine through other colours as a soft blue shade. I usually have an idea about the pattern before I start working, deciding which colours and techniques to employ and the main direction of the design. The rest is improvised. I try to make the vessels express different moods. The inspiration comes from erosion, nature and the material itself. I try to take advantage of any happy coincidence. The base layers may be added in various ways depending on their softness or plasticity. I can roll out very thin coloured slabs between two sheets of linen, scratch and draw on them, and stretch them carefully before attaching them to the base slab. I may paint or pour liquid slips directly on to the slab, dry it out with a piece of linen and fix it with a rolling pin.

Another, more unusual method used by Andreassen is to paint slips and water-based stains on to canvas attached to plywood or plasterboard. According to the tools used and the fluidity of the colours, she can make soft shades or precise line drawings to be applied, once the moisture *shine* has gone, to the base slab as a kind of 'transfer' pattern and the design is fixed by rolling. The vessel can then be constructed in the usual way with its pattern already in place.

fairly complex process. Finally, the slip decoration is covered by a transparent, matt glaze based on feldspar and barium, reduction fired to 1360°C in a gas kiln. The globular, swelling shapes of her bowls in particular seem as if they are stretching these patterns almost to bursting point, adding to their feeling of tension.

Kristin Andreassen (Norway) handbuilds using a porcelain body from Limoges (TM 10/LPB). She begins by pinching out a base and pressing this into a plaster mould to ensure it has a steady bottom and leaves it to stiffen until leatherhard. A cylinder made from a previously decorated, rolled out slab is then attached to the pinched section in the mould. Pressure is applied from the inside to fit the clay

Printed decoration

Ceramic transfers and printing methods have long been used in decorating pots for mass consumption but it is an aspect that has received only scant attention from studio potters. However, the techniques do present opportunities for painting or printing extremely detailed designs on to porcelain either in the leatherhard and the bisque state or on top of glaze. **Paul Scott** (UK) is one who has exploited this method on both tile panels and vessel forms. He uses a photocopier to make transparencies of drawings which he intends to reproduce as a ceramic print and then transfers this image on to a silk screen coated with a light sensitive film. The silk screen, with its light sensitive face, is placed down on to the transparency drawing and exposed to light from a mercury vapour lamp for about five minutes, making a contact print to fix the image. Then the screen is washed out with warm water to remove the areas not fixed by the exposure, i.e. the drawn images, and checked to ensure that the mesh is cleared of gel ready for printing. Screens made in this way can be used for printing directly on to tiles and slabs (Scott prefers to print on porcelain when the clay is becoming leatherhard) or for producing ceramic transfers for use on glazed pieces.

For printing underglazes on unfired clay, Scott mixes an 'ink' consisting of 10 parts of stain with 5 parts of powdered porcelain body (finely sieved) to 10 parts of a

water-based print medium using a palette knife to blend the material thoroughly on a flat glass plate. The mixture is thinned slightly to increase its volume with the addition of between 5 and 10 parts of a textile printing medium. He points out that the consistency of the prepared 'ink' is critical to printing successfully but this can only be judged through a process of trial and error. Finally, the 'ink' is forced through the mesh of the silk screen and printed on to the leatherhard tiles. Powdered glaze replaces the clay for making transfers and this is mixed with an oil-based medium and printed on to decal paper, a special paper coated with gum. When the printed images have dried, they are covered with a layer of transparent solvent-based resin applied through a blank silk screen. The transfers can be cut up when the 'covercoat' is dry. Soaking them in

Porcelain Bowl, 30 cm × 26 cm, by Susanne Fagermo (Norway), 1993. Slipcast, with transparent glaze coloured with vanadium pentoxide, fired to 1400°C in reduction. Decorated with silkscreen decals containing cerium oxide, vanadium pentoxide, uranium pentoxide, cobalt oxide and black ceramic stain and refired to 1280°C.

Below 'Pots No.32', porcelain panel with pen and ceramic 'ink' and underglaze colours, 60 cm × 40 cm, by Paul Scott, 1993. *Photograph by Andrew Morris.*

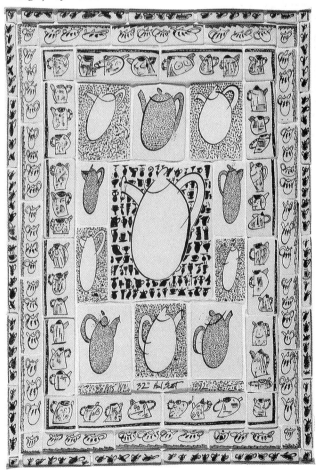

Porcelain Bowl, slipcast, with silk screened decal decoration containing uranium pentoxide and opaque glaze, fired to 1280°C in oxidation (multiple firings), 30 cm × 26 cm, by Susanne Fagermo, 1993.

warm water allows the transfers to float off the paper ready for immediate application to glazed ware. Detailing his processes in an article written for *Ceramic Review* No. 140, Scott places great emphasis on safety when handling these materials. 'If you do make ceramic transfers, ensure that you get safety datasheets on the oil-based medium and the covercoat. Use good ventilation at all times, and store products safely.'

Airbrushing

The airbrush is a wonderfully versatile tool. There are many different types available from which to choose one best-suited to the work in hand. The most basic models provide a constant spray pattern but far greater control is obtained with those having a trigger action. The latter model can produce an infinitely variable spray from very thin lines to the coverage of broad areas and with textures anywhere between coarse and fine. Passing ceramic materials at quite high pressure through these instruments does have a more abrasive effect than used with inks etc. and they require careful maintenance. It is necessary also to keep them meticulously clean while the work is in progress as well as after work is finished for they can easily clog up with compacted pigments, slips, lustres or glazes which stop them functioning correctly. Perhaps the most annoying and frustrating thing that can happen when pigment accumulates around the needle or when solid particles build up within the nozzle, is the sudden splattering of uncontrolled colour. This will most often occur, in my experience, when I have become so absorbed in the more expressive design aspects that I have neglected this elementary precaution and am approaching the final stage of the work! Since the main attraction of airbrushed colour is the smooth graduations that can be achieved, unintentional splatters or blobs will destroy the effect and illusion for which one aims.

I take the precaution of putting all my stains, whether commercially-prepared or mixed myself with an underglaze medium, through a 200s mesh cup sieve to ensure even dispersal with no lumps. The airbrush is dismantled and thoroughly cleaned after each session. While the work is in progress, also, clean water is frequently passed through the instrument so that no build up of hardened material is allowed to impede the free flow of colour. The nozzle cap must be regularly removed and the aperture checked for the same reason. Great care is necessary during this procedure because the needle point is so fine that it can be easily damaged. A bent needle will affect the performance of the airbrush quite badly and delicate work will be ruined by uneven splattering of colour. It is advisable to always keep a spare needle handy as a replacement. A bent needle can sometimes be repaired by gently rotating the point against a smooth board in a stroking movement.

Underglaze stains are well-suited to airbrushing on to porcelain at any stage from dry to bisque or over unfired glaze. Bright coloured stains that will withstand high temperatures and remain close to their appearance when first applied have become readily available over recent years. Colours and patterns can be applied freehand but, more frequently, masks of one kind or another are used to control the exact placement of the medium. Hand-held shapes cut from paper or card are simple masks to use. They can be oversprayed repeatedly as they are moved about the surface to build up multiple marks having a distinctive quality. Rich visual textures and tonal variations are thus possible with economy of means, provided that the mask does not become too wet so that the medium runs off and mars the design. Similarly, fixed masks made from paper tapes or other material must be dried out between successive appli-

Porcelain Bowl, 'Skies Series', 11 cm high × 27.5 cm diameter, by Peter Lane, 1993. Wheel-thrown and airbrushed with ceramic stains on the bisque. Fired to 1260°C in an electric kiln.

'Mountain Dawn' (Skies Series), wheel-thrown, translucent porcelain, airbrushed on the bisque with underglaze stains, fired to 1260°C in an electric kiln and polished, 13 cm high, by Peter Lane, 1993.

cations if bleeding of one colour into another at the edges is to be avoided.

Masking tape of the kind used in the automobile industry and for protecting window glass when the frames are painted is ideal for use with an airbrush and I, and many other potters, have used it extensively. It can be purchased in different widths which can be cut and reshaped to suit most aims. Some brands are slightly less adhesive than others and this is an undoubted advantage when applying tape to areas previously sprayed with underglaze stains so that another colour can be added. Coloured stains are best prepared with a good binding medium which fixes the colour firmly to the pot and prevents smudging. A number of excellent underglazes mixed with a suitable medium are commercially available for this purpose. My own preference is to work directly on bisqued ware (previously sanded smooth) by airbrushing the lightest colours first and to proceed with progressively darker colours until finally, perhaps, black is reached. This may mean that the piece is almost completely covered with tape, obscuring the design, until peeled away. I use a hot air gun to dry the colours and stop the tape from becoming saturated to overflowing with liquid medium when building up complex patterns with tapes. (Tapes made from any kind of plastics must be used with discretion because they quickly become too wet. They have the added disadvantage that they will shrink under excessive heat and so cannot be force dried.) With care, the colour remains clear and unblemished when, eventually, the tape is removed. Working in this way from light to dark rather than the reverse process avoids the problems encountered when removing a tape that leaves a residue of adhesive on an area still to be oversprayed. (Sasha Wardell works in the opposite direction, from dark to light colours when decorating her bone china with underglaze stains and she refers to the risk of pigment or glaze particles settling on traces of glue to become fixed in the final firing. See page 44.)

Unless masks of one kind or another are used with the airbrush, the spray pattern will always produce a soft edge even when the needle is set at the smallest aperture. This can be turned to advantage by combining soft and hard edges within the overall design. Colours can be merged gradually into one another so that the hues alter in the transition. Underglaze stains also offer the added convenience of remaining fairly true to their unfired colour when applied to pure white porcelain. It is easier, therefore, to assess the success or otherwise of the surface design before committing it to the kiln.

145

Translucent porcelain bowl mounted on an earthenware base by
Patrick Piccarelle (Belgium), 1993. The bowl is thrown and trimmed to
a very thin section, carved, bisque fired and then engraved and
pierced using dental tools. The holes are filled with a high viscosity
glaze and then glazed overall with various feldspathic glazes and fired
to 1300°C in a gas kiln. The bases for this series of pieces are fired
between 850°C and 950°C depending upon the kind of black surface
required.

Slips and glazes are less amenable to airbrushing,
although not impossible to use successfully, due to their
nature and larger particle size. They tend to take longer to
dry naturally. The hot air gun speeds this process but
glazes usually remain friable to some extent and liable to
disturbance while handling. Handheld masks are more
appropriate in this case since tapes cannot be applied to
unfired glaze. Resin-based lustres can also be used to good
effect providing that the airbrush is thoroughly cleaned
between each application of colour.

Clear glazes over stains make the colours appear
brighter but many people find that a glossy, reflective surface lessens the visual impact while matt glazes tend to
mute the colours. High-fired porcelain, therefore, is frequently left unglazed. Instead, pieces are polished smooth
at several stages in the making process. Rubbing down any

slight irregularities that appear after bisque firing can be
done with a fine grade of sandpaper (I use a zinc-based
type) and the surface is sponged clean of dust so that airbrushing can begin. (Sandra Black prefers to polish her
porcelain bisque, after soaking it in water to avoid the usual
build up of dust, by using firstly a 300 grade of wet and dry
sandpaper and then the finer 600 grade.) Following the
final firing to 1220°C or above, the work is thoroughly
polished with a very fine grade of silicon carbide paper,
'wet 'n dry'. This action removes any hard particles which
may have emerged as the clay contracted further in the
kiln, spoiling the smooth surface.

Carving and piercing

Porcelain is especially amenable to carving and piercing at
various stages of making but, perhaps, it is at its most
seductive when the clay has lost some of its moisture.
Carving when the clay has dried out completely has its
attractions for some potters but it does present a very real
risk to health through inhalation of clay dust. For this
reason I would not recommend carving unless a degree of
moisture remains and that it is sufficient to bind the cut
waste together as it is removed. *This waste clay should not be
permitted to fall on the floor and be trodden to dust as it dries.*
Another important reason for working the clay while it is
still damp is that it retains a certain flexibility and is thus
less likely to crack or split under the pressure of carving
tools.

I frequently left pieces to dry out completely when I first
began carving porcelain in the early 1970s and often suffered considerable frustrations as a result. It is much more
difficult to cut smoothly into bone-dry porcelain even with
the sharpest of tools. I have found that the perfect condition for most carving applications in my own work is when
the clay has dried to a rather stiff, 'leatherhard' state. Distortion is far less likely to occur when this point is reached.

Many different tools can be used and each will impart its
own character to the work. Bent wire loop tools having a
round section produce a slightly softer edge to cut channels than those made with a flatter section. Solid blades,
whether metal or wooden, meet with greater resistance in
the clay and can leave more obvious chatter marks. Both
open and solid tools can be used to carve channels of
varying width and depth in one movement in a rather
calligraphic manner. Needle points give thinner linear
marks which usually remain constant in width. Multiple,
repetitive marks made in the surface of a pot with any tool
produces a strong rhythmic texture. I have made some of

Eggshell porcelain slipcast in two layers with part of the outer layer carved away to increase translucency. Multiple glazes were applied and fired several times in an oxidising atmosphere. 26 cm diameter. By Jeroen Bechtold, 1993.
Photograph by R. Gerritsen.

walls were pierced proved critical for their physical survival. If too much clay was removed below a certain level relative to any given profile, the walls would be weakened and unable to maintain their shape. It is always of the utmost importance to give sufficient support to the wall of a bowl with one hand while the other applies pressure in carving. This is especially so when working from the inside outwards because all the stress is centred over very small area. Carving from the outside inwards is slightly less risky because, to some extent, the pressure is distributed more evenly around the circumference. I had to work fairly rapidly in order to counter the problem of the clay drying out as I worked. I have never liked to see carving which merely pierces through the wall leaving a crude cut edge as a sharp

'Ring of Trees', porcelain bowl, wheel-thrown, carved and pierced, with satin matt white glaze, fired to 1260°C in an electric kiln, 16 cm diameter, by Peter Lane, 1982.

Vessel Form with carved top and pierced decoration, reduction fired to 1280°C in a gas kiln, 16 cm high, by Horst Göbbels.
Photograph by Wolf Böwig.

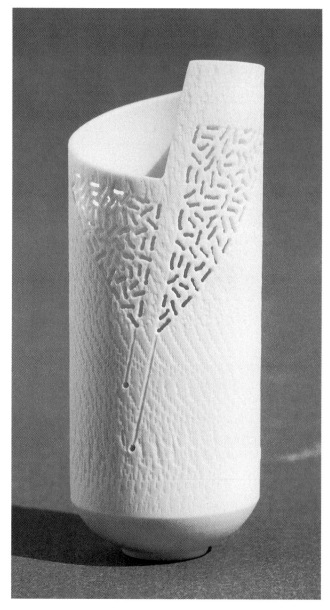

my favourite tools from metal strips used in the building industry to bind parcels of bricks to a wooden pallet. These strips can often be found lying around on building sites or dumped in skips. Reduced into short lengths (10–15 cm) (4–6 in.) and cut across diagonally at one end, they can be sharpened on a grindstone to make ideal tools for incising porcelain. Vee-shaped linear incisions with one side of the vee longer than the other can produce surface effects rather like those to be seen on beautifully carved Chinese vessels with celadon glazes from the 10th and 11th centuries.

Greater care is necessary when piercing right through the clay wall not only in its execution but with proper regard to the fired strength of the finished piece. If piercing is done without sufficient understanding of the stresses which the form will suffer in the kiln, serious deformation can occur. The risk of slumping is reduced where the wall of the piece is vertical but special care is necessary where holes are cut through on sharply curved sections which have to support the weight of the clay above. Faults of this nature are more likely to be revealed in large forms. I well remember problems I had to overcome with a series of porcelain bowls I used to make on the theme of 'Trees'. This entailed cutting away a fairly extensive part around the circumference of a bowl. Each of those thinly-thrown bowls stood on quite narrow footrings from which they swelled up and outwards to the rim. The point at which the

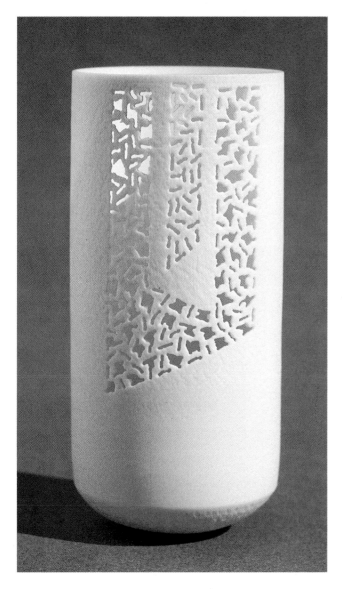

Cylindrical Vessel Form, porcelain, carved and pierced and fired to 1280°C in reduction in a gas kiln, 13 cm high, by Horst Göbbels.

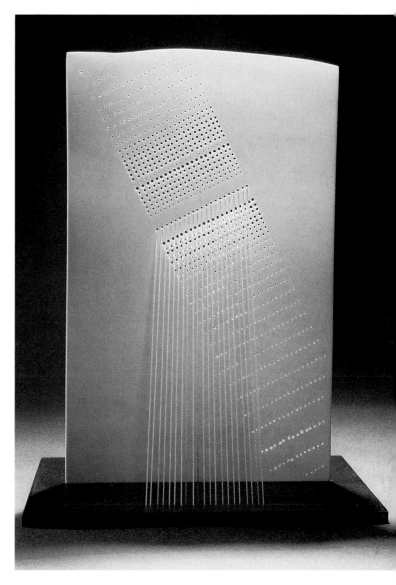

Translucent porcelain slab sculpture, pierced and threaded with red strings. Reduction fired to 1280°C in a gas kiln, 38 cm high, by Horst Göbbels, 1991.
Photograph by Wolf Böwig.

right angle within its thickness so I would always bevel the edges with the narrow-bladed scalpel immediately after completing the pierced shapes. These would be softened further with a fine grade of steel wool when the piece was completely dry (see illustration on page 148).

Some of the finest filigree carving of porcelain in recent years has been done by the German potter, **Horst Göbbels**. He has produced work of great delicacy and with much intricate, highly-ordered detail. Many of his vessel forms have only minimal contact with the surface on which they stand. Bottoms are rounded or raised on small foot-rings or elevated on integral pedestals. These devices contribute even more to the appearance of weightlessness and ethereality. At the same time, the mathematical precision

of both the design and of the carving conveys a feeling of strength as much as fragility. There is little sense of fragmentation because that which has been removed is balanced by and of equal value to that which remains. The relationship of the inside and outside surfaces is accentuated. Colour and glaze are of secondary importance in such pieces and many are left unglazed. All his vessel forms are thrown using the KPCL porcelain from Limoges in France. Carved and perforated sections of the design are done with a broken saw blade when the piece has dried to the consistency of hard leather. The work is fired to 1280°C in a gas kiln with a reduction atmosphere.

'Deco Bowl' and 'Bird and Fish Bowl', porcelain carved and pierced with surgical blades, fired to cone 10 (1300°C) in an electric kiln, by Sandra Black.

Sandra Black from Western Australia has long been recognised for her carved and pierced porcelain and bone china vessels. Her designs are sometimes reminiscent of the angular patterns of the Art Deco period. Geometric carving in relief often has elements of the pattern cut away completely, giving emphasis to the rhythmic decoration and revealing the inner wall. Such pieces are frequently polished smooth but left unglazed. Her chosen motifs (e.g. 'fish and birds') are often interlinked or juxtaposed rather like an Escher drawing without the transmutation (see illustration above). She likes to make about 20 or more pots on the wheel and stores them in an old refrigerator to keep them damp. She stresses the importance of turning or trimming them to an even thickness of about 2 mm ($\frac{1}{16}$ in.) rather than leaving them too thick so that they lose translucency or making them so thin that they risk being cracked while carving or slump in the kiln. Black restricts herself to just four tools in the carving process. There are a surgical blade in a cane holder, a soft brush, a sponge and a water sprayer. Designs are first drawn on to the pot with the tip of the blade and then cut into about half the wall

Teapot, 'Time Gate', series made in black bone china with applied gold leaf by Sandra Black, 1990. The bone china slip is stained with iron chromate 7%, black iron oxide 7% and cobalt carbonate 3.5% and, as these are strong fluxes, the normal firing temperature is lowered to cone 4–cone 5 depending on the firing schedule. *Photograph by Victor France.*

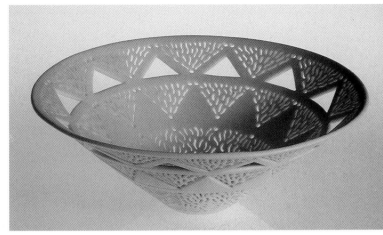

Bowl, slipcast porcelain, carved and pierced at the leatherhard stage and cleaned up when dry, fired to cone 7 in an electric kiln, by Sandra Black.
Photograph by Victor France.

'Deco Vase', by Sandra Black. Wheel-thrown porcelain, carved with surgical blades, lightly sanded at the dry stage and polished after bisque and final firings with silicon carbide pads. Fired to cone 10 in an electric kiln.
Photograph by Victor France.

thickness. The same blade is used on its side to remove excess clay and establish the relief. The soft brush is used to dislodge small particles without damaging the design and, finally, a damp sponge softens the edges and smooths the surface. The work is bisque fired to 950°C and those that are to remain unglazed are soaked in water and sanded down, first with a 300 grade then a 600 grade of silicon carbide paper until they are completely smooth. Polishing the pieces while they are wet prevents dust flying around and from clogging the silicon carbide grit.

Karl Scheid's carving shares the control and precision that is evident in the work of Horst Göbbels and Sandra Black but, although abstract, it is usually more organic in nature. His vessel forms are not pierced but instead the carving flows around and embraces his forms making them objects for quiet reflection. Glazes pool in the depressions. Ridges, although crisply cut, are softened and less severe. Repeated, rhythmic movements with the carving tool endows his work with an unforced, naturally rhythmic pattern that encompasses and complements the form in an expressive way that makes it unique.

A more powerfully demonstrative kind of carving can be seen in the porcelain pieces by **Rolf Bartz** (Australia). His interest in carving was aroused initially by the work of prominent ceramicists using this technique and being heavily influenced by products of the Art Nouveau and

Oval Shaped Vessel, 14 cm high, by Karl Scheid, 1989. Porcelain with cobalt slip and relief decoration under a copper red, feldspar/petalite glaze. Fired to 1360°C in a gas kiln with a reducing atmosphere.
Photograph by Rolf Zwillsperger.

151

Slab-built vessel form 20 cm high with the top square 9 cm × 9 cm, by Karl Scheid, 1993. Mounted on a square base, porcelain, painted with green slip, partly unglazed and part with copper red feldspathic glaze fired to 1360°C in reduction atmosphere (gas kiln).
Photograph by Rolf Zwillsperger.

Bowl, wheel-thrown porcelain with diagonally carved relief decoration on copper slip under a feldspar-petalite glaze, fired to 1360°C in a reducing atmosphere. 10.9 cm diameter × 7.2 cm high, by Karl Scheid, 1990.
Photograph by Bernd Gobbels.

Bottom right Porcelain bowl with fluted carving under a copper red glaze, fired to 1360°C in a reducing atmosphere, diameter 11.9 cm × 9.8 cm high, by Karl Scheid, 1989.
Photograph by Peter Lane.

Art Deco movements. The growth and shapes of plants provide him with ample subject matter to embellish a variety of vessel forms. Pieces are wheel-thrown with unusually thick walls because he likes to carve deeply and to suggest different layers and overlapping shapes. No further clay is added to these pieces and the eventual form is decided purely by the amount of clay which is removed during the carving process. Having thrown a piece and allowed it to become firm and easy to handle, he trims it to perfect the shape, especially for his vase forms. Normally, he throws about six pieces in one session and this provides him with enough basic material for carving to keep him fully occupied for two weeks or more depending on the complexity of the design. Incising and excising is carried out when the clay has dried to a fairly hard state. Various tools are used for this work but his favourite for carving is a nib-shaped tool with a curved head and shaft, sharpened on the edges and fitted into a handle. The abrasive action of the clay causes this to wear down very quickly. The flat wire type of modelling tools are particularly useful for smoothing and scraping between raised areas of the design. He has found that some dental tools are excellent for dealing with tight corners and narrow sections while flexible aluminium scrapers are ideal for smoothing away unwanted carving marks on larger areas. It can take anything between four and ten hours to complete a single carved form. 'Probably the hardest part of all is handling the pot while carving, especially in the latter stages as it becomes more fragile. On a number of occasions I have cracked a piece while carving the last part and seen several hours of work come to nothing.'

When the pieces have been thoroughly dried, Bartz uses a fine grade of steel wool to finish smoothing the whole surface and then applies colours (commercially-prepared underglaze stains) painted with a brush or sprayed through an airbrush. The work is once-fired to 1260°C in an electric kiln before being given a final polish with wet 'n dry emery paper. This gives the work a smooth, tactile finish which he feels is more sympathetic to the carved design than a glaze.

Most potters who choose to carve porcelain refer to the problems experienced in the latter stages when the pieces are drying rapidly and too much pressure applied while carving or piercing the thin walls can cause cracks which may not be evident until the work has been fired. **Margaret Frith** (UK) mentions losses suffered in this way and also other frustrations encountered in several commercially-prepared bodies when iron specks appeared in the otherwise pure white surface. This encouraged her to prepare her own porcelain body, made by the 'slop' method, and that particular problem has now been eliminated. She throws all her bowls and then turns them upside down on the wheel to obtain an even thickness throughout the length of the wall before adding a thickly thrown ring to the base. This is re-thrown *in situ* to match the pot. 'This method has stopped any 'S' cracks appearing in the base of the bowls.'

Potters often complain about 'S' shaped cracking in the

'Lily Bowl', 14 cm high, by Rolf Bartz, 1991. Wheel-thrown and carved porcelain, with airbrushed and painted underglaze colours. This piece is unglazed but it has been polished with silicon carbide paper after firing to 1260°C in an electric kiln.
Photograph by Grant Hancock.

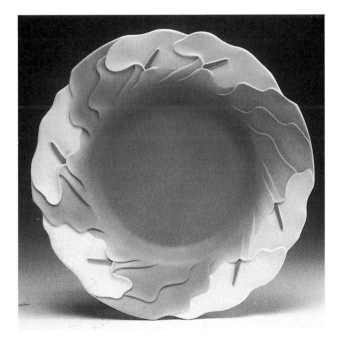

'Lily Plate', 23 cm diameter, by Rolf Bartz, 1992. Wheel-thrown and carved porcelain with airbrushed and painted underglaze colours and once-fired to 1260°C in an electric kiln. Unglazed but polished with wet and dry silicon carbide paper.
Photograph by Michal Kluvanek.

'Lily Vase and Plate', wheel-thrown and carved porcelain with airbrushed underglaze stain in pale blue, fired in an electric kiln to 1260°C, unglazed but polished, by Rolf Bartz, 1989.

bases of their porcelain pots but this is a problem that I am rarely troubled by in my own work. I find that bowls, especially, can be thrown while leaving sufficient thickness in the base to provide a footring which can be turned out from the inverted pot at the leatherhard stage. The pressure of the turning tools (I always use small, strapwire tools for this purpose) helps to compress and align the clay particles sufficiently to avoid cracking occurring. Bowls are usually left to dry naturally, inverted on their rims. However, on occasions when time is of the essence, I have dried out quite damp bowls with their footrings in direct contact with our Rayburn cooker-cum-central heating boiler in the kitchen without loss. I check the state of dampness in each piece by holding its foot against a mirror which reveals a ring of condensation until completely dry.

Porcelain Bowl, 28 cm diameter, by Margaret Frith, 1993. Wheel-thrown, with wax resist decoration and painted with coloured pigments and glazes (blue, black, purple, orange and white). Fired to 1280°C in a reducing atmosphere (gas kiln).
Photograph by Nick Broomhead.

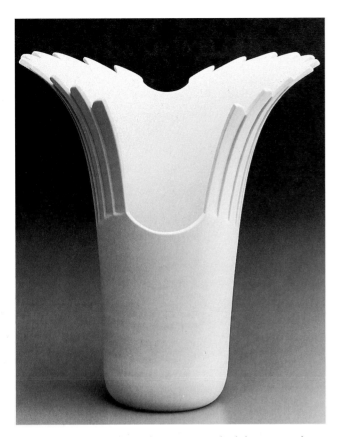

Porcelain Bowl, 24 cm diameter, by Margaret Frith, 1993. Wheel-thrown and carved with floral design under a blue celadon glaze which pools in the depressions to emphasise the carving. Fired to 1280°C in a reducing atmosphere.

'Fan Vase', 22 cm high, by Rolf Bartz, 1986. Wheel-thrown porcelain, deeply carved, unglazed but polished with wet and dry silicon carbide paper after firing to 1260°C in an electric kiln.
Photograph by Grant Hancock.

Margaret Frith likes to commence carving while the clay is at the softer end of leatherhard because she says that 'after handling for an hour or two it dries quickly and you have to be very careful not to break it as you near the end of the work'. She carves with metal tools made from old hacksaw blades by her husband, David, who is a stoneware potter. The blades are given wooden handles to make them more comfortable to work with.

I like to use them like drawing with a pencil so they must be nice to hold. The smoothness of the porcelain body makes it ideal for carving on open bowls and jars. These designs are mainly floral. I draw beforehand but I like to work directly on to the clay without copying so that I can achieve greater spontaneity and flow. Every imperfection shows on a pale blue celadon, carved piece and losses can be frustratingly high. A piece of soft, malleable clay, nurtured through all its processes and carefully placed in the fire and coached to orange heat, never ceases to amaze me at the cooling of the kiln. A wonderful transformation takes place which can last for thousands of years. This is the force that drives me on!

Lidded Ginger jar with Bird Knob, by Margaret Frith, 1993. Wheel-thrown porcelain, wax resist decoration with coloured pigments and glazes (blue, black, pink, white and orange). Fired to 1280°C in reduction (gas kiln).
Photograph by Nick Broomhead.

Incising

Traditional celadon-type glazes have long been favoured by those who incise and carve porcelain. Every mark, even the smallest scratch in the clay surface is emphasised and revealed under these delicately coloured, transparent glazes. In the hands of a skilled carver today, pieces made in this way still possess the same seductive qualities that have charmed countless numbers over hundreds of years. Some of the most expressive incised work being produced in porcelain in the 1990s comes from the American potter, **Elaine Coleman**. Her fluent drawing of cranes incised on a large porcelain plate under a pale, turquoise blue celadon

'Two Jars with Elephant Lids', 14 cm and 12 cm high, by Margaret Frith, 1993. Wheel-thrown porcelain with carved decoration under a blue celadon glaze, fired to 1280°C in a reducing atmosphere.

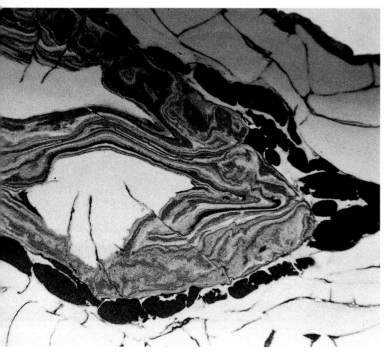

Surface detail of a laminated agateware dish 'Rocks and Minerals Series (1988–1989), porcelain, unglazed but polished, by Maggie Barnes.

Porcelain Plate, wheel-thrown and incised with a pattern of cranes under a turquoise blue celadon glaze, 40 cm diameter × 6.5 cm high, by Elaine Coleman, 1993.

158

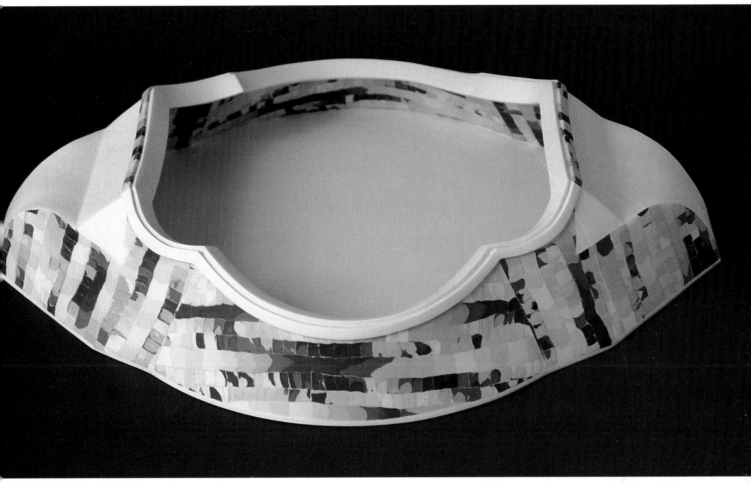

'Mediterranean Mosaic', handbuilt from multi-coloured, laminated and inlaid porcelain slabs and fired to 1280°C in an electric kiln, 41.5 cm × 31 cm, by Saskia Koster, 1991.

glaze demonstrates the possibilities of the technique extremely well. It is essential to make positive movements with any tools used for incising because a tentative or hesitant approach results in clumsy, awkward work that will be ruthlessly exposed under the glaze.

Neriage and inlaid techniques

Porcelain can be easily coloured with commercially-prepared stains or combinations of metallic oxides to povide the potter with a reliable and scintillating palette. Marbling is the simplest way of using compound mixtures of coloured clays but the patterns produced are fairly random. Such mixtures are usually wedged together before use and they inevitably develop linear patterns in a spiral formation around a wheel-thrown pot. If the potter wishes

Porcelain Vase, wheel-thrown and incised with 'leaf' decoration completely covering the surface, under a dark green, celadon glaze, 45 cm high, by Elaine Coleman, 1993.

Bowl made from mainly white and blue/black-stained porcelain laminated and pressed into a mould, 23 cm × 16cm, by May An Go 1993.

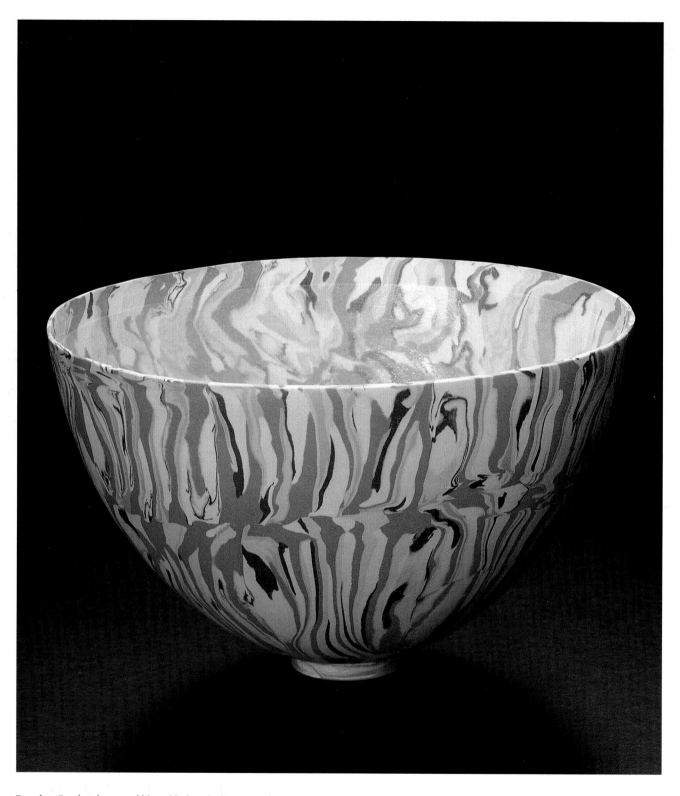

Porcelain Bowl, in laminated blues, black and white, press formed in a
mould, 26 cm × 20 cm wide and 17 cm high, by May An Go, 1992.
In the collection of Boymans Museum, Rotterdam.

'Flying Home', 20 cm high × 45 cm wide × 10 cm deep, by Curtis Benzle, 1992. Vessel form with inlaid and incised, multi-coloured porcelain. The extremely thin walls of this piece allow light to pass through enhancing and revealing both inner and outer decorated surfaces at the same time.
In the collection of The University of Miami.

to keep the inner surface white while the outside becomes a striated pattern of inlaid clays the white porcelain 'host' body is first centred on the wheel and then sliced open in two or three places around the circumference for coloured clays of the same plastic consistency to be inserted. The form is then opened up in the normal way and pulled up to the required height and shape. Any 'muddy' slip created in the process of throwing is carefully removed from the surface with a sharp tool (flexible kidney-shaped steel tools are ideal for this purpose) towards the end of the throwing process. Subsequent turning will help to increase the clarity of the colours. Further visual interest can be given to pots thrown in this manner by rhythmic, vertical fluting with a wire tool when leatherhard.

When researching my first book *Studio Porcelain* in 1979, I found only a few potters specialising in the technique of neriage or marquetry which entails the use of multi-coloured porcelain sliced up and assembled so that the pattern becomes an integral part of the form. This method allows the potter much greater control than is possible in marbling. It also requires far more care in the construction and a great deal of patience. Drying of forms made this way must be extremely gradual if cracking and separation of the constituent pieces is to be avoided. The slow building process has a certain advantage in that the maker can

Bowl in porcelain stained yellow, black and white, laminated and pressed into a mould, 23 cm × 19 cm, by May An Go, 1992.

adjust the design as work proceeds. In addition, what you see is what you get, allowing for slight variations in the intensity of the colours in the final firing. Problems can arise, however, where stains or oxides cause uneven fluxing of the body so that some pieces shrink more than others pulling the joints apart. This can be overcome by (a) carefully testing the proportions of colour stain added to the base body to ensure compatibility and (b) firing very slowly to the optimum temperature. Some forms may need to be supported in bisque moulds during firing to help them keep their shape without distortion due to the different fluxing effects of added stains.

Potters such as **Dorothy Feibleman** (UK), **Curtis Benzle** (USA) and **Thomas Hoadley** (USA), whose work has been featured in my previous books, have continued to refine the art of neriage while many others are now producing exciting and high quality work by the same method. In particular, three Dutch potters, **Saskia Koster**, **May An Go**, and **Judith de Vries**, and **Mieke Everaet** from Belgium have all chosen to use variations of this technique with considerable success.

Bowl Form, porcelain, 29 cm × 19 cm × 19 cm, by Judith de Vries, 1993. The base is wheel-thrown and then pushed into an oval form and slabs of laminated and inlaid coloured porcelain are added to it. The inside has a transparent glaze but the outside is polished with very fine silicon carbide paper. Fired to 1200°C in an electric kiln.

Left Bottle Form inlaid with coloured porcelains, evoking a landscape theme, burnished exterior with glaze only on the inside. Fired to 1280°C in reduction, 30 cm high, by Sony Manning (Australia), 1994. *Photograph by David McArthur.*

Vase, 'Spring', approximately 35 cm high, by Judith de Vries, 1993.
Constructed from separately made 'leaves' of laminated, coloured
porcelain built up piece by piece. Fired to 1200°C in an electric kiln.

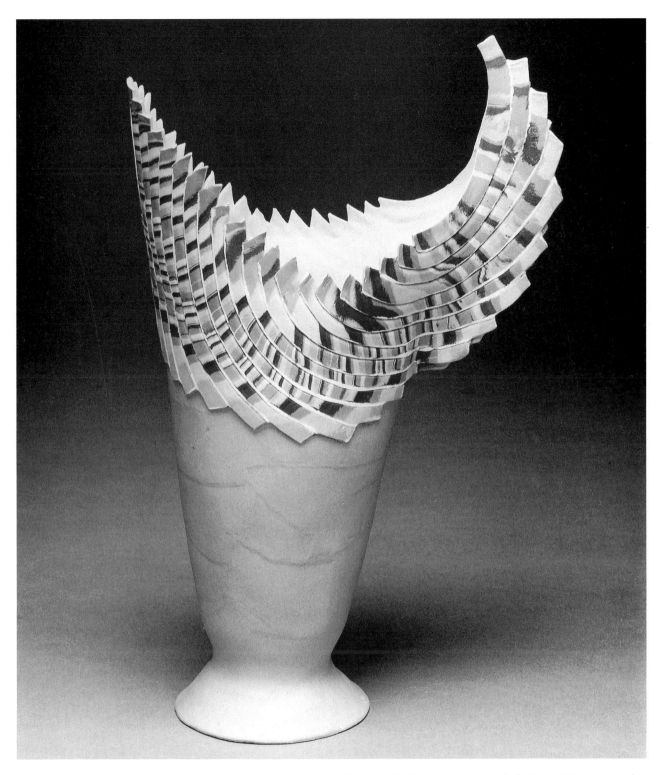

Vase form, 42 cm high, by Judith de Vries, 1992. Made from laminated strips of coloured porcelain. A multi-coloured, laminated slab is laid on top of a white porcelain slab and the two are joined together by rolling. The inside is glazed but the outside is polished. Fired to 1200°C in an electric kiln.

Vase, 'Bluebird', 35 cm high, by Judith de Vries, 1992. Constructed partly in a mould and partly by handbuilding with slabs of laminated, coloured porcelain. Two layers of clay are rolled out together (so that the inside remains white and without pattern) and then cut into strips and assembled, overlapping each other, with slip. The lower part outside is sprayed with a porcelain engobe mixed with 6% bodystain (blue) while the inside is celadon. Fired to 1200°C in an electric kiln. *Photograph by Claude Crommelin.*

Above
Laminated Parian vessel form, 20 cm × 11 cm approx., by Dorothy Feibleman. Built as a flat slab and then put in to a mould. Distortion and further changes in shape take place in the firing (1120°C in an electric kiln) due to overloading with chemicals.
Photograph by Thomas Ward, courtesy of Bonhams, London.

(a) Pair of earrings, laminated and carved porcelain mounted on cast and constructed 18 ct gold. Ceramic beads made by forming around a needle and cutting with a surgical scalpel. The gold beads are cut from 18 ct gold tube on a lathe, the arrows are cast 18 ct gold. 4.5 cm.
(b) Multi-strand necklace with cast 18 ct gold arrows and had cut ceramic arrows. Ceramic beads made around a needle and cut with a surgical scalpel. 18 ct gold beads cut and carved on a lathe. Spacers of 18 ct gold and carved and ground agate porcelain. Side slide clasp constructed of 18 ct gold and cut and ground agate turquoise porcelain set in bezels. 30 cm.
(c) Single strand porcelain necklace with laminated and carved beads and end pieces with 18ct gold cast beads and 18 ct hinged, moveable clasp. 'The end pieces are meant to be worn at the back but people tend to wear them at the front.' 30 cm. By Dorothy Feibleman.
Photograph courtesy of Christies, London.

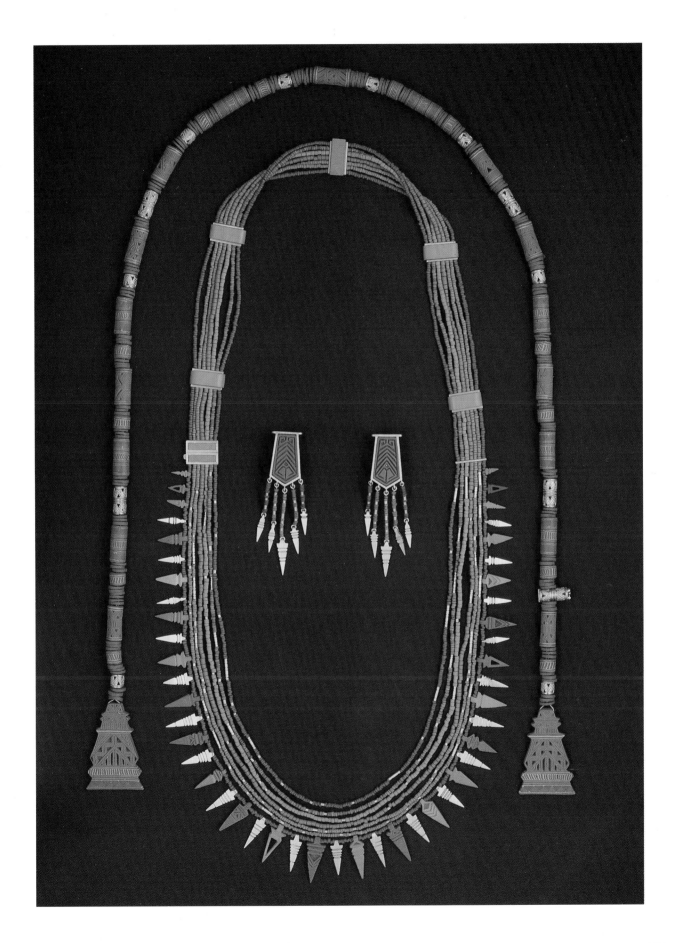

Three vessel forms, 'L'Afrique', handbuilt with laminated, multi-coloured porcelain, fired to 1280°C in an electric kiln, 23 cm, 22 cm and 22 cm diameter, by Mieke Everaet, 1993.

Two Bowl Forms, 20 cm and 7.5 cm diameter, by Mieke Everaet, 1992. Handbuilt with laminated, multi-coloured porcelain with their translucency enhanced by 'eggshell thin' walls. Fired to 1280°C in an electric kiln.

Saskia Koster makes architectural 'vessel' forms in which she tries to impart a sense of harmony through 'space and silence'. Inspiration for much of her work comes from the flat, empty and rather monotonous landscape around Groningen in the north west of Holland. She makes many sketches and describes attempting to translate her feeling for the 'extensive space and silence of my flat country' with its patchwork and stripes of fields and dykes, the movement of clouds across the landscape, and atmospheric conditions generated by the changing seasons. Form and colour are inseparable in her work. Colour contrasts with and accentuates elements within the object. Her abstract vessel forms are often based on combinations of circles and squares because she wants to 'create unity between forms of different qualities' and this offers opportunities 'to make unexpected objects with a tension' through their interaction. Koster makes models of part or all of her pieces in paper first. This is necessary for her to determine how slabs will fit together. Generating and rearranging geometric

forms she is always conscious of her wish to 'design an individual (three-dimensional) object having no direct reference to existing shapes'.

She introduces colour into the white porcelain two different ways. Sometimes colours are mixed thoroughly throughout the body which allows her to produce well-defined patterns. The other method requires the preparation of coloured porcelain which is then dried completely and ground into powder. A slab of plastic white porcelain is then covered with the coloured powder and rolled into the surface. The powder absorbs moisture from the damp clay and ensures a perfect marriage between the two.

The method of joining strips and slabs of porcelain with slip is common to all handbuilding, but where coloured stains are likely to cause varying rates of shrinkage, and this problem is further compounded by using slabs made up of many different elements, then drying becomes the most critical stage of the whole process. Koster says that experience has taught her 'to be very patient, *very, very* patient' and this statement is echoed by others. She says that the drying period can take as long as four months to one year according to the form and whether it is constructed as a single or double walled piece.

170

The extremely complex decorative patterns seen in the work of **Judith de Vries** are made piece by piece with multiple strips of coloured clays. These are rhythmically arranged in overlapping layers which, to some extent, dictate the evolution of the forms and produce a strong sensation of movement. The coloured stains and oxides are mixed with water before kneading and wedging into the white porcelain. Occasionally, she uses moulds to support the bottom, or bottles or cans as props inside vertical vessels while she is working on them. Some of the forms also require supporting in moulds while in the kiln if they are not to suffer deformation.

Dorothy Feibleman refers to her particular technique of assembling sections of poly-coloured porcelain as millefiore. In one of her methods she rolls out, separately, several thin, even slabs of clay of different colours on finely textured cloth. The slabs are coated with thin layers of slip between them and then bonded together using a rolling pin. A sharp knife is used to cut a slice vertically through the layered slab and each strip is then turned on its side to reveal the striped surface. These are rejoined with slip (often of a contrasting colour) and pushed tightly together to make into a new slab which can itself be re-cut in a variety of directions and reassembled until a particular design is achieved. Eventually, the new slab with its pattern appearing on both sides can be cut to fit a plaster mould into which it is gently coaxed. The whole is then wrapped in polythene to allow gradual drying to take place. Any smudging of the colours occurring during assembly are scraped carefully away when dried to a leatherhard state and, finally, smoothed when the pot is bone dry.

Glazes are rarely used by potters using neriage techniques because the clarity of the patterned surface could be obscured or become too reflective. The crisp designs and bright colours to be seen in the work of **Mieke Everaet**, for example, would be, in a sense, cheapened by a covering of shiny, transparent glaze. This young potter, born in 1963, has developed a uniquely personal style that brought her international recognition soon after completing her studies in Antwerp. Despite some unexpected results and failures caused by technical difficulties with uneven shrinkage of porcelain mixed in different colours, she has produced many exquisitely beautiful designs. Her pieces are well-conceived and executed with a remarkable liveliness considering their graphic complexity, while colours are carefully coordinated to unify pattern and form.

Everaet speaks of the forms, composition and colours of her pieces as evoking 'exotic influences, emotions inspired by nature or the memories of recent styles transcribed into

Bowl with strong, diagonal pattern in lines of different coloured porcelain laminated together and fired to 1320°C in a reducing atmosphere, 15 cm diameter × 8 cm high, by Rainer Doss, 1993.

Bowl with strong diagonal pattern of multi-coloured, laminated porcelain, fired to 1320°C in a reducing atmosphere, 17.5 cm diameter × 15 cm high, by Rainer Doss, 1993.

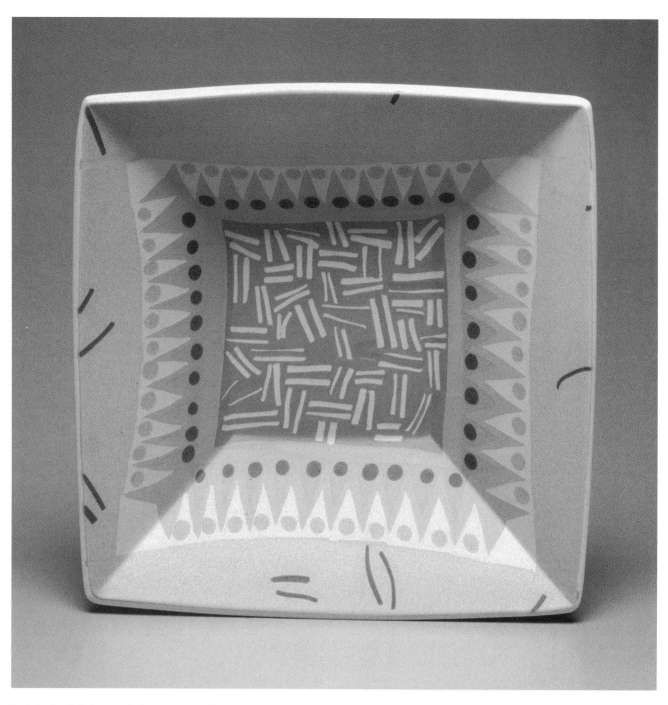

Rectangular Dish form made from press-moulded, laminated, coloured porcelain, fired to cone 8 (1250°C), 34 cm × 34 cm, by Anne Mercer, 1993.

artistic language'. The bowl is a favoured shape with its open character offering both inner and outer surfaces to view and, since the design is echoed precisely within and without, there is little room for confusion. The simplicity of these basic forms can support complex graphical imagery to a degree that would overwhelm a more consciously articulated shape. Light, especially when strategically placed, is gathered and diffused through extremely thin walls, and adds a certain magical quality. Black slip used to join the fragments of coloured porcelain appears as black boundary lines of varying thickness. The density of the black contrasts delightfully with the variable translucency of the coloured areas. Many of her bowls have thin strips of colour alternating with thinner black lines rising up vertically and radially from a small base to form a broad encircling band. This often constitutes a large part of the bowl which supports another band with contrasting colours and

Porcelain Vessel, handbuilt from different coloured clays laminated together, by Thomas Hoadley, 1987.

Three handbuilt bowls with laminated sections, porcelain, tallest 25 cm high, by Thomas Hoadley, 1993.
Photograph by Paul Rocheleau.

tones around the rim which defines the personality of the piece. The work is fired in an electric kiln to 1280°C.

Rainer Doss (Germany) exploits diagonal rhythms in many of his inlaid bowls. Stripes of different colours and widths from wide to narrow swirl upwards, sharply angled around the forms in a strong pattern mirrored inside and out.

Of course, another way to make precise placements of colour is to inlay slips and stained plastic clay made from the same body to ensure compatibility. I use some of the dried trimmings from my wheel-thrown work as the base material. This is thoroughly dried and reduced to fine powder ready to be weighed for the additions of carefully measured percentages of stains or colouring oxides. After mixing with water this is then sieved several times through an 80s and 100s mesh to obtain even dispersal of colour throughout the mix. Unless the mixture is required to be used as a slip for painting, spraying or inlaying, I pour the slip mixture into a plaster mould previously lined with a fine muslin cloth and leave it to stiffen to a plastic state. The cloth enables the clay to be easily removed from the mould without sticking. It can then be kneaded to a workable consistency as a coloured body for inlaying or assembling into neriage-type patterns or for making one-piece forms.

Coloured porcelain can be placed directly on top of slabs of the same body and in the same condition, whether white or coloured, and then pressed into the parent slab by rolling. This method causes the applied pieces to spread under pressure of the roller and allowances must be made for that in the design. The inlaid slabs may be used in various ways to build any kind of form but one of the most suitable is to lay the rolled slab face down over a plaster or bisque hump mould to create a dish or bowl with its decorated surface uppermost. An example of this technique can be seen in the 'Bug Plate' by **Anne Mercer** (Australia).

Inlaid slabs made by the rolling method offer other possibilities when they are stretched in the opposite direction. Instead of bending the decorated surface inwards as described above, the slab can be bent round into a cylindrical shape with the pattern outside. This movement causes the inlaid elements to separate slightly from the parent slab so that a narrow crevice appears around the outline. This fissure can itself be inlaid with slip, oxides or stains. Rolling white into white porcelain and painting a dark colour in the cracks is particularly effective. Any excess colour is removed with a metal scraper or steel wool when the work is dry.

For even greater control of the placement of colour, the completed object can be incised (up to half the thickness of the wall) or areas removed from the surface and then inlaid with slips or with plastic clay only slightly damper than the underlying form. Slow drying is usually necessary to prevent separation or cracking. Again, excess clay is cleaned up when the piece is dry. Slips must be applied until the inlay stands proud of the surface to allow for shrinkage as it dries out. Compressing the slip into the incisions when it has stiffened helps to ensure a good bond.

Tom Hoadley (USA) cites the countless variety of patterns to be found in nature as providing his primary source of inspiration but other influences 'range from fabric designs to styles of contemporary music, to painting and graphic design'. His distinctive bowl forms are begun by draping a disc of soft clay, whether patterned or a solid colour, over a bisqued hump mould. When it has stiffened enough to hold its shape, it is removed from the mould and turned upright on to a batt with the outer edge supported by wads of clay. The rim is then moistened and scored so that slices taken from variously patterned, laminated blocks can be attached and built up into the main walls of the pot. The sides are then paddled on the outside while a cloth-covered wad is used for support on the inside. Gently beating the pot in this way helps to strengthen the seams, compressing the patterns, and also stretches the form into the required shape. This forming process is followed by slow drying, scraping with a metal rib at the leatherhard stage, and several sandings both before and after the bisque and high firings.

Inlaid coloured porcelains which are polished with silicon carbide grits rather than glazed have a special visual and tactile appeal. Without a 'skin' of glaze distancing the observer from direct contact with the piece, the colours remain clean and clear. Matt glazes tend to obscure the patterns while transparent glossy ones produce reflections which disturb the form. It is hardly surprising to find so many potters in the 1990s who are attracted to working with techniques such as neriage and inlays do so because their work in most respects is little changed in appearance after firing. They have reduced the number of variables due to glaze composition and body fit or the uncertain effects of atmosphere adjustments in the kiln during firing. An electric kiln may not give them those delightful surprises (and occasional disasters!) which can be the reward of reduction firing in a live flame kiln but it does provide them with an enviable degree of reliability.

'Bug Plate', made from press-moulded, laminated, coloured porcelain, fired to 1250°C (cone 8), 22 cm × 22 cm, by Anne Mercer, 1993.

GLAZES FOR PORCELAIN

The chemistry of glazes is a vast subject and open to limitless possibilities far beyond the scope of this book to deal with in any detail but a suggested reading list will be found at the end of the book. It is a subject that is of only passing interest to those ceramicists who either use no glaze at all or who prefer to rely on commercially-prepared glazes that they know will perform reliably for their purposes. However, it is an area of ceramics which, despite many publications covering every aspect of the technology involved, continues to fascinate or mystify many.

The colour response of white porcelain has been previously mentioned with regard to stains, oxides and slips but even the most simple of glazes on porcelain can have unequalled luminosity. A classic example is a glaze composed of just two natural materials:

Porcelain Bowl, trimmed and altered, with a matt feldspar glaze fired to cone 9 (1280°C) in an electric kiln, by Gwen Heffner, 1993. *Photograph by Ron Forth.*

Cornish stone	85 parts by weight
Whiting	15 parts by weight

Cornish stone is a feldspathoid containing feldspar, quartz, kaolinite, mica and a small amount of fluorspar so it consists of enough of the right constituents to melt into a glassy state on its own but to produce a reliable glaze other materials are normally added. A number of alkalis such as potash, soda, calcia and magnesia are introduced into a glaze composition by Cornish stone but in the above recipe further calcia is added in the form of whiting (calcium carbonate) to act as a flux. This well-known glaze is one which I have used extensively for its ability to craze evenly over porcelain. The resulting fine network of lines can be stained in various ways to emphasise the crackle pattern. Experience has taught me that the thickness of the glaze coating dictates the nature of the crackle. The more thickly glaze is applied, the wider apart the (initial) crackle lines will be. The converse is also true but if the glaze is too thin no noticeable crazing will occur. However, if the combined thicknesses of glaze on inner and outer surfaces exceeds that of the body wall it can cause cracks and splits around the rim of a bowl. Crazing is likely to continue for a while and so the resulting crackles can be stained with one or more colours. Ink is normally used for this purpose but finely ground oxides of iron, copper, cobalt or manganese can be mixed with a medium and rubbed into the lines and the piece refired to produce further visual texture. New crackle patterns occur on cooling and these can then be stained with inks for extra interest. This glaze has a fairly wide firing range and I have used it successfully at temperatures between 1220°C and 1300°C. Without additions of colouring elements and in the relatively clean atmosphere of an electric kiln, the glaze becomes a glossy, slightly warm white, but under reduction conditions in a live flame kiln, it is affected by minute traces of iron present in the materials making up body and glaze which produces a cooler, bluish tint. This simple glaze offers many possibilities for use under or over other coloured glazes, over coloured slips or when stains are added to it. One can take it as a starting point for further development and experi-

Translucent porcelain bowl, by Patrick Piccarelle (Belgium), 1993.
Wheel-thrown and trimmed several times, carved and bisque fired and
then engraved with dental tools. The holes are filled with a high
viscosity glaze (Cornish stone 85, whiting 15) and then glazed overall
with a palette of feldspathic glazes. Fired in reduction to 1280°–
1300°C (gas kiln).

Loosely thrown porcelain vase with a crackle glaze applied over a
different, solid glaze and fired to cone 10 in a reduction atmosphere,
30 cm high × 40 cm wide, by Tom Coleman, 1993.

ment. Adjustments can be made by progressively substituting small amounts of china clay for some of the Cornish stone, for example, to produce a satin rather than a glossy surface. Natural oils in human skin can impede the application of water-based inks into the crackled glaze so pots destined to be stained should be handled carefully and protected with cloth until the process of inking has been completed.

Glaze chemistry is something of a mystery to many amateur potters and there is also a surprising number of professionals who admit to having little knowledge or interest in the subject. The search for an ideal, reliable glaze that will transform pots with its magical qualities certainly occupies a large proportion of pottery students around the world. Glaze tests are often fitted into odd spaces in the kiln as part of this quest. Ultimately, most sensible potters rely on very few glazes which they get to know and understand intimately.

Crystalline glaze experiments

A great deal of effort is sometimes put into trying to grow crystals in glazes. The oxides which act as crystallisers and opacifiers in a glaze are provided by baria (BaO), calcia (CaO), magnesia (MgO), tin (SnO_2), titania (TiO_2), zinc (ZnO) and zirconia (ZrO_2). Porcelain bodies are particularly well-suited to crystalline glazes, which can have a kind of mystical quality, but they are not universally popular. Large, flamboyant crystals spreading over the surface of a pot can tend to dominate and distract from the form. The maker's satisfaction is often in achieving these random effects irrespective of whether they properly complement the form. The nature of the glaze composition and the degree of control exercised during the firing cycle will, to some extent, condition the results but a good deal must be left, inevitably to chance. **Hein Severijns** (Holland) has had extensive experience of crystalline glazes over many years and he warns ceramicists who do not fully comprehend glaze technology against adventuring into the crystalline field. It is not his intention to discourage experiments with such glazes but he feels that it is too easy to be seduced by them and that too often excellent crystalline effects are used in the 'embellishment of imperfect inappropriate pots'.

Severijns has studied many articles dealing with the subject and has been surprised to find the same glaze recipes appearing in which the main component is an American Ferro-frit, difficult to obtain in Europe, without suggesting alternatives. He rarely uses the brighter, shiny

Bottle Vase, 43 cm high × 20 cm diameter, by Hein Severijns, 1993. Wheel-thrown porcelain, with matt crystalline glazes coloured with cobalt, iron and titanium and fired to 1280°C in an electric kiln. The kiln is cooled slowly for 12 hours for the temperature to drop to 980°C to encourage crystal growth.
Photograph by Peter Bors.

'Bottle Vase', 43 cm high, by Hein Severijns, 1993. Wheel-thrown porcelain with matt crystalline glazes fired in an electric kiln to 1280°C and cooled slowly for 12 hours down to 980°C to encourage crystal growth.
Photograph by Hein Severijns.

crystalline glazes because he prefers the silky touch of satin matt surfaces even though they provide more of a challenge to produce. They are more unreliable and, he says, their success depends on many more factors than those that influence the glossy types. They are more aesthetically appealing to him with their smaller, rounder crystals embedded within the surface 'like a starry sky'.

The development of crystals within a glaze is dependent upon (a) the chemical composition and its physical properties and (b) the temperature and duration of the firing and cooling cycles. In his excellent book on *Ceramic Glazes* (see bibliography), Parmelee stresses the important role played by the nature of the glaze.

Chiefly because it must serve as a solvent for the silicates which are later separated during cooling and because its physical properties, notably the viscosity during that period, must be favourable to the growth of the crystals. This is shown by the widely different types of glazes in which zinc silicate, for example, may be induced to crystallise. The reaction of the glaze and the body, in so far as the solution from the latter is concerned, may be important in some instances since a fundamental relationship is thereby disturbed

Severijns' glazes are based on 'the crystallisation of zinc-barium-silicates with quite complex crystal structures whereas the shinier glaze crystals are mainly composed of willemite Zn_2SiO_4 with colouring oxides taken into the crystal matrix'. The basic formula for his glazes varies within the following limits based on the molecular or unity method devised by Seger:

KNaO 0.15—0.20
ZnO   0.35—0.50
BaO   0.20—0.40 Al_2O_3 0.15—0.20 SiO_2 1.5—2.2
CaO   0.05—0.15
MgO   0.05—0.10

His glazes are applied in several layers.

For the first layer of glaze I add 5% of SnO_2 and 5% of TiO_2 plus some quartz to make it somewhat stiffer and reduce the risk of running. (I always fire my pieces on a thin disc of soft refractory brick to absorb any glaze runs which can be ground away and polished later if necessary.) This layer is applied quite thickly. Subsequently, glaze is put on with a brush or by spraying very thin layers of the base glaze coloured with natural oxides from cobalt, copper, iron, manganese and titanium. Up to six layers may be used. It is interesting to note that base glazes with less than 0.35 ZnO and more than 0.35 BaO give rose-red colours with 2% nickel oxide, while the same percentage of nickel oxide in a glaze containing less than 0.20 BaO and more than 0.45 ZnO produces blue crystals against a light brown background. Thin layers of glaze rich in zinc silicates are applied in between and the final layer contains compounds of molybdenum, tungsten or vanadium to influence and improve the crystallisation.

Limoges porcelain bodies (mixtures of TM10, TM18 and 45937) are used for Severijns' wheel-thrown vessels. Bisque firing is taken to the slightly higher than usual temperature of 1100°C to reduce the eventual reaction between body and glaze. The final glaze firing is first taken up to 1260°–1280°C and then the kiln is rapidly cooled to 1080°C to assist the formation of nuclei before raising the temperature again to be held at 1150°C for three hours. This is followed by a gradual firing down process which involves dropping the temperature in a series of cooling steps to 1120°C, 1100°C, 1050°C, then back up to 1100°C, 1070°C, 1040°C and 1000°C for periods each varying between half an hour and three-quarters of an hour. He has found that the firing cycle contributes as much as the glaze composition to the ultimate success of crystalline glaze development but he insists that it is for every potter to discover his own personal 'signature' through the many variables involved.

I prefer to work empirically with dry batches of glaze materials measured by weight rather than to work out formulae by molecular equivalents. As long as careful and thorough records are kept, not only of the materials used but also concerning the placement of pots in the kiln, the kiln atmosphere, the pattern of firing and cooling and the temperature reached, this method can suffice for most potters. A crystalline glaze recipe, which resulted from such practical experiments I conducted several years ago, has a silky smooth surface similar to those favoured by Hein Severijns. This glaze proved well-suited to porcelain, providing that it was applied to the right thickness, without such a lengthy cooling programme. Doubtless it would have produced more consistent crystalline results had I not lacked sufficient patience to watch over the kiln and had

'Drop Form', 22 cm high, by Hein Severijns, 1993. Wheel-thrown porcelain with matt crystalline glazes fired in an electric kiln to 1280°C and cooled slowly to 980°C in 12 hours to encourage crystal growth.
Photograph by Hein Severijns.

attempted a longer period of cooling to allow time for the crystals to grow! The recipe for my glaze could be used as a starting point for further exploration so I give the details as follows:

Nepheline syenite	50	parts by weight
Barium carbonate	15	parts by weight
Zinc oxide	20	parts by weight
Flint	15	parts by weight
	100	

Up to four per cent light rutile should be added to the above (or titanium dioxide which gives slightly different results) to 'seed' the crystals. Colouring carbonates of copper (0.5 per cent–2 per cent) or cobalt (0.25 per cent–1 per cent), or oxides of iron (2 per cent–4 per cent), manganese (up to 4 per cent) or nickel (up to 2 per cent) can be added also singly or in combination (to a suggested total maximum of 4 per cent colourant) for a variety of coloured crystal formations when fired in an electric kiln to 1260°C. Bungs and spyholes should be left closed and the kiln unopened until completely cold. Crystalline glazes are under a great deal of compression and if the above glaze is applied too thickly, it can cause thinly thrown porcelain to fracture, but if too thin few crystals will appear. This is very much a matter for trial and error experiments as with all the recipes printed in this book.

Another potter who has conducted extensive tests and experiments with crystalline glazes, **Derek Clarkson** (UK), differs in his approach to the subject from that of Severijns although they share much common ground. Clarkson wrote an article published in *Ceramic Review* (No. 137 in 1992) describing his methods in some detail and he has generously supplied further information for the purposes of this book. He declares that he can offer no rational explanation for the attraction crystalline glazes holds for him. 'It can be a passionate, obsessive affair overriding one's good sense!' His practical work, after several years, is still experimental with each glaze having a different firing cycle. The use of a fairly small (2 cu. ft.) electric kiln with a programme controller and containing no more than six to

Porcelain Vase, 20 cm high, by Derek Clarkson, 1993. Wheel-thrown, with crystalline glaze producing large green crystals (copper carbonate with titanium dioxide). Fired to 1280°C and cooled slowly from 1078°C to 1030°C in five and a half hours.

Porcelain Bottle, wheel-thrown, with dark green crystalline glaze (refer to text for details of recipe and firing programme), 21.5 cm high, by Derek Clarkson, 1993.
Photograph by David Seed.

eight pots per firing makes this a practical, economical proposition. His 12 cu. ft. gas kiln is 'much more inhibiting' for these experiments.

Clarkson uses a chemical balance to accurately measure and make up just sufficient glaze for each pot. Colouring oxides are sieved through a 120s mesh cup sieve before adding to the glaze, and the complete mixture is twice passed through an 80s mesh sieve to ensure even dispersal. The glaze, mixed to a creamy consistency, is brushed on to the pot with a one inch brush, applying the bulk of it on to the top third (most of his crystalline glazes are used on narrow necked 'bottle' forms and approximately 100 g dry weight is used to coat a bottle form 26 cm high with the inside left unglazed). Wider necked forms are glazed inside with a non-crystalline glaze in order to avoid cracking the piece by the pooling of glaze in the bottom were a crystalline type to be used. A further layer of crystalline glaze is applied by brush over the first for 5–6 cm down the neck of the piece. 'This glaze flows down over the first giving a linking crystalline effect.'

For the development of large crystals on a plain background, the glaze has to be quite fluid. This can create problems with glaze running off the pot and on to the kiln shelf. In order to deal with this occurrence, Clarkson uses a flat-bottomed saucer (bisque fired from the same porcelain body to equalise the shrinkage) to contain any excess glaze, and a pedestal about 3 cm high is also made from the same body to lift the pot above that pooled glaze in the saucer. The pedestal is made to fit *exactly* to the diameter of the footring in the base of the pot. After bisque firing, a mixture of 2/3 flint and 1/3 china clay is generously applied between the pot and its pedestal to assist separation after the glaze firing. Separation is then achieved by first scratching through the glaze surface all the way around the junction with a glass or tile cutter and then tapping gently with a chisel around this line. The footring is then smoothed with a flint tungsten carbide disc mounted in an electric drill and finished off with carborundum paper or block.

The colouring oxides mainly used by Clarkson are cobalt carbonate, copper carbonate, manganese dioxide and red iron oxide in different combinations using all four or just one in amounts from 0.05 per cent to 6 per cent. A limitless range of colours, varying in subtlety, are possible

Porcelain Bottle, 26 cm high, by Derek Clarkson, 1993. Wheel-thrown, with crystalline glaze (silvery blue crystals on a speckled tan background). Details of this glaze recipe and its firing programme are given in the text.
Photograph by David Seed.

Covered Jar, porcelain with dry, wood ash glaze, salt fired to cone 10, height 18 cm × 20 cm wide, by Neil Moss (USA), 1993.

and which can be repeated accurately. He finds that there need be no end to experimenting in the search for more matt glazes, more muted colours, the introduction of a wider range of materials into the glazes, and in 'seeding' to obtain the crystal formations. 'The number of crystals forming in the glaze and their location on the pot cannot be controlled precisely. However, with careful attention to every detail of the making process, some repetition of fairly similar characteristics can be achieved. The clay, the glaze composition, its application and the firing cycle all play a vital part.'

Clarkson conducts the usual bisque firing but takes his glaze kiln up to 900°C as for a normal glost and proceeds from that point to fire up to around 1260°–1290°C as quickly as possible before switching off the kiln. The temperature is then encouraged to drop rapidly by opening vents and spyholes (to prevent glaze running too much) until 'somewhere between 1150°C and 1020°C at which temperature crystals develop'. All openings in the kiln are then closed and the electricity switched on again to hold the temperature steady within this range for up to five hours. The kiln is then switched off and allowed to cool naturally. 'Periods of moving to higher and/or lower temperatures will produce concentric bands within the crystals.'

Titanium dioxide is an important ingredient for aiding crystal formations in glazes. Amounts about five per cent tend to make the glaze less shiny and the background becomes a darker, opaque tan colour and above 10 per cent larger crystals begin to beak up into the more familiar mottled surface obtained in many glazes with titanium/rutile compositions.

Zinc oxide also encourages crystal growth and it often contributes about 25 per cent of the glaze recipe. Clarkson has found that the high shrinkage problems associated with zinc oxide can be reduced by calcining it in a bisque-fired bowl to about 1000°C. Its volume will decrease but its weight will be reduced only slightly by calcining.

Crystalline glaze recipes

The glaze recipe and firing cycle used by Derek Clarkson for the porcelain bottle illustrated on page 183 is as follows:

Ferro Frit 3110	42.0	*This glaze was fired in 2 hrs. 5 min from 900°C to*
Calcined zinc oxide	31.5	*1260°C, then cooled to 1095°C and held there for*
Flint	20.0	*1 hr. 25 mins, then cooled to 1065°C and held there for*
Titanium dioxide	5.5	*1 hr. 30 mins, then cooled to 1055°C and held there for*
Alumina hydrate	0.4	*15 mins, then cooled to 1045°C and held there for*
China clay	0.6	*15 mins, and allowed to cool completely.*

+ 6% Copper carbonate

The recipe and firing cycle for the porcelain bottle illustrated on page 184 was:

Ferro Frit 3110	43.0	*This glaze was fired in 1 hr. 50 mins from 900°C to*
Calcined zinc oxide	29.0	*1260°C then cooled to 1093°C and held there for*
Flint	19.0	*1 hr. 25 mins then cooled to 1069°C and held there for*
Titanium dioxide	8.0	*1 hr. 45 mins then cooled to 1053°C and then held there for*
Alumina hydrate	0.5	*1 hr 30 mins then cooled to 1041°C and held there for*
China clay	0.5	*25 mins and then allowed to cool completely.*

+ 0.4% Copper carbonate
1.2% Manganese dioxide

The variables are infinite but the meticulous record-keeping shown in these two examples by Derek Clarkson indicate the importance he attaches to noting every detail of the process involved in the successful creation of crystalline glazes.

Further glaze recipes for porcelain

Sandra Black uses the following glaze for 1260°–1280°C which has a 'dry' surface:

Whiting	50 parts by weight of dry material
China clay	50 parts by weight of dry material
Feldspar	50 parts by weight of dry material

Colours are produced by adding different glaze stains up to a maximum of 10 per cent to obtain the intensity of colour required. Glazes are sieved through at least an 80s mesh. For her carved pieces where she wishes to give greater emphasis to the design, she used a clear glaze 'originally developed for hotel china' with a firing range of 1220°–1300°C but which performs best between 1260°–1280°C. This glaze has proved to be very reliable and it has a low

Large porcelain pot, 75 cm diameter, by Paul Davis, 1993. Wheel-thrown, with a black crystalline glaze composed of feldspar, the local Albury slip (similar in nature to the well known Albany slip from the USA) and a high proportion of manganese dioxide. Fired to between cones 10 and 11 in a reducing atmosphere. (The full recipe for this glaze is potash feldspar 67.3; whiting 2.79; talc 1.35, kaolin 4.45; silica 3.6, red iron oxide .76; manganese dioxide 20.5, all parts by weight.)

rate of thermal expansion. Its quality can be improved further by ball milling and, of course, it can be coloured in the usual way or made opaque by the addition of five per cent tin oxide:

Nepheline syenite	29.3	parts by weight
Whiting	9.7	
Barium carbonate	6.4	
Zinc oxide	7.9	
Talc	3.9	
China clay	10.1	
Ball clay	5.0	
Silica	27.7	

Paul Davis offers the following recipes which he uses for reduction firings to 1300°–1320°C:

Celadon Glaze (for cone 10)

Potash feldspar	61.26
Talc	.04
Whiting	10.22
China clay	2.57
Silica	26.41
Iron silicate	4.00
Red iron oxide	.02

Apricot Lustre Shino Glaze (for cone 10)

Nepheline syenite	50.9	
Potash feldspar	39.2	Spray over top of glaze
Terracotta clay	6.1	with pine ash for rich
China clay	9.2	lustrous orange.
Salt	3.6	

Porcelain Vase, 30 cm high × 42.5 cm diameter, by Elaine Coleman, 1993. Wheel-thrown and incised (using dental tools) with cranes around the upper part under a green, celadon glaze which pools in the depressions giving emphasis to the design.

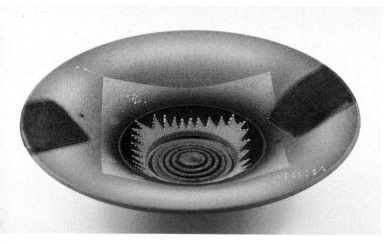

Porcelain Bowl, 45 cm diameter, by Paul Davis, 1993. Brightly coloured, with glaze containing a large proportion of calcined alumina which produces a sandy textured surface. This is fired to 1320°C in a reduction atmosphere and then reworked with a maiolica type glaze, stained with various colours and refired to 1100°C.

Chun Glaze (for cone 10)

Potash feldspar	61.25
Soda feldspar	1.70
Talc	1.24
Whiting	18.29
Bone ash	.57
Silica	16.90
Red iron oxide	.28
Yellow ochre	1.60

Johan Broekema offers the following glazes for reduction firing at 1320°C:

(a) Matt black glaze:

Feldspar	25	
Whiting	11	
Magnesite	15	add 8% black body stain
China clay	14	
Quartz	25	

Vessel Form, wheel-thrown porcelain with copper red glaze fired in reduction, 16 cm high × 11 cm wide, by Johan Broekema, 1993.

(b) Clear porcelain glaze:

Feldspar	24.5
Whiting	24.0
Magnesite	3.0
China clay	19.0
Quartz	29.5

(c) Copper red glaze:

Soda feldspar	42
China clay	8
Whiting	15
Quartz	33
Calcium borate	5

+ zinc oxide 2%, tin oxide 2%, copper cabonate 1%.

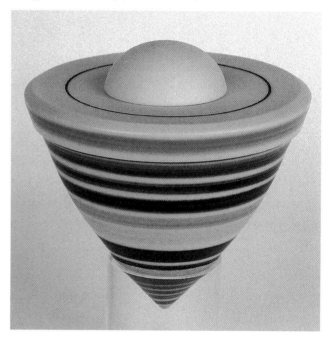

Left   Lidded Vessel, wheel-thrown porcelain with black and white banded glazes, 13 cm high × 8 cm wide, by Johan Broekema, 1993.

Right   Porcelain Vase, 36 cm high × 21 cm diameter, by Hein Severijns, 1993. Wheel-thrown, with matt crystalline glazes coloured with cobalt, titanium, nickel, copper and iron. Fired to 1280°C in an electric kiln and cooled very slowly to encourage crystal growth. *Photograph by Peter Bors.*

Below   Cone-shaped vessel form with domed lid, wheel-thrown porcelain banded with various colour stains on a satin white glaze, 9 cm high × 9 cm wide, by Johan Broekema, 1993.

Hein Severijns offers two crystalline glaze recipes with the amounts given as percentages for quick reference. Both are for 1260°–1280°C.

Matt–semi matt base glaze

Potash feldspar FFF or B411	33	
Soda feldspar F7 Ventilato	12	'Add colouring oxides and apply
Zinc oxide	15	many layers. In between these, very thin
Barium carbonate	18	layers of glaze having 80 per cent $2ZnO.SiO_2$
Lead bisilicate frit	5	(zinc silicate), quartz, whiting and talc,
China clay	3	eventually with 5% iron oxide.'
Talc	5	
Quartz	5	
Whiting	4	
	100	

Shiny–brilliant base glaze

Frit (Reimbold & Strick A2120)	34	
Frit (Reimbold & Strick A3389)	16	'Add colouring
Zinc oxide	25	oxides and
China clay	2	apply thickly!'
Titanium dioxide	5	
Quartz	18	
	100	

Glaze application

Derek Clarkson gives the following recipe for his favourite celadon glaze:

Cornwall stone	80
Ball clay AT	5
Molochite	5
Wollastonite	10
Talc	6
Bentonite	1
Red iron oxide	1

Clarkson applies his crystalline glazes by brushing but dips pots into his ash glaze. This glaze needs a generous thickness but requires careful application because any unevenness in the glaze will remain after firing. He holds his bottles at the rim/neck and dips them, base first, into the glaze up to the narrowest part of the shoulder. As soon as the glaze is dry enough to touch (almost immediately) the top of the bottle is then glazed down to meet up with the previously glazed area. The inside is left unglazed. Brush decoration is carried out whilst the applied glaze is still damp because dry glaze on the porous porcelain body sucks the water-mixed oxide pigment too quickly from the brush, thus making long thin brush strokes difficult. 'Inadequate brush strokes cannot be "touched up" but it is possible to scrape off a little pigment (shortening a too long brush stroke or slimming one too fat). However, this should be kept to a minimum.'

I prefer to spray all my glazes because I want to have an even layer with no 'runs' or fingermarks to mar the surface. It is essential to do this in a properly vented spray booth. Porcelain bisque is notoriously difficult to dip glaze because it can become easily saturated and take a very long time to dry. Some potters try to overcome this problem by dampening the bisque slightly to lessen the absorption, but it is better either to adjust the glaze suspension with the right amount of water or to fire the bisque to a higher temperature to reduce its porosity. Double dipping of glazes is much easier to accomplish on stoneware bisque. Overlaying one or more glazes offers interesting possibilities. This is especially true when, for example, a 'dry' or matt glaze is applied on top of a more fluid one. The first glaze melts and begins to flow dragging and breaking the surface of the drier glaze. When one glaze is dark in colour and the other light, even greater visual interest can develop. One method which I have found very rewarding to explore is a kind of glaze sgraffito. This entails spraying one glaze which, can be drawn into, as soon as it is dry, with a sharp tool (not necessarily pointed, almost any shape will do) right through to the underlying body. Traces of glaze will be left and, even with a white glaze, there will be a marked difference between the sgraffito and the glaze when fired. The first layer of glaze and sgraffito can itself be oversprayed (preferably before it is *completely* dry in order to lessen the risk of lifting off the first layer which can cause 'crawling'), with another glaze different in character, colour or tone and the two will interact but the design will remain clear to see. This is a very direct way of working that can be extremely satisfying (see examples on page 193). I have achieved some of my best results when using this glazing method with a clear, transparent glaze under a matt, or even dry, glaze stained with various oxides. Rich blues, greens and reds (from cobalt and copper in combination or with other oxides) can appear where the

Porcelain Mug, 10 cm high × 12.5 cm wide, by Gail Russell, 1993. Wheel-thrown, with applied sprigging taken from antique lace and a press-moulded handle from a silver tray. Green celadon glaze.

Porcelain Teaset by Joanna Howells (UK). Each piece is wheel-thrown as a complete sphere and then altered into the various forms. Celadon glaze fired to 1280°C.

two glazes merge together and the more linear sgraffito design is picked out with contrasting, darker colour.

I rarely do more than make simple, experimental 'line blends' when working out new glaze compositions. Since I use a spray booth to apply all my glazes, the 'waste' glaze which gathers on the inner walls is added to that which is fettled from the bases of pots to mix together into new glazes. These are usually fairly predictable in colour and texture but I make regular tests, nevertheless, and am occasionally surprised by the results. More often, adjustments are made to each batch of any size until I am satisfied with its appearance and performance. It is a simple matter to increase the flux content of any glaze which is too dry, or to add china clay to those which would benefit from a more matt surface. This seemingly haphazard procedure reduces the waste that would otherwise occur when sprayed glazes of different kinds are in constant use in a small workshop.

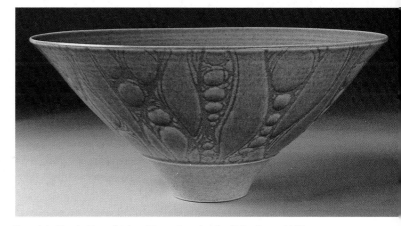

Porcelain Bowl, 13 cm high × 29 cm diameter, by Peter Lane, 1990. Wheel-thrown porcelain, with glossy, transparent glaze incised through to the body and then oversprayed with a matt barium glaze containing cobalt carbonate and iron oxide. Fired to 1280°C in a reducing atmosphere (Liquid Propane Gas kiln).

Bottle Form, wheel-thrown porcelain, with satin matt white glaze incised through to the body prior to firing to 1260°C in an electric kiln 20.5 cm high, by Peter Lane, 1991.

One of my favourite glazes works equally well for porcelain in both oxidation and reduction firings and the recipe and also for others better-suited to oxidation are as follows:

1260°C–1280°C

Potash feldspar	65	Add (a) 0.75% copper carbonate and 0.25% cobalt
China clay	5	carbonate or (b) 0.25% cobalt carbonate and 2% red iron
Barium carbonate	20	oxide or (c) 0.75% copper carbonate and 2.5% rutile or
Dolomite	10	other combinations for colour.

Smooth matt *1250°C (Oxidation)*

Nepheline syenite	45	Smooth matt surface with crystal inclusions. Interesting
Barium carbonate	13	variegated colour from additions of 3–4% rutile together
Zinc oxide	20	with up to 2% copper carbonate or up to 1% cobalt
Flint	20	carbonate. Titanium dioxide may be used in place of rutile
Lithium carbonate	3	with slightly different results. Slow cooling will aid the growth of crystals. *Too thick an application of glaze can cause runs and risks cracking thinly made porcelain.*

Shiny porcelain glaze *1260°C. (Oxidation)*

Nepheline syenite	70	Shiny glaze studded with tiny crystals. Inclined to run above
Whiting	9	1260°C if applied too thickly. The addition of 2–4% rutile
Zinc oxide	9	or titanium dioxide in combination with up to 2% copper
Flint	10	carbonate gives good results but it is worth experimenting
Lithium carbonate	2	with small amounts of cobalt, iron, manganese also.

Cane-handled Teapot with wooden stand and four cups, 26 cm diameter, by Bryan Trueman, 1992. Wheel-thrown porcelain with wax resisted glazes (Chun, copper, iron and chrome) fired in reduction to 1300°C and the gold lustre applied and refired to 740°C in oxidation. *Photograph by Uffe Schulze.*

Bryan Trueman (UK) uses a variety of overlaid glazes with wax resists to produce rich visual textures. He has always tried to use glazes in a very personal way, calling upon his previous experience in painting and printmaking, with masking techniques that allow him

to convey my sensory responses to things around me. By orchestrating an exotic collection of high temperature glazes and anticipating their movement, distortion and interaction with each other and experimenting with different temperatures and kiln atmospheres have been the most significant aspects of my work. The challenge has always been the 'freeze frame' effect of shutting down the kiln at the precise moment when all the melting and colour maturation has taken place and you think that you have achieved what you had set out to do. These refined critical judgements are the results of numerous firings in which failures as well as successes combine to establish parameters that enable me to develop greater understanding of the process.

'Frederick Henry Bay Window Series', 45 cm diameter, by Bryan Trueman (UK), 1992. Large porcelain platter, wheel-thrown, decorated with multiple glazes (Chun, copper, iron, rutile and chrome) poured over wax resist design. Fired to 1300°C in reduction atmosphere (ceramic fibre, downdraught LPG kiln). *In the collection of University of Tasmania. Photograph by Bryan Trueman.*

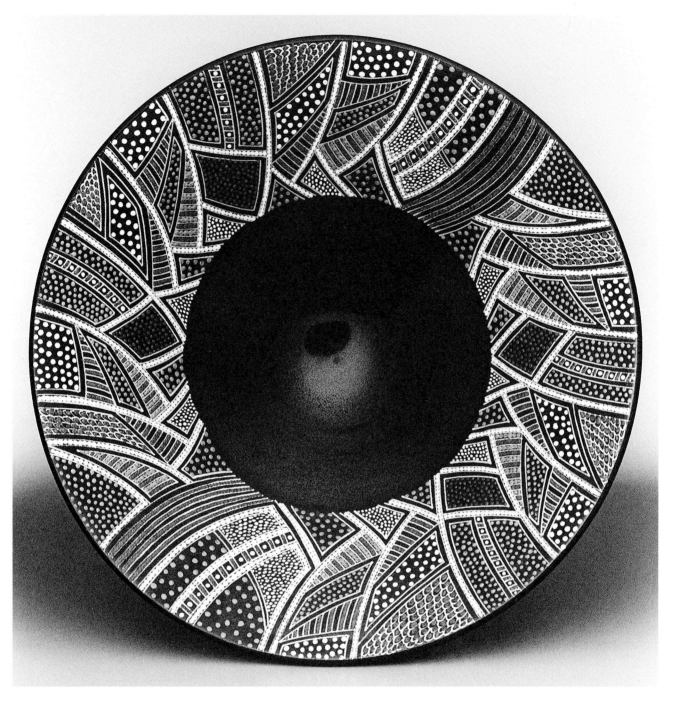

Porcelain Bowl, 'Australian Outback Series', diameter 45 cm, by Marianne Cole, 1993. Wheel-thrown, with shiny black glaze fired to Orton cone 9 in an electric kiln, and then decorated with painted liquid bright gold lustre and coloured enamels and refired to cone 018.
Photograph by Michal Kluvanek.

Trueman's images are produced by using opalescent and opaque glazes overlapping and interlapping (edge to edge) over a black glaze. The base glaze is a dark tenmoku formulated to remain stable at cone 10. This stability prevents subsequent glaze layers from running and distorting too much. A wax resist is brushed over parts of the tenmoku prior to pouring more fluid glazes. Interlapping parts of the design are controlled by painting wax to mask areas of one glaze where it is due to meet another edge to edge. The unwanted section of glaze can then be sponged off and left to dry before pouring another glaze in its place. This method ensures a clearly defined boundary between the two glazes.

The two main opalescent glazes used by Trueman are a pale blue Chun and a copper red.

The Chun glaze is responsive to various oxides applied over images painted in wax resist, particularly chrome and cobalt. Rutile over the tenmoku provides an opaque effect which can be controlled by the thickness of the rutile painted on. I use several methods of applying glaze over the wax images but pouring, brushing, sponging and slip trailing are the most common. Each provides different linear and textural qualities to the finished piece.

Bryan Trueman offers the following glaze recipes for cone 10 reduction firing:

'Novelty II', 21 cm × 6 cm × 18.5 cm, by Dianne Peach, 1993. Semi-functional teapot, slipcast porcelain assembly with thrown knob. Decorated with underglaze colours and glaze brushwork, fired to cone 5 in an electric kiln.

Chun glaze 1

Potash feldspar	52.40
China clay	.75
Magnesium carbonate	2.55
Whiting	3.55
Silica	24.00
Zinc oxide	5.50
Bone ash	.90
Red iron oxide	.75

Chun glaze 2

Potash feldspar	50
Silica	23
Whiting	14
Zinc oxide	11

Tenmoku glaze:

Potash feldspar	46.50
Whiting	14.25
China clay	8.75
Silica	19.50
Red iron oxide	8.50

Copper red glaze:

Potash feldspar	36
Silica	36
Borax frit	10
Whiting	15
Tin oxide	2
Bentonite	1
Black copper oxide	0.5

Tom Turner (USA) has experimented with crystalline inclusions in his copper red 'oxblood' and 'flambé' glazes. He tries to encourage the growth of crystals in the glaze in his normal reduction firing schedule without a special cooling programme. Another glaze which has proved to be of considerable interest is made from a natural clay found beneath his house in Delaware, Ohio. The clay is ball-milled and one per cent iron oxide is added to it. 'It's a gorgeous, natural *hare's fur* glaze with crystals where thick.' He has named this slip glaze 'Peachblow' after the road in which he lives. All his pots are wheel-thrown porcelain and reduction fired to cone 10 in ten hours. 'The reduction period starts at 1850°F (1010°C) with an ACI oxy-probe reading of .70 and no changes or adjustments are made until the kiln is turned off and the damper closed.

We use no clean up period nor do we quick cool. The kiln is cooled in about forty hours and unloaded without gloves.'

Tom Turner suggests the following glaze recipes as *starting points* for experiment ('never before published because chemicals and kilns vary so much. I doubt whether they will work for anyone else. When I lived in Florida, I did not protect the copper red pots during firing but when I moved to Ohio and put my kiln inside tall barns, the taller chimneys required that we semi-saggar them. By this I mean that soft bricks are set alongside the pots on the fire side (*to act as baffles to divert the direct action of the flames*). Other formulae don't require this adjustment either BUT MINE DOES. My copper red is a product of years of experiment with the Chun base glaze given in Carlton Ball's books.'):

198

'Dome Jar', 25.5 cm × 15 cm, by Tom Turner, 1993. Wheel-thrown porcelain, with copper red glaze and zinc glaze with rutile inlaid on the lid. Fired to cone 10 in reduction with no special cooling cycle.

Covered Jar, 25.5 cm high × 17.5 cm wide, by Tom Turner, 1993. Wheel-thrown porcelain with assimilated wood ash glaze, part thick and part thin, fired to cone 10 in a reducing atmosphere.

Satin celadon glaze:

Cornish stone	25	'This is a variation of the David Leach
Silica	25	recipe with additional clay and some
EPK china clay	34	alumina hydrate to promote a satin
Whiting	25	surface that appears frosted. VeeGum T
Alumina hydrate	1	is the whitest and most plastic material I've
VeeGum T	1	ever found. It's a plasticiser and lubricant
Iron oxide	1.7	that does not burn out.'

Teapot, wheel-thrown porcelain with faceted sides and copper handle, with 'Peachblow' glaze (refer to text for details of this glaze), fired to cone 10 in a reducing atmosphere, by Tom Turner, 1993.

Lidded Casserole, diameter 19 cm × 15 cm high approx., by Gail Russell, 1993. Wheel-thrown porcelain with satin celadon glaze and blue ash glaze brushed over. Then an iron/rutile wash decoration brushed on top and dots of white glaze applied. Reduction fired to cone 10.

Tom Turner oxblood glaze:

Kingman feldspar	72
Silica (325 mesh)	45
Whiting (low Mg)	25
Kaolin	4
Gerstley borate	8
Magnesium carbonate	7
Barium carbonate	7
Zink oxide	3
Tin oxide	1.5
Copper carbonate	.75
Frit 3134	1.25

Tom Turner flambe glaze:

Kona A3 feldspar	150
Silica	90
Whiting	30
Kaolin	6
Gerstley borate	40
Dolomite	20
Barium carbonate	14
Zinc oxide	6
Tin oxide	3
Copper carbonate	1.5

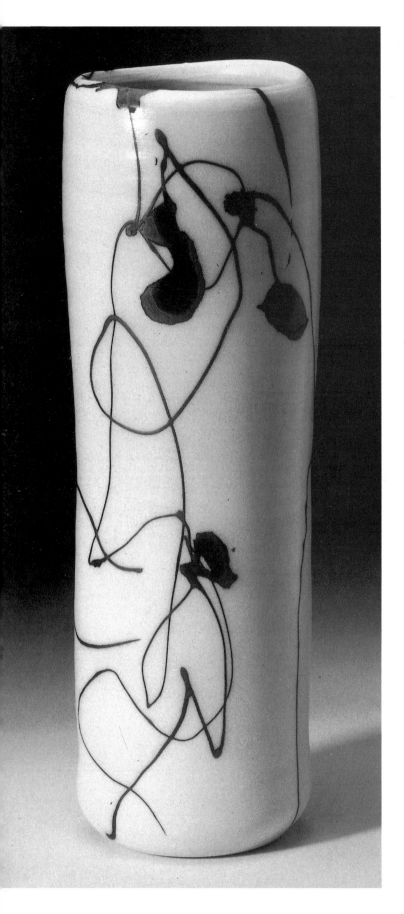

Firing methods

Reducing atmospheres can be introduced into live flame kilns extremely easily by altering the ratio of fuel and air. Cutting back on the air supply alone encourages the excess carbon from unburnt fuel to search out oxygen from the metallic elements contained in bodies, slips and glazes and thus altering the colour and appearance of the pots. The drama and additional involvement experienced by potters working with reduction glazes in live flame kilns is quite different from the more detached, almost clinical, practice

Above 'Dragon Teapot', 28 cm high, by Marianne Cole, 1993. Wheel-thrown Limoges porcelain with pulled handle, fired in an anagama kiln for 72 hours to Orton cone 13/14. *Photograph by Michal Kluvanek.*

Left Porcelain Vessel, 35 cm high, by Emil Heger (Germany), 1993. Wheel-thrown, painted with ceramic stains and reduction fired in a gas kiln to cone 7 (1230°C approx.) with saltglaze.

Right Porcelain Vase, 39 cm high, by Masamichi Yoshikawa, 1991. Slab-built, incised decoration stained with cobalt under a satin glaze with a pale blue tint. Fired in a reducing atmosphere. *Photograph by Wolf Böwig.*

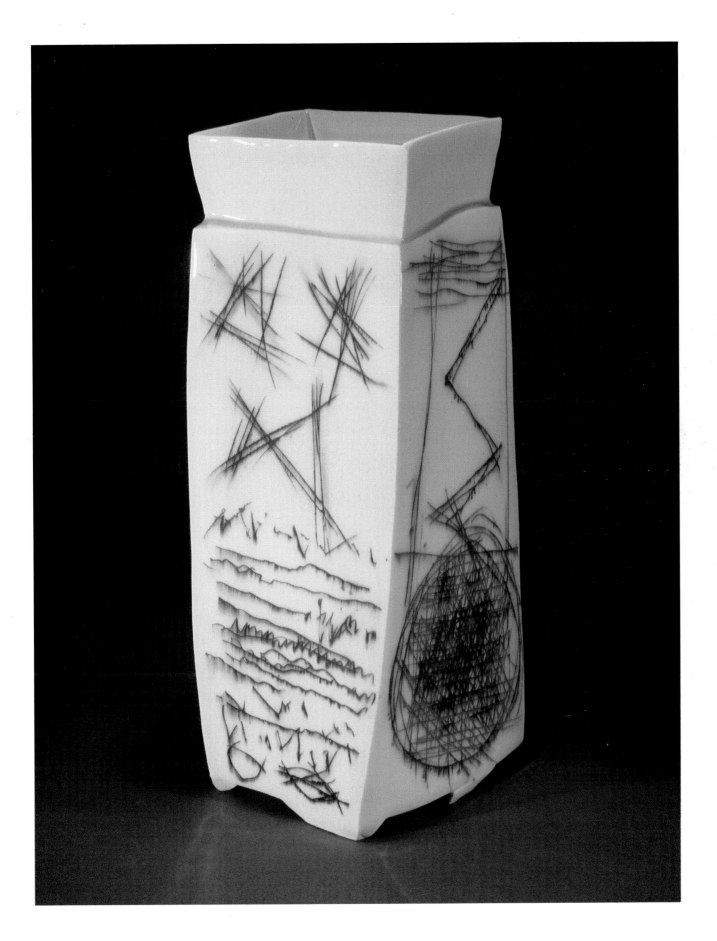

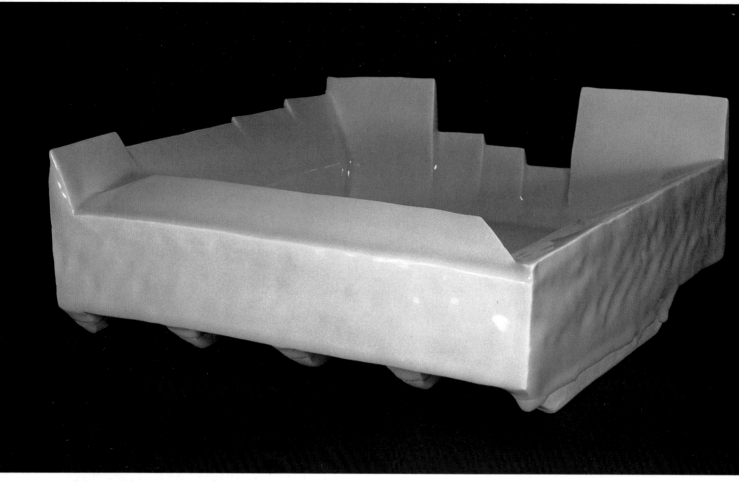

'Architecture II', slab-built porcelain with pale blue, celadon-type glaze, 14 cm high × 26 cm × 26 cm, by Masamichi Yoshikawa, 1991. *Photograph by Wolf Böwig.*

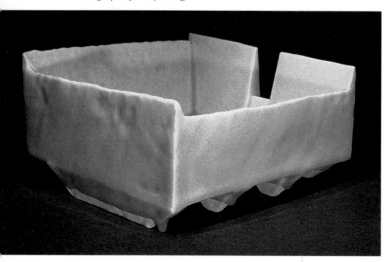

'Architecture I', 16 cm high × 19 cm × 38 cm, by Masamichi Yoshikawa, 1992. Slab-built porcelain with pale blue, celadon-type glaze. This artist makes all his pieces from assembled slabs of varying thickness. Most pieces are quite thick and solidly built in asymmetrical way. He aims at a 'well-balanced irregularity'. *Photograph by Wolf Böwig.*

of firing with electricity. It is possible to introduce similar conditions in electric kilns for short periods but with some risk to the life of the wire elements and this is not normally advisable. However, one method used by Derek Clarkson to achieve respectable copper reds in some of his crystalline glazes, without the same degree of risk to the elements, is worthy of mention. He discovered that he could obtain fine copper red glazes (containing between 0.25 per cent and two per cent copper carbonate) just by pouring old or used vegetable cooking oil from a tablespoon through the top central vent of his kiln. The vent was restricted to a hole no more than $1\frac{1}{2}$ in. (10 cm) wide (closed with a bung) and a bisque saucer was placed on the floor of the kiln directly under the hole with pots arranged around it. A spoonful of oil in every few minutes, and the bung replaced, over a period of an hour and a half while the temperature was dropping from 850°C to 650°C. At this stage the kiln is no longer switched on but is cooling naturally. Approximately half a litre of cooking oil was used in the process. The main disadvantages to this method appear to be, firstly the constant attention required during the

Porcelain Teapot, wheel-thrown and altered, with yellow wood ash glaze fired to cone 10 in reduction 28 cm × 26.5 cm, by Tom Coleman, 1993.

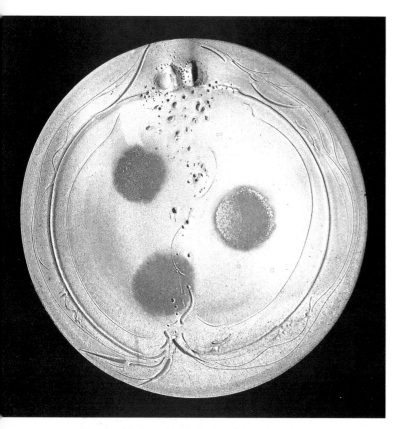

'Flatfish Dish', porcelain with incised decoration, fired in an anagama kiln, 35 cm diameter, by Terry Davies (Australia), 1993.
Photograph by Michal Kluvanek.

The most simple of familiar, traditional, oriental porcelain glazes can acquire a fresh and exciting appearance when applied to contemporary ceramic forms. Copper reds of different shades have long been a challenging and popular choice for many potters. Likewise, celadons ranging from the palest blues through greys to pale and deeper olive greens are frequently chosen to enhance incised work and surface carving. The grey-green version of this glaze, so revered by the Chinese from the T'ang period onward for its jade-like appearance, is generally accepted as the original and, therefore, proper colour for 'celadon', although there is some confusion over the origin of the name. The delicate colour variations and soft luminous quality of Chinese celadons comes from differing amounts of iron present in the glaze and/or body together with countless undissolved particles and tiny bubbles held in suspension within the glaze. Fired in a reducing atmosphere, even small amounts of iron are sufficient to contribute colour to the glaze. The Japanese potter, **Masamichi Yoshikawa**, clothes his monumental slab-built pieces with a particularly sumptuous, pale blue celadon glaze. Made from very thick slabs of porcelain, his work is sometimes decorated with incised, linear drawing picked out with cobalt. The visual power of these forms is in complete harmony with the glaze that seems to flow with great depth over them.

Reduction firing, however, is not always possible for those who live in an urban conurbation. The greater predictability of electric kiln firing has proven perfectly satisfactory for the needs of a considerable number of potters whose work is illustrated in this book. Porcelain bodies are relatively inert compared to those more commonly associated with stoneware and which rely for effect on their positive contribution to the final results achieved through the reaction between body and glaze. Iron spots burning out from stoneware bodies to enliven even the dullest reduction glaze would, in most cases, be inappropriate blemishes on porcelain.

Without the need to make ceramics that must conform to fit functional, domestic requirements, potters are no longer bound to make vessels watertight. In this book are illustrations of the work of potters who have chosen to dispense with firing porcelain to the high temperatures necessary to mature the body. This liberty has allowed them to produce objects of beauty and interest serving purely decorative purposes. Others may fire their pieces many times with multiple glazes at both high and low temperatures. The options are infinite and the directions chosen for exploration are the decision of each individual. That which appeals to one will be anathema to another.

period of reduction and, secondly, the unpleasant smell that clings to the workshop for several days afterwards!

Nothing can quite match the excitement of firing with living flames. When we moved to our present address in Hampshire, it proved impossible to take my excellent gas kiln with me and the glazes which I had perfected for reduction firing lacked the attraction and element of surprise when transferred to the more detached and predictable firing by electricity. There seems little point in trying to imitate those uniquely attractive effects of reduction firing in an electric kiln, although many potters try to do so. Both oxidation and reduction offer ample opportunities to experiment and to achieve very satisfactory results with or without glazes. In either case, it requires a supreme act of faith on the part of the potter to commit the result of his or her labours, perhaps the work of several months, to be transformed by such intense heat. The most radical changes, of course, are wrought by the glazes which will be no more than dull, powdery coverings to the underlying ceramic objects. Hence the excited anticipation which accompanies many glaze firings, especially when experimental work is involved.

The freedom from any traditional constraints has encouraged fresh, adventurous approaches to working with clay. There can be little doubt that the enormous variety of forms, surfaces and expressions which we see today in porcelain and ceramics generally, will continue growing, enriching our environment and adding to our cultural heritage with each succeeding generation.

Porcelain Form, by Ingvil Havrevold, 1993. Wheel-thrown and handbuilt, with impressed texture inlaid with coloured nepheline syenite glazes and parts left unglazed. Fired to 1280°C in oxidation. *Photograph by Jan Enoksen.*

CONCLUSION

It is never easy to evaluate the true worth of works of art created in one's own time because it is virtually impossible to become detached enough to appraise them with a totally objective eye. The inevitable question that arises when assessing works which may be held in high regard today or which grab the attention for one reason or another is *will they survive the test of time*? So often in the past that which seemed so fresh and exciting soon palls through lack of substance. Contemporary work preserved in museums and in serious private collections does acquire a certain status by association. In this respect the selection policies followed by public institutions, especially, present them with an enormous responsibility. Auction houses too, by their approval and increasing sales of work by living ceramicists, have the opportunity to influence public taste as well as the standing of individual artists and the commercial value of their works. Recent prices at auction of pieces by Hans Coper or Lucie Rie, and others in England have been so high that increasing numbers of collectors have been encouraged to look upon contemporary ceramics as worthy of serious investment. Nevertheless, in comparison with other branches of the art market, ceramics still offers a relatively inexpensive purchase for anyone wanting to possess original works.

For many people the term 'pottery' implies the making of functional vessels intended primarily for domestic use

Bowl form, 52 cm diameter, by Thomas Naethe (Germany), 1993.
This piece is a composite form made in a *stoneware* clay with painted coloured slip banding. Porcelain slip is sprayed over the bisque and then a white feldspathic glaze reduction fired to 1250°C in a gas kiln.
Photograph by Foto Strenger.

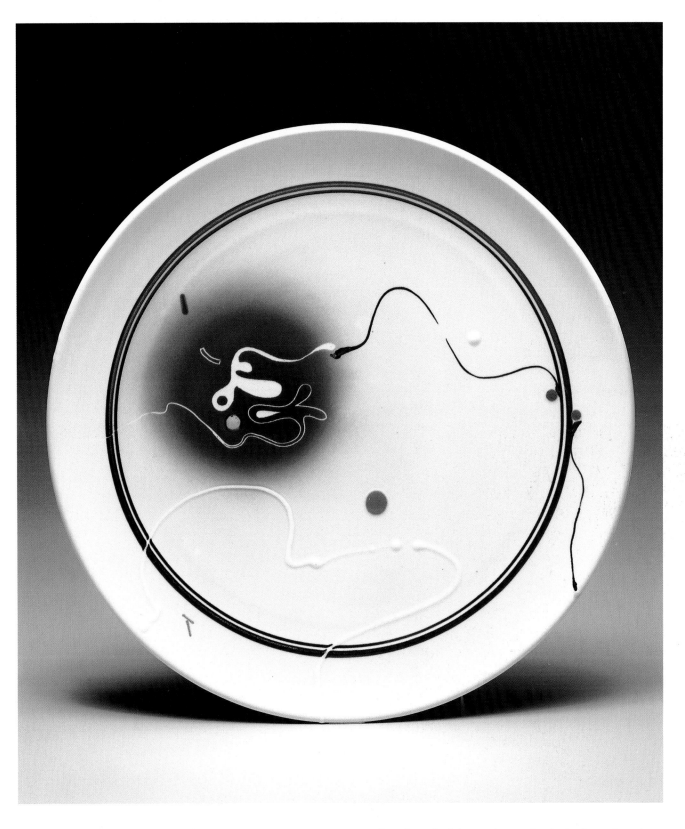

Porcelain Plate, wheel-thrown, decorated with metallic oxides and a chun glaze (cone 10 approximately 1300°C), 40 cm diameter, by Tom Coleman, 1993.

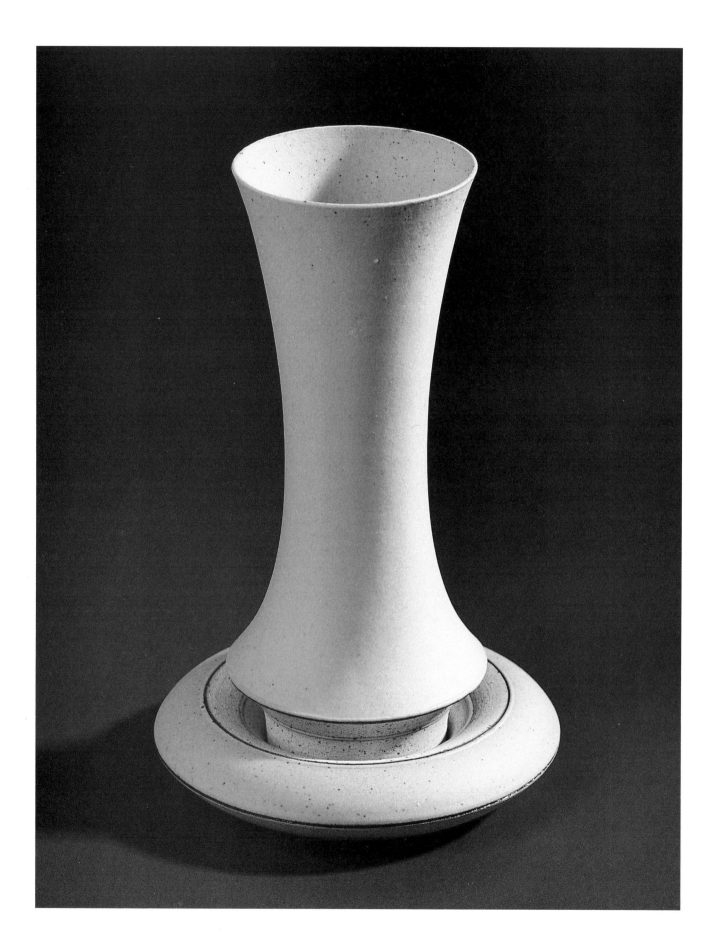

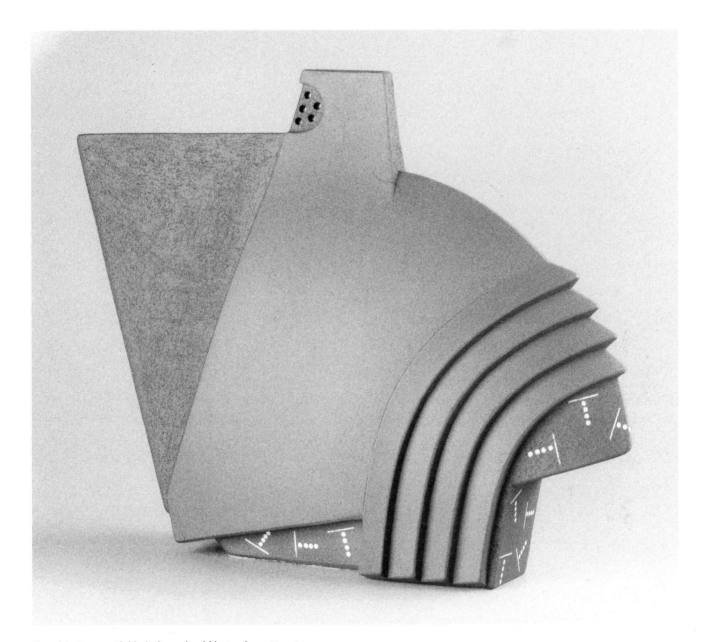

Porcelain Form, with black slip and gold lustre decoration, 31 cm
35 cm × 10 cm, by Brigitte Enders, 1992.
Photograph by Klaus Moje.

Left
Vessel form, 21 cm high, by Thomas Naethe (Germany), 1993. This
piece is a composite form made from wheel-thrown sections in a
stoneware clay, partly painted with coloured slip. Porcelain slip is
sprayed over the bisque and then a white feldspathic glaze reduction
fired to 1250°C in a gas kiln.
Photograph by Gros-Photographie.

but we have seen that the majority of those individuals
whose work is represented in this book are more concerned with expressing personal feelings in response to the
various stimuli that impinge upon their lives. In some cases
'function', in the recognised sense, remains an important
element. In others, vessel forms provide a springboard for
fresh explorations and invention. The reworking of traditional forms in porcelain like bowls, vases or teapots etc.,
need never be a dull exercise, especially when translucency, delicacy and purity contribute their cherished
qualities to the final appearance. Expressions possessing
subtlety and sensitivity can create long-lasting impressions
while demonstrations of extrovert flamboyance may soon
be forgotten. Anyone who takes an interest in ceramics

Raku fired porcelain bowls (1100°C) with lustres containing gold, silver and copper, by David Jones.

learns to recognise even the simplest objects as being from the hand of a particular craftsman or woman. Their identity may be revealed through extremely subtle visual clues. Slight nuances in the profile, the way in which the form rises up from its base, perhaps the style of decoration or maybe just the choice and arrangement of colours will provide enough information for instant recognition. No more than a quiet, restrained elegance may suffice. Recog-

nising the indefinable quality that gives a ceramic object a kind of 'presence' irrespective of any label or category assigned to it is an ability which becomes more refined as experience in the field grows. In *Studio Porcelain* (1980) I wrote that, 'a simple bowl may possess a quiet, unassuming "presence", no less impressive than the most complex sculpture, whether designed for use or otherwise. The best solutions to aesthetic problems are often remarkable for their simplicity.' But, whatever form the work may take, it can express the very essence of considered ideas as well as revealing something of the emotional involvement of the individual who made it.

Unusual images or surprising uses of a traditional material may capture the imagination but without substance or, perhaps, further development, they are unlikely to prove much more than a passing fancy. Sculptural objects created in ceramics by modern potters have often been underrated or dismissed as being of little significance. In part this may be because they are difficult to categorise. Should they be labelled as 'fine art' or *merely* pottery? Indeed, does it really matter? Undoubtedly, it is often easier to accept and absorb that which conforms to traditional concepts. Anything which appears to violate normal boundaries may need more time to become familiar and, therefore, acceptable. The new can excite but it may also offend sensibilities. Therein lies a dilemma, for entrenched attitudes impede the progress of thought, ideas and expression. One can cultivate an 'open' mind without necessarily conceding personal principles or granting *carte blanche* approval to a work merely on the basis of its 'originality'. Each object whether as a vessel form or as a figurative or abstract sculpture is the concrete realisation of multiple and complex strands of human feeling. The reso-

Handbuilt ceramic forms combining earthenware bases surmounted by porcelain cups decorated using the neriage technique, 26 cm and 32 cm high. These pieces were produced through the collaboration in design and execution by two Belgian artists, Frank Steyaert and Chris Scholliers in 1994.

A group of four related slab-built vessel forms 20 cm high, by Karl Scheid, 1992. With angled top sections, porcelain, decorated with different coloured slips applied by brush. Glaze fired to 1360°C in a gas kiln (reduction).

lution and production of each ceramic piece requires the artist to work with ingenuity and sensitivity, to have a thorough understanding of materials and processes, and a sincerity of purpose if it is to successfully appeal to a wide audience. We may choose to deny *any* worth in work which does not happen to coincide with our own personal taste or does not conform to some perceived ideal but if we try to value any genuine human endeavour we can learn to judge each piece on its individual merit and become enriched in the experience.

GLOSSARY

Agateware
Ceramics assembled from layers of different coloured clays (usually prepared with body stains or metallic oxides), laminated and sliced through.

Airbrush
An instrument which operates with compressed air to propel a fine, adjustable spray of coloured material (stains, slips, glazes, lustres) onto the ceramic.

Albany clay
An American clay from Albany, New York, containing a high proportion of fluxes and a fine grain size, which is used as a brown/black slip glaze at temperatures above 1240°C.

Albury clay
An Australian clay having similar characteristics as Albany clay.

Alkali
Opposite to acid. Potash, soda and lithia are strong fluxes. Potters also use alkaline earths such as calcium, barium, magnesium and strontium as fluxes.

Alumina
Aluminium oxide. An important ingredient in clays and glazes. It provides the plasticity in clay and acts as an opacifier, stiffener and matting agent in glazes. Usually added in the form of china clay.

Applied decoration
Often describes additions of pieces of clay to the main form. Can also be decoration with slips, oxides, stains and glazes used in various ways.

Ash glaze
A glaze containing a proportion of ash from burnt organic material, mainly trees, straw, grasses, etc.

Ball clay
An extremely fine-grained, light coloured. sedimentary clay, sometimes used as a plasticiser in porcelain bodies.

Ball mill
A porcelain jar filled with pebbles and used to grind minerals and glazes to a fine particle size.

Banding
The application of horizontal stripes of oxide, stain, slip, glaze or lustre to pots on a rotating wheel.

Barium
An alkaline earth. Barium carbonate (poisonous) is used in glaze recipes for particular surface and colour effects (notably with copper and nickel).

Batt
This can be a kiln shelf, a removable wooden disk attached to the wheelhead for throwing making it easier to remove freshly thrown pots, or a slab of plaster or low-fired bisque used to dry wet clay.

Bentonite
A clay with a very fine grain, used to plasticise porcelain and added to glazes in small amounts around two per cent to aid suspension in the slop state.

Bisque
Unglazed ware, usually porous.

Bisque firing
The first firing of clay into ceramic. Usually conducted prior to glazing or other treatment because it is easier to handle than in the raw state.

Blunging
Mixing clay with water in a blunger to produce a smooth slip.

Bodies
Any clay or mixture of clays. Few clays are used by potters 'as dug'. Normally they use mixed clay bodies with different qualities for specific purposes.

Body stains
Colours prepared from metallic oxides to mix into slips and clay bodies.

Bone ash
Calcium phosphate made from calcining cattle bones. It is used in certain glazes to give a milky quality and is a major constituent of bone china.

214

Bone china
A very translucent white ware with a high proportion of bone ash.

Bung
A ceramic stopper to fit in the spyhole of a kiln.

Calcine
To heat materials to a sufficiently high temperature to drive off chemically combined water.

Calcium
The carbonate form is extensively used as a flux in glazes.

Carborundum
The trade name for silicon carbide, a hard grit used for polishing ceramic and, occasionally, added to glazes to cause local reduction in electric kilns.

Carving
Cutting into and removing clay from the surface of (usually) leatherhard clay.

Casting slip
Deflocculated mixture of clay and water in suspension for pouring into moulds.

Celadon glaze
A high-fired, grey-green glaze often used over incised or carved decoration. Blue and grey glazes having similar characteristics are sometimes described as 'celadon' types.

China clay
Kaolin, a pure form of primary clay, high in alumina and extremely refractory.

Chun glaze
A thick, opalescent glaze and bluish tint caused by scattered blue light waves.

Cobalt
Small amounts of the oxide and carbonate forms of this mineral give strong blue slips, bodies and glazes.

Coiling
Coils are made by rolling clay between the fingers or by extruding through a machine. Forms can be built up with coils joined together.

Cones
Elongated, three-sided pyramids composed of ceramic materials graded to measure the actual 'heat work' in a kiln and designed to collapse at specific temperatures. Cones can be observed through the spyhole during the firing.

Copper
The oxide and carbonate forms are used to give greens, blues and reds in slips and glazes according to their composition and the kiln atmosphere.

Copper red glazes
In reduction firing small amounts of copper produces red in reduction.

Crackle glaze
A glaze designed to craze by shrinking more than the body. The pattern of crackle lines is often stained after firing to give them greater emphasis.

Crazing
This occurs when the glaze does not fit the body due to uneven expansion and contraction. Either can be adjusted by the addition of silica.

Crystalline glaze
Glaze with crystals visible in and on the surface. Usually 'seeded' with titania, zinc or zirconium to encourage the growth of crystals. Slow cooling also helps.

Cup lawn
A small, cup-shaped sieve with a fine mesh.

De-airing
The removal of all air bubbles in a plastic clay prior to working.

Deflocculation
The dispersal of fine clay particles suspended in a slip prepared for casting. Soluble alkalis are added so that the slip can contain a high proportion of clay to a small amount of water without loss of fluidity.

Dolomite
A natural mineral, containing calcium and magnesium, used as a flux and crystalliser in high temperature glazes.

Dunting
Cracking of the body during firing or cooling.

Earthenware
Porous pottery usually fired to temperatures under 1100°C.

Engobe
Slip applied to pots at either the unfired or the bisque stage.

Engraving
Shallow incisions made into the surface of a ceramic at any stage.

Extruded
Plastic clay can be shaped into various sections by forcing it through a metal dye.

Feldspar
One of the most useful material in ceramics. Used as a flux in bodies and as a natural frit in glazes.

Feldspathoid
Mineral with similar properties to feldspar e.g. Cornish stone and nepheline syenite.

Fettling
Trimming away excess clay, slip or glaze before firing.

Flambé
A bright, glossy glaze streaked with reds produced by the use of copper in reduction.

Flint
Silica for bodies and glazes.

Fluting
Cutting vertical or diagonal grooves in the surface of a pot.

Flux
An oxide which lowers the melting point of a glaze mixture and aids vitrification in bodies.

Footring
The thrown or turned ring of clay supporting a bowl.

Frit
Glass or glaze which has been ground to be added to a glaze or body recipe. Frits are often prepared to make soluble materials insoluble for use in glaze mixtures.

Fusion
The melting of ceramic materials.

Glaze stain
Pigments made from oxides and added to give colour to glazes.

Grog
Fired clay body ground and graded to pass through various mesh sizes. It is added to bodies to provide extra wet strength and reduce shrinkage.

Inlay
Clays and slips, usually of different colours, inlaid into the porcelain body.

Iron
An important source of colour in ceramics. Rust reds, browns, tans, blues, greens and blacks can all be produced from different forms of iron oxide in various compositions and kiln atmospheres.

Kaolin
China clay.

Kidney steel
A small piece of flexible steel shaped like a kidney and used for shaping and scraping clay.

Kneading
Mixing plastic clay to an even consistency by hand.

Latex resist
A liquid rubber solution which can be painted or trailed on to a pot. When dry it resists water-based mixtures of colour, slip or glaze.

Lawn
A fine mesh of wire or fibre for sieving wet materials like slip or glaze etc.

Leatherhard
Clay in a stiffened condition but with sufficient moisture content to accept carving, piercing, inlaying and slipping.

Lithium carbonate
A strong alkaline flux used in glazes.

Lustre
Metallic salts of copper, gold, silver, platinum, bismuth and tin are mixed with resin and oils to deposit pure metal on the surface of pots in a localised reduction firing at a relatively low temperature around 750°C.

Magnesia
Used in bodies and glazes. Contributes opacity and mattness when percentages between 20%–30% are used in high temperature glazes. Often added in the form of dolomite.

Manganese (carbonate or dioxide)
Used as a colourant in bodies and glazes giving browns, blacks and purples.

Molochite
A refractory grog made by English China Clays in Cornwall.

Neriage
A form of decoration where slabs of contrasting coloured clays are laminated together, cut into strips and reassembled into patterns pressed into moulds.

Onglaze enamels
Soft, coloured glass with a low melting point for painting on top of fired glaze.

Opacifier
Materials in a glaze composition which remain suspended in the fired glaze. Tin, oxide, titanium dioxide, zinc oxide and zirconium dioxide are the principal agents.

Oxidation
This occurs when there is an ample air supply in the kiln during firing.

Oxide
A chemical compound formed between oxygen and another element.

Oxidising atmosphere
A clean kiln atmosphere where plenty of oxygen is present.

Paper porcelain
Porcelain slip mixed together with paper pulp and cast and rolled into sheets.

Plasticity
The essential property that allows clay to be shaped and reformed, but excess plasticity can make a clay unworkable or increase the amount of shrinkage when fired.

Polishing
This term is used to described the method of smoothing fired porcelain with silicon carbide 'sandpaper'.

Potash (potassium oxide or carbonate)
A strong alkaline flux and an important constituent of porcelain bodies and glazes.

Press mould
A hollow mould, made from plaster or from fired clay, used to form clay pressed into it.

Pyrometer
An instrument to measure temperature in the kiln.

Quartz
Silica. Used in body and glaze composition.

Raku
A Japanese word used to describe a particular type of low-fired ware made from a refractory clay able to withstand the shock of removal from a red hot kiln with tongs and rapidly cooled in water, or covered with combustible materials to create reducing conditions for special effects.

Reducing atmosphere
An excess of carbon is introduced into the kiln, usually about 900°C, so that oxygen atoms are extracted from the oxides present in the ceramics to produce often radical colour changes in glazes, notably from copper and iron.

Reduction firing
See reducing atmosphere.

Refractory
Resistant to high temperatures.

Rib
A tool usually made of wood or metal and used in throwing or for shaping.

Rutile
A natural titanium dioxide used to modify other colouring oxides. Alone, it has small traces of iron which produce tan colours. It is also used to give mottled colour effects in glazes. It is often used in crystalline glazes.

Salt glaze
Common salt thrown into the kiln fire at high temperatures decomposes and volatilises to combine with the alumina and silica in the clay body to produce an uneven glaze surface resembling orange peel in texture.

Satin glaze
A semi-matt glaze.

Sgraffito
Decoration scratched through the surface of slips or glazes or painted oxides.

Silica
All ceramics contain silica. It occurs as flint or quartz or sand. It is the essential ingredient of glass and glazes. Clay is a combination of silica, alumina, and water.

Silicon carbide
A compound of silica and coke used for its refractory properties and in grit form, as a powerful abrasive.

Slip
A creamy mixture of clay and water. The potter's *glue*. Can be coloured and used to completely cover a pot, or used for inlay and other decorative purposes.

Slip glaze
A fusible clay which melts to form a glaze at high temperatures.

Soak
A period during which the kiln temperature is kept constant to allow glazes and body to mature.

Soluble salts
Chlorides, nitrates and sulphates of metals commonly used as colourants in ceramics.

Sprigging
Adding pieces of clay as relief decoration.

Stannic oxide
White tin oxide, used as an opacifier in glazes.

Stoneware
A vitrified ware, usually fired to temperatures in excess of 1200°C with low porosity (no more than 5%).

Talc
Magnesium silicate. Used as an insoluble form of magnesia in bodies and glazes.

Tape resist
Paper masking tape used to protect areas of a design when painting, spraying and dipping slips, glazes and coloured stains.

Tenmoku
A high-fired glaze containing a large amount of iron oxide. It is usually brown to black in colour with streaks of rust, especially where thin on rims and carved edges.

Throwing
Making hollow pottery forms by hand on a rotating wheel.

Tin glaze
An opaque, white glaze containing tin oxide. This glaze forms the base for painting coloured pigments as seen in maiolica and delftwares.

Titanium
A creamy coloured opacifying agent which also produces crystals in a glaze.

Trimming
Turning or trimming waste clay away from a pot rotating on the wheel. This is usually done at the leatherhard stage.

Turning
See *Trimming* above.

Underglaze stains
Prepared ceramic pigments applied to the raw clay or bisque and normally covered with a transparent glaze. Colours which are capable of withstanding high temperatures are often used on porcelain without a glaze coat.

Vanadium oxide
A rare metallic oxide used to produce yellow pigments with tin oxide or zirconia, and blue pigments when combined with zirconium silicate.

Viscosity
Without the property of viscosity, glaze runs off a pot as molten glass. Viscous glazes hold their position due to internal friction between the particles of their composition. The alumina content in a glaze is one of the factors affecting viscosity.

Vitrification
The point at which the glassy materials within a body melt and flow into and fill the spaces between the clay particles and interact with them fusing them together. The vitrified state is the furthest point at which the body will hold its shape prior to deformation.

Wax resist
Molten wax or a wax emulsion design painted or trailed onto unfired clay, bisque, or glaze, resists water-based colours, slips and glazes with great clarity.

Wedging
The preparation, or restoration, of plastic clay by kneading into a smooth, homogeneous mass, free of air bubbles ready for use.

Whiting
Calcium carbonate. A material which is frequently used as a flux in glazes and as a source of calcia in clay bodies.

Wollastonite
Calcium silicate. A natural mineral used in glazes as a source of calcia.

Zinc oxide
Used as an auxiliary flux in glazes. It has a strong effect on certain colouring oxides and is generally best with copper or cobalt. Zinc oxide is often an important constituent of crystalline glazes.

Zirconium oxide
Used as an opacifier in glazes, often as a substitute for the more expensive tin oxide. Helps to promote crystal formation and mottled colours in glazes.

SUGGESTED FURTHER READING

Books

Åse, Arne, *Water Colour on Porcelain* (Norwegian University Press, 1989)

Axel, Jan and Karen McCready, *Porcelain: Traditions and New Visions* (Watson Guptill, 1981)

Billington, Dora, *The Technique of Pottery*, (Batsford, London, 1966)

Blackman, Audrey, *Rolled Pottery Figures* (Pitman/A&C Black, London, 1978)

Casson, Michael, *The Craft of the Potter* (BBC Publications, London, 1977)

Clark, Kenneth, *The Potter's Manual*, (Macdonald, 1983)

Clays and Glazes (The Ceramic Review Book of Clay Bodies and Glaze Recipes, 1988)

Colbeck, John, *Pottery: Techniques of Decoration* (Batsford, London, 1983)

Cooper, Emmanuel, *Electric Kiln Pottery* (Batsford, London, 1982)

Cosentino, Peter, *The Encyclopaedia of Pottery Techniques* (Headline Book Publishing, 1990)

Flight, Graham, *Ceramics Manual* (Collins, London, 1990)

Fournier, Robert, *Illustrated Dictionary of Practical Pottery* (A&C Black, 1973, 1977, 1992)

Fraser, Harry, *Glazes for the Craft Potter* (Pitman/A&C Black, London, 1973)

Gibson, John, *Pottery Decoration: Contemporary Approaches* (A&C Black, London, 1987)

Godden, Geoffrey, *Encyclopaedia of British Porcelain Manufacturers* (Barrie & Jenkins, London, 1988)

Gompertz, G. St. G. M., *Chinese Celadon Wares* (Faber and Faber, London, 1968)

Grebanier, Joseph, *Chinese Stoneware Glazes* (Pitman, London, 1975)

Green, David, *Understanding Pottery Glazes* (Faber and Faber, London, 1963)

Green, David, *A Handbook of Pottery Glazes* (Faber and Faber, London, 1978)

Hamer, Frank and Janet *The Potter's Dictionary of Materials and Techniques* (A&C Black, London, 1975, 1986, 1991, 1993)

Hamilton, David *Stoneware and Porcelain* (Thames and Hudson, London, 1982)

Hopper, Robin, *The Ceramic Spectrum* (Chilton Book Company, USA, 1984)

Lane, Peter, *Studio Porcelain* (Pitman/A&C Black, London and Chilton Book Company, USA, 1980)

Lane, Peter, *Studio Ceramics* (Collins, London and Chilton Book Company, USA, 1983)

Lane, Peter, *Ceramic Form: Design & Decoration* (Collins, London and Rizzoli, New York, 1988)

Leach, Bernard, *A Potter's Book* (Faber and Faber, London, 1945)

Medley, Margaret, *The Chinese Potter* (Phaidon, Oxford, 1976)

Nelson, Glenn C., *Ceramics* (Holt, Rinehart & Winston, New York, 1978)

Parmelee, Cullen W., *Ceramic Glazes* (Industrial Publications, Chicago, 1951)

Rhodes, Daniel, *Clay and Glazes for the Potter* (Chilton, USA and Pitman/A&C Black, London, 1973)

Rhodes, Daniel, *Stoneware and Porcelain* (Chilton, USA and Pitman, London, 1960)

Rhodes, Daniel, *Kilns: Design, Construction and Operation* (Chilton, USA, 1969)

Savage, George, *Porcelain through the Ages* (Penguin, London, 1954)

Scott, Paul, *Ceramics and Print* (A&C Black, London, 1994).

Wood, Nigel, *Oriental Glazes* (Pitman/A&C Black, London, 1978)

Periodicals

American Craft (Published by the American Crafts Council, New York)

Ceramics: Art and Perception (35 William Street, Paddington, Sydney NSW 2021, Australia)

Ceramics Monthly (Columbus, Ohio, USA)

Ceramic Review (Published by The Craft Potters' Association, London)

Crafts Magazine (Published by the Crafts Council, London)

Pottery in Australia (Published by The Potters' Society of Australia, Sydney)

La Revue de la Ceramique et du Verre, (France)

INDEX

Page numbers in italics indicate illustrations